TOTAL ELECTRIC GUITAR TUTOR

THIS IS A CARLTON BOOK

Copyright © Carlton Books Limited 2002, 2011

First published in 2002 by Carlton Books Limited
20 Mortimer Street
London W1T 3JW

A CIP catalogue record for this book is available from the British Library

ISBN 978 1 84732 761 1

Editorial Manager: Lorna Russell
Art Editor: Adam Wright
Music editor: Mike Flynn

Designed and edited by The Orgone Company

Production: Janette Burgin
Photographs by Paul Mattock and Terry Burrows

CD Produced by The Orgone Company
Printed in Dubai

TOTAL
ELECTRIC
GUITAR TUTOR

Terry Burrows

CARLTON
BOOKS

INTRODUCTION
GETTING STARTED

Before we launch into the nitty gritty of playing the guitar, let's spend a few pages looking at the guitar and its associated hardware. A better understanding of how the instrument has developed, how it works, and what the various components actually do should provide you with a sound basis for making decisions when you reach for your wallet to make that all-important purchase.

THE ROOTS OF THE GUITAR

The origins of the guitar is one of mystery and is the subject of dispute among music historians. The guitar as we know it dates back to the Renaissance period, but the earliest evidence we have can be traced back to clay reliefs found in Asia Minor, dating back to almost 2000 BC, that clearly show images of musicians playing instruments from which the guitar *might* have evolved. The volatile cultural shifts within this region – as well as the movements of the early merchants and traders – are likely to have been largely responsible for the spreading of these mysterious early instruments.

The direct precursors to the guitar are likely to have found their way into Europe via Spain – unquestionably the home of the guitar. The development of the instrument in the south of the country resulted from the invasion of the Arabic Moors in AD 80, who introduced stringed instruments such as the ud. From there they spread northward where, in the hands of the indigenous European instrument makers, instruments such as the lute and gittern gradually evolved. Until well into the 16th century, the lute was the dominant musical instrument throughout Middle Europe and Great Britain.

Renaissance Europe saw the birth of an early lute known as the *guitarra moresca*, but the earliest true guitars – appearing at the end of the 15th century – were closer in size to the smaller lute. Until the late 16th century, the guitar was viewed very much as a crude relation to "nobler" stringed instruments, such as the lute and vihuela.

TORRES AND BEYOND

The first important stage in the guitar's modern evolution came in the middle of the 19th century when Antonio de Torres Jurado began experimenting with new larger dimensions and production techniques at his workshop in Seville, Spain. The instruments he manufactured created a template for the modern classical guitar.

Torres became the maker of choice for the finest classical players of the second half of the 19th century. In particular, it was Francesco de Tárrega who, more than any other, brought respectability to the guitar. Although some of the finest players of the early 20th

---

THE CHANGING FACE OF THE GUITAR

The early guitars of the Renaissance were considerably smaller than their modern-day counterparts. Oddly enough, a more popular instrument of the period, the now-extinct Spanish vihuela, was far closer in shape and size to the instrument we now know. The vihuela was considered every bit the guitar's superior – there remains a considerable body of work composed for the instrument – and yet by the mid-17th century it had all but vanished.

There are many other surprising and significant differences. For example, instead of having six strings, these instruments featured sets of four or five "courses" – pairs of strings tuned to the same note and plucked at the same time. It wasn't until the mid 18th-century that a sixth course was added, and not until the early 1800s that courses were replaced by single strings.

The most radical difference, perhaps, was to be found on the fingerboard. Instead of there being a series of fixed metal bars, the frets were made from pieces of gut, which were bound around the neck. The number and position of these frets depended on the nature of the music being played. This meant, of course, that before performing, the 16th century guitarist had to ensure not only that each pair of course was in tune, but also that the frets were positioned for correct intonation.

THE SOLID-BODY STARS

Although country musicians such as Merle Travis and Les Paul were among the pioneers of the solid-body electric guitar, it was the R&B/rock and roll boom of the 1950s that helped to establish their role in modern music. In particular, the sounds of the electric bluesmen like Muddy Waters, B.B. King and Howlin' Wolf had a major impact on the first wave of young rock players of the early '60s, such as Eric Clapton, Jeff Beck and Jimmy Page.

The greatest star of the solid-body electric guitar was Jimi Hendrix. In his short life he gave a glimpse of the potential for the instrument in rock music that made him every bit as influential as Charlie Christian – the first truly great electric guitarist – had been to jazz players at the end of the 1930s.

The past three decades have seen the emergence of a number of fleet-fingered pyrotechnicians, such as Eddie Van Halen, Stevie Ray Vaughan, Steve Vai and Joe Satriani.

With the growing popularity of metal in its various forms during the first decade of the 21st century, a new generation of bands has emerged for whom a guitarist able to mix dazzling technical skills with the creation of new and interesting sounds is a basic necessity.

century had been pupils of Tárrega, it was a self-taught musician named Andrés Segovia who established the guitar firmly as an international instrument. Segovia's achievements as a virtuoso performer on the international stage attracted a worldwide following.

THE GUITAR IN AMERICA

The guitar has been at the heart of most of the popular music since the end of the 19th century – from folk and country and western to rock and pop. The roots of the guitar in popular music can largely be traced back to the way in which the guitar developed in the United States, most significantly through the work of European emigres Charles Frederick Martin and Orville Gibson. Their companies would both play a major role in the future of the guitar in America.

THE FIRST ELECTRICS

By the 1920s guitars were commonly being used in jazz and dance bands, with famous models like the Gibson L5 having usurped the traditional role of the banjo. However, compared to the other acoustic instruments, the guitar's naturally low volume meant that in most circumstances its use had to be restricted to providing a rhythmic backing.

In an attempt to solve this problem, one of Gibson's engineers, Lloyd Loar, began to experiment with magnetic coils, and in 1924 developed a very basic pickup that could be fitted to a standard six-string acoustic guitar.

A significant breakthrough came in 1931, when Adolph Rickenbacker produced the first in a series of cast-aluminum lap-steel "Hawaiian" guitars. Known as the "Frying Pan" because of its shape, this was the first commercially produced electric instrument. Four years later, Gibson launched the ES-150 – the first great electric guitar.

THE SOLID-BODY ELECTRIC GUITAR

One problem that resulted from fitting pickups to an acoustic guitar was that if the amplifier volume was too high, the sound would cause the body of the guitar to vibrate. This created howling "feedback". The solution was to give the instrument a solid body, thus reducing its capacity to vibrate.

During the 1940s a number of musicians and engineers experimented with this idea, producing prototype models. Among them was the popular guitarist Les Paul. But it was in 1950 that Californian Leo Fender set about creating the first production-line solid-body electric guitar: the Fender Telecaster (originally launched as the Broadcaster).

Following Fender's runaway success, Gibson recalled Les Paul and asked him to take part in the development of a rival instrument. The resulting guitar, launched in 1952, bore his own name – the Gibson Les Paul Standard. Fender replied two years later with the Stratocaster, perhaps the most famous guitar of them all.

Although Fender and Gibson are the best-known makers of electric guitars, there have been other notable US companies, such as Gretsch and Rickenbacker, or in more recent times, Jackson, Parker and PRS (Paul Reed Smith). Over the past 20 years, however, rivals have emerged. Initially producing inferior copies, Japanese manufacturers such as Ibanez now sell some of the finest production-line guitars found anywhere in the world. To counter this assault, Fender offered cheaper versions of their own guitars, built in Korea and Mexico. These remain popular since they allow novices or those with less money to own genuine Fender guitars – just not the top-of-the-range models built in the USA.

THE GUITAR AND ITS PARTS

Let's begin with a look at the instrument itself. In spite of the many different designs and production techniques employed, the vast majority of electric guitars comprise very similar components. The main differences affecting sound are the quality of the woods used. Most bodies are made from kiln-dried hard woods, such as mahogany, ash, maple, walnut or alder; some manufacturers have also experimented with carbon fibres in their construction. The neck is usually bolted on separately, although Gibson solid-body electrics famously have their necks permanently "set" – glued to the body.

HOW A GUITAR WORKS

All stringed instruments use a similar principle to create and project sound. By striking the string with the fingers or a pick, the vibrations disturb the surrounding airwaves. On an acoustic guitar, these soundwaves pass this energy into an acoustic chamber – THE SOUNDBOX – via the BRIDGE SADDLE (the point where each string comes into direct contact with the body). An audible sound is created, as it vibrates in sympathy with the strings.

It was the followers of the mathematician/philosopher Pythagoras who figured out that the pitch of a vibrating

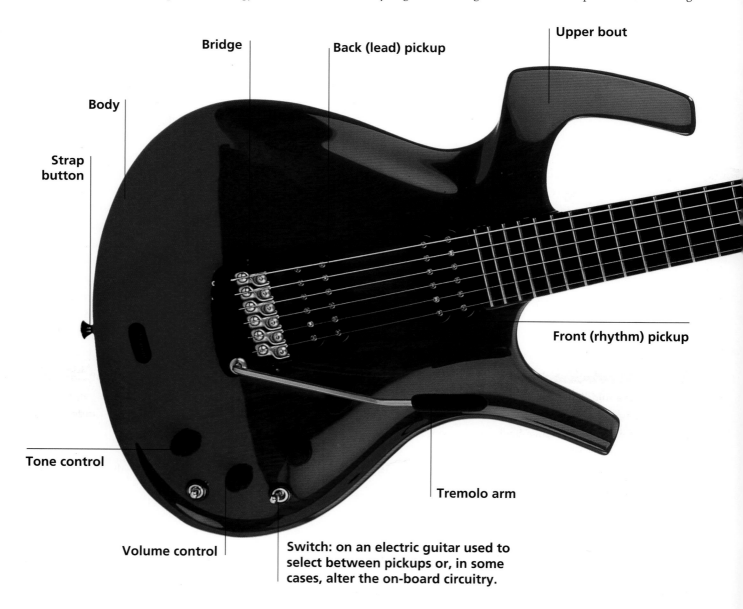

Bridge

Back (lead) pickup

Upper bout

Body

Strap button

Front (rhythm) pickup

Tone control

Tremolo arm

Volume control

Switch: on an electric guitar used to select between pickups or, in some cases, alter the on-board circuitry.

string altered according to its length, and according to strict mathematical laws. It's this fundamental law that governs the pitch of the sound when a guitar string is pressed against a fret and plucked.

ELECTRIC GUITARS

Although the basic principle is the same, electric guitars are slightly different in that they don't have a natural sound chamber. When you strike the string, the sound it produces is not usually very loud. For an electric guitar to produce any useful sound it must first be connected via a cable to an AMPLIFIER and LOUDSPEAKER. The part of the guitar that channels this sound is called a MAGNETIC PICKUP.

Pickups are made up of a series of magnets tightly wound with copper wire. This creates a magnetic field. They are positioned directly beneath the strings on the body of the guitar. Each time a string vibrates, it disturbs this magnetic field. These disturbances are passed to the amplifier via the guitar lead where they are converted into electrical impulses. Following amplification and alteration (by tone and volume controls), the signal arrives at the loudspeaker, causing the cone to vibrate. This results in a disturbance of the airwaves, which creates a sound.

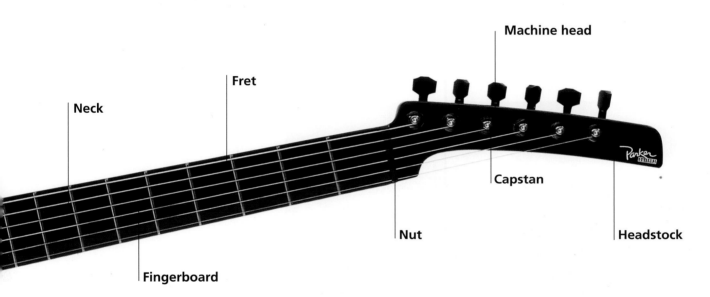

PERFECTION ACHIEVED?

During the middle of the 20th century, the guitar went through a period of radical revolution, with the development of electronic pickups and solid-bodies. Since then, innovations have been on a far more modest scale.

Makers have experimented with new shapes: the Steinberg "headless" guitar became briefly popular in the 1980s, and Ovation's round-backed guitars have largely defined the electro-acoustic genre.

Manufacturers have also tried out new materials: Dan Armstrong produced instruments with plastic bodies, and Kramer used aluminium necks, both claiming that levels of

sustain would be improved. Ultimately, however, players continued to prefer their instruments to be made of the traditional wood.

In the early 1980s, many felt that some kind of hybrid instrument involving the synthesiser was the next stage in the guitar's evolution. But few players bought into the idea.

Yet it seems that for the vast majority of players, the perfect format has already been established. In fact, the first production models, launched almost half a century ago – the Fender Telecaster and Stratocaster and the Gibson Les Paul – remain the most popular instruments.

AMPLIFIERS AND EFFECTS

If you are using an electric guitar you need a combination of an amplifier and a loudspeaker to produce any useful sound. Apart from boosting the volume of the guitar, amplifiers can also alter the way a guitar sounds. Indeed, your choice of amplifier may be as important as your choice of guitar in the impact it has on your sound. There are also numerous electronic effects available with which you can radically alter any basic amplified guitar signal. The most commonly used of these are distortion, delay and reverberation.

THE AMPLIFIER – IN BRIEF

The first electronic amplifiers were built in the 1930s. These enabled instruments fitted with pickups to be heard over the louder acoustic instruments found in the dance bands of the time. Their output was laughably low by modern standards – rarely exceeding 10 watts – and they used valve radio technology to project sound through a tiny loudspeaker.

As the idea of electrified acoustic guitars took off during the decade that followed, the demand grew for higher volumes. The first company to respond with dedicated guitar amplifiers was owned by a man named Leo Fender. In 1949, his small manufacturing operation produced the Fender Super Amp. Two years later he would create history with his revolutionary range of solid-body guitars, which resulted in an explosion in demand for electrified instruments.

THE ACCIDENT OF DISTORTION

By the end of the 1950s, now-classic amplifiers such as the Fender Twin Reverb and the British-built Vox AC30 dominated the marketplace. These models were popular with the early rock musicians, not only because of the lush warmth of their tone, but also because of the pleasantly distorted sound that emerged when the valves were overdriven. This was not a deliberate feature – designers sought to keep distortion to a minimum – but it was a happy accident that in part has defined the classic rock guitar sound.

THE ROCK ERA

As rock music started to be played in larger venues, power once again was an issue. Until, that is, British engineer Jim Marshall designed a 100-watt amplifier that could be connected to a stack of four 12-inch speakers. The "Marshall Stack" was used by just about everyone during the early days of heavy rock, among them giants like Jimi Hendrix (*left*) and Jeff Beck.

By the start of the 1970s, as far as hi-fi manufacturers were concerned, valve technology was already 20 years out of date. Instead, the cheaper and more predictable solid-state transistorised technology had taken over. Traditional guitar amplifier manufacturers quickly followed suit. This cheaper technology quickly became popular, especially with beginners and semi-professional users.

ALTERING THE SOUND

It's possible to achieve a wide array of sounds just by altering the controls of the amplifier. However, an infinite number of possibilities can be considered by inserting one or more electronic effect units between the guitar and the amplifier.

The first effect to take off in a big way was the fuzz box foot pedal. Appearing in the early 1960s, they could create artificial distortion, and were popular with guitarists who played instruments that were less well suited to overdriving an amp (such as Fender guitars, which used single-pole pickups).

Also famous during this period was the wah-wah pedal. A tone filter control, the sound could me manipulated by rocking back and forth on a foot pedal. The greatest exponent of this effect (and much else, for that matter) was Jimi Hendrix. The wah-wah drops in and out of fashion every few years.

The other important classic effect is the echo unit. Using loops of magnetic tape to play back a signal, "slap-back" echoes or longer delays could be created. In the modern era, echo is produced digitally, which can not only create echoes, but other delay effects such as phasing, chorus, or pitch-shifting. These units are easily affordable and – above all – programmable, so complex settings can be stored and recalled whenever they're needed.

THE GREAT DEBATE

There was one big problem with transistors: when they overloaded, they made a deeply unpleasant howling noise. Designers tried to compensate by introducing distortion circuitry, but it just wasn't as effective as the "real thing".

Most modern guitarists prefer the classic valve sound, characterized by a warmth and smoothness of tone, even if, unlike solid-state circuitry, the valves themselves can come loose, or may need periodic replacement. Different valves can also produce different sounds, so can be worth experimenting with different combinations.

Solid-state amplifiers have a sharp, brittle character and since they distort less at higher volumes, they are best suited to "pure" amplification purposes, such as PA systems or studio monitoring. Indeed, few modern guitarists would actively choose a solid-state option, and, as such, transistor guitar amps are now only found at the bottom end of the market.

A popular alternative to emerge in the 1990s was a hybrid of both types of system, typically utilising a VALVE PREAMPLIFIER to provide the basic "character" of the sound, which can then be amplified using a SOLID-STATE POWER AMPLIFIER. For some players this represents the best of both worlds.

Since the beginning of the 21st century, technological development has centred around MODELLING – the use of on-board computer software to simulate the sound characteristics of different types of amplifier, speaker cabinet and effects. In practice this may mean that at the press of a button it may be possible to create something that sounds like a 1960s Fuzz Face distortion pedal being played through a Vox AC30 combo; press another button to get the sound of a Marshall valve amplifier with a closely-miked four-by-twelve speaker stack. This technology is versatile, convenient and highly usable, but the key is in the phrase "sounds like" – it will never sound as "real" as the equipment it is simulating.

A recent development has seen some of the manufacturers of modelling technology integrate their software into genuine valve guitar amplifiers. This enables the musician to combine the staggering sound programming possibilities of the software with the age-old benefits of a valve amplifier sound.

COMBOS, HEADS, STACKS AND RACKS

The traditional guitar amp combines an amplifier and loudspeaker in a single cabinet. Such units are called COMBOS. They are compact and easy to transport. When the two components are separate, the amplifier is usually referred to as the HEAD and the speaker cabinet as the STACK. This can potentially produce greater volume than a combo, although this won't be much of an issue if the venue has a powerful PA system. Separate components do, however, allow the player the luxury of choosing a bespoke combination of amplifier and loudspeaker.

Some manufacturers produce preamplifiers and power amplifiers that fit into a standard 19-inch studio rack. Many of these models feature USB or MIDI connections to allow different settings to be stored and selected externally.

Line 6 Spider Mark II combines valve and modelling technology.

CHOOSING YOUR EQUIPMENT

OK, the time has come. You've got your cash or credit card in your wallet and you're about to march purposefully into a music store. Hold on for a moment. Choosing a guitar or amplifier can be a nerve-wracking time – especially if you haven't done this kind of thing before. So before you set out it's worth trying to involve someone with at least a little experience in these matters (especially if you intend buying used equipment). If you first check out the guidelines shown over the next few pages, you shouldn't go too far wrong.

TEN TOP TIPS FOR BUYING A GUITAR

1 BUY THE BEST YOU CAN AFFORD
So long as your pockets can stretch to it, try to get hold of a quality product. It will be both more playable and more reliable. You may not want to hear this, but compromise at this stage is guaranteed to be a false economy. You'll have no trouble at all finding something cheap, but ultimately it may prove to be hard to play.

2 CHECK FOR FINGERBOARD WARPING
If the fingerboard is severely curved or warped the intonation will be poor, making the guitar difficult to play. To test the quality of the neck, hold the guitar as if you were aiming a rifle and align your eye with the top surface of the neck. It should appear to be very even. If the top of the fingerboard appears to be at all twisted, DON'T BOTHER WITH IT. The intonation will be unreliable (the guitar will not stay perfectly in tune across the whole fingerboard). These problems can be repaired, but are likely to be costly. If you align your eye with the side of the neck, you are likely to notice a very slight curvature halfway down the neck, around about the 7th to 9th frets. This is normal, and can be controlled using the truss rod.

3 CHECK THE INTONATION
The note on the 12th fret should ALWAYS be exactly one octave higher that the open string. You can make a more direct comparison between the note and harmonic on the 12th fret. To do this, gently rest one of your fingers on the string above the 12th fret (at that position there are usually noticeable marker inlays on the fingerboard). If you pluck the string, you should hear a delicate bell-like tone. If the notes do not match, then the guitar will gradually go out of tune the further you play along the neck. Although this can easily be rectified, ask someone in the shop to do it for you. You don't want to be messing about with this kind of business before you begin playing.

4 CHECK THE ACTION
Now take a look at the distance between the top of the 12th fret and the bottom of the string above. This height is known as the ACTION. A low action means that the strings are closer to the frets, so that your fingers don't have to press hard to play a note. This is important for fast solo work. A high action will make it harder for you to learn, so is best avoided. Make sure that you also play EVERY note on the fingerboard. This is to check that the frets are all sitting at the same height. If they are not, it will result in buzzing or rattling sounds when some notes are played. This is not pleasant.

WHICH GUITAR?

Guitars come in three different "flavours": there are acoustic guitars, which don't require any amplification at all; electric guitars, which most certainly do require an amplifier; and then there is the electro-acoustic – the "inbetweeners" of the guitar world. Which of those will best serve your purpose is entirely up to you, and the kind of music you plan to play.

Most rock music is oriented toward the electric guitar, although there clearly are many famous acoustic examples that one could bring to mind. So which instrument should you buy? One false assumption is that an electro-acoustic guitar can cover both bases. Most of these are basically steel-string acoustic guitars with pickups fitted. They are mostly used to supply an amplified acoustic guitar sound without the problems of dealing with a microphone.

There are other electro-acoustics that fall at the other end of scale: these are "hollow-body" electrics. Although they have something approaching a soundbox, they don't function as acoustic guitars – the sound chamber simply provides a different kind of electric sound.

If you're going to choose just one guitar – and buying a new instrument can be a surprisingly addictive habit – go for a classic solid-body electric.

5 CHECK THE ACTION

The machine heads are the six winding mechanisms on the headstock at the top of the neck which control the tension of each string. If the capstan (the pin that holds the string) turns too easily, then the strings may slip, making the guitar difficult – or even impossible – to keep in tune. This is not quite so important if you are buying an instrument fitted with a locking tremolo unit, since it is the nut mechanism that clamps the string in place.

6 CHECK THE SUSTAIN

The quality of sustain – the length of time a note rings naturally before it fades away – is a direct result of the design and construction of the instrument. The best guitars have the longest sustain. It's therefore a sensible idea to play every note on the fingerboard to ensure that all notes sustain equally. Avoid acoustic instruments on which "dead" notes can be heard. These so-called "wolf notes" sometimes occur as a result of an instrument's natural frequencies.

It's a good idea to buy (or haggle) a carrying case for your guitar: it will protect the instrument from damage, and keep it dust free.

NAME OR NO-NAME?

There are some very famous names in the realm of guitar manufacture: instruments such as the Fender Stratocaster or the Gibson Les Paul have developed an iconic status. These instruments can be viewed much the same as a car with a desirable marque, and so are not cheap. So is it really worth the expense of a "name" guitar? In my view, the answer has to be "if you can afford it". Such an instrument is *generally* a sign of quality – and it'll make playing more enjoyable. Name guitars also have better resale value, with some models even appreciating over time. And what other modern instrument or piece of technology can that be said about?

7 CHECK THE PICKUPS

Plug the guitar into an amplifier. Now check the relative volumes of each string. If there are significant variations, the height of the pickups need to be adjusted. If each pole of the pickup (the node beneath each string) has an individual height adjustment, then this can be done easily. If not, the whole pickup may need to be replaced. (Note: make sure that the amplifier controls are in a fairly neutral position – if there is too much bass or treble it may be difficult to judge relative volumes across all six strings.)

8 CHECK FOR NOISE

While the guitar is still plugged in, stand it close to the amplifier and listen to the sound. It should be silent. Unpleasant, whistling feedback may indicate that the pickups are not well isolated, which may pose problems when playing at high volumes. Now strum the strings and turn all of the potentiometers (the tone and volume controls) and switches on the guitar. If you hear crackling sounds, they may be damaged. This is not difficult to repair, but – once again – it's something that you shouldn't have to worry about.

9 KNOW WHAT YOU'RE HEARING

Make sure that the amplifier in the store is not enhancing the quality of the guitar. Ask for any effects to be switched off so that you hear only the amplified guitar.

10 FALL IN LOVE

Every guitar has a sound and feel of its own. Just as two people are sometimes drawn together seemingly for reasons that can't easily be described, if you are lucky you will find a guitar that produces a similar kind of magnetism. It can't be stressed strongly enough that it's important that you feel happy with the instrument. This relationship will play a major part in your development as a guitarist.

CHOOSING AN AMPLIFIER

Here are some additional tips to help you take on the mysteries of buying an amplifier or speakers.

1 POWER
Before you choose an amplifier, put a little thought into what you may want to do with it ultimately – or how loud you want to be able to play. If you intend playing in even the smallest live venue, you are likely to need at least 50 watts of power. Most guitar amplifiers (combos, at least) are rated at between 50-100 watts. Word of warning: A HIGH OUTPUT IS NOT NECESSARILY A SIGN OF HIGH QUALITY.

2 COMPATIBILITY
Any amplifier will work with any guitar, in as far as it will amplify the signal, but some combinations work better than others. Consequently, it's always a good idea to take your own instrument along when you test an amplifier. This is the only way you will really know if it's the right piece of equipment for your sound.

3 KNOW YOUR NEEDS
Some amplifiers may offer you a good deal more than just boosting a signal. Some come complete with electronic effects, multiple input channels and complex graphic equalizers. Try not to be too dazzled by the "bang-for-your-bucks" factor: think about whether you really need those additions. Like their counterparts in the guitar world, some of the best and most popular valve amplifiers are variations on very simple models designed in the 1950s. It's usually a reasonable idea to start out with a pared-down system, and then build it up as new requirements emerge.

DO I *HAVE* TO HAVE AN AMPLIFIER?

If you want to be able to hear yourself playing then most definitely you do. BUT, if you're not planning to play live, or you simply can't afford the expense just now, there is an alternative. If you have a hi-fi system then you already have an amplifier. If it's capable of taking LINE INPUTS, then you can simply plug your guitar into one of the channels, press the MONO button (so it comes out of both speakers), and start to play. It isn't ideal, and it probably won't sound great, but at least you'll be able to hear yourself. Don't crank up the volume too high, though: sensitive hi-fi tweeters can easily be wrecked.

---

4 SIZE
Amplifiers can vary greatly, both in size and weight. If you are buying an amplifier head with a "four-by-twelve" speaker cabinet, make sure that you have sufficient room to store it in your home. Damp basements or garages are not ideal places to keep delicate electrical equipment. And be practical: having to lug a massive piece of kit up and down eight flights of stairs before and after every rehearsal and gig is guaranteed to dampen your enthusiasm.

5 STATE
Buying used equipment is an attractive proposition to many novices. If you go along this route, take special care when you encounter models that seem to have taken a heavy battering. It's just like buying a car – a model that barely left it's owner's garage is usually more desirable than one which has driven around the word a dozen times. It's quite obvious that if the amplifier has been heavily used or badly treated, its longevity might just be affected.

6 SILENCE
Listen out for excess buzzing or hiss, both before you plug the guitar in and when you are not playing. This may indicate that some of the circuitry is worn, or components need to be replaced.

7 SPEAKER
Always check the speaker. Remove the covering grille and give it a serious inspection. The cone is especially delicate, so you should ensure that it is not torn or dented. Also check the periphery of the cone because this is where natural wear occurs. All of these elements can affect the sound. Although methods of production have improved over the years, it should be pointed out that loudspeakers don't last forever. If you are buying an old or vintage piece of gear you might want to budget for buying a replacement speaker.

8 ELECTRICS
THOROUGHLY TEST ALL OF THE SWITCHES, AS WELL AS THE VOLUME AND TONE CONTROLS. Make sure that they all do all the things they are supposed to, and – above all – without making extraneous clicks or crackling noises. Once again, you will find that some of these components do simply wear out, but having a volume control potentiometer replaced by a professional servicing engineer is not likely to set you back a fortune. Quite frankly, if you think you're on the verge of a real bargain, you should still consider buying.

9 STOMP

With the amplifier switched on, but not connected to a guitar, stamp your foot on the ground next to the model. If you hear any electrical noise as a result, there may be loose valves or other circuitry. This is likely to cause you problems eventually. (Note: if the amplifier has a built-in spring reverb, this will start to clang if you do this – that's completely normal.)

WHAT ABOUT EFFECTS?

While shopping for guitars and amplifiers, it's always tempting – cash permitting – to add the latest in electrical gadgetry to your newly acquired armoury. At first, you'll have your work cut out just getting your fingers to obey your instructions, without the added distraction of worrying about strange and exotic sounds coming out of the loudspeaker.

If you've just GOT to get your hands on an effect at this stage, choose something simple, classic and versatile, such as reverb or delay – or, above all, distortion if you don't have an amplifier that can produce such sounds.

Since many musicians now have home computer recording set-ups, one alternative might be to buy a studio-quality rack-mounted effect or modelling unit *(see page 11)*. These can

10 TAKE YOUR AMPLIFICATION SERIOUSLY

Some guitarists are more than a little blasé about amplification. Don't forget that it's not just about boosting the guitar's volume, an amplifier also colours your sound. Don't just take the first model that you see. Try out different makes and types – the differences will quickly become very apparent.

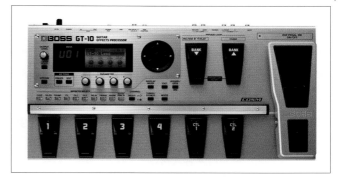

Boss GT-10 programmable digital effects foot pedal.

offer a huge variety of different sounds, many of which can be used simultaneously. This approach has the advantage of giving you a decent set of effects that can be used either live or as part of a studio.

WHERE TO BUY

The obvious place to look for guitars, amplifiers and effects used to be by taking a visit to your local music store. And it's still the best. Most reasonable-size towns have at least one such place, and you'll find that many of them also trade in used equipment. These places are also invariably staffed by musicians, so (assuming you can actually get the guy who should be behind the counter to stop playing Zeppelin/Nirvana/Mastodon [delete according to your "era"] licks, put his guitar down and serve you) then it can also be a useful source of advice and other information – finding local gigs, for example.

If you are looking for second-hand gear, the classified adverts in guitar and music technology magazines make a good starting point, or your local newspapers if you don't fancy travelling.

But the obvious place to find a bargain these days is, of course, on the Internet. If you're buying new, you may even find that you can get a better price buying from a shop's website than by visiting in person. And, of course, it's also an absolutely invaluable research tool – *everything* you

could want to know about guitars and amplifiers is on there somewhere – if you can find it!

Now for the thorny issue of buying a guitar online. When the first edition of this book appeared back in 2002 I took a pretty firm line on this area – one that could more or less be summed up by saying that anyone buying a guitar without first playing it would have to be insane! Maybe my mind was changed when I *finally* found that elusive 1960 Gretsch Anniversary in smoke green going on a Texas website for about a third of what I would have expected to pay in London. I went for it, it arrived safely and it's a lovely guitar. But it *was* undoubtedly a risk. So my official line now shifts to *caveat emptor* – "let the buyer beware". If you're after a brand new "name" guitar from one of the big online sellers you'll probably be fine, especially as most offer a reasonable returns policy. If you exercise caution and a little common sense you should be fine. The bottom line is that if a deal seems too good to be true (like those eBay sellers – usually based in China – who offer "genuine", "brand new" Gibson Les Pauls for £100!) then it probably *is*.

CHAPTER 1
UP TO SPEED

To be completely honest, this book wasn't conceived with the complete novice in mind. We figured that there are plenty of people out there who already know how to hold a guitar, and can strum a few chords, but who want to take things a little further. That said, however, if you are starting from scratch, this chapter should get you up to speed pretty quickly. Work methodically through the steps outlined over the next 24 pages. At the end of the chapter review what you have learned, and make absolutely sure that you've grasped each of the concepts before attempting to move on. If you already have some experience of playing the guitar, this chapter might serve as a useful refresher.

A BIT ABOUT THE BOOK

Total Electric Guitar is more than just a book about playing rock guitar. It has been designed so that you learn the fundamental mechanics of music and immediately put them into a practical context. You can do this by playing the exercises over a series of specially composed backing tracks. To make things more interesting (and to appeal to the broadest number of readers) a variety of different musical styles has been used: some you may like; some you may not – but they're all in there for a good reason, so stick with it.

Sometimes the book teaches some pretty serious stuff, but hopefully, we can make it fun. For example, learning scales can be a very tedious business, but if you're playing over a backing track written specifically with that purpose in mind, it should be a more enjoyable experience.

So here is a flavour of what you should be able to achieve by the end of the course if you work methodically through each chapter:

- A basic understanding of the evolution of the guitar, the various components that make up the instrument, and which type of guitar will be most appropriate to the music that you want to play.

- A reasonable understanding of the fundamentals of music theory, including sight-reading standard musical notation, and tablature.

- A chord vocabulary that should be sufficiently developed to enable you to play pretty well any song that's ever been written – and in any key.

IN THIS CHAPTER YOU'LL LEARN...

- Holding the guitar in the standing position
- Fingerboard positioning
- Tuning to a set of reference tones – keyboards, electronic tuner or the accompanying CD
- Holding a pick
- Naming the notes on the fingerboard
- The basic open-string major chords:
  E major, A major, D major, G major, C major
  and F major
- Understanding rhythm

- Holding the guitar in the seated position
- Fretting technique
- Tuning to a single reference tone
- Fingerpicking
- Basic music theory
- Naming the notes on the music staff
- Open-string minor chords: E minor, A minor, D minor
- Compound time
- Tempo
- Time signatures

HOW TO USE THIS BOOK

This book aims to provide a truly interactive experience. Not only will you find a variety of visual cues to get across its ideas – photography, diagrams, written music and guitar TAB – but many of the exercises and examples can be heard on the accompanying CD.

This is a very simple system to use. The first ten tracks on the CD take are named according to the chapter. Within each lesson, individual tracks are given what are known as "index points". The CD symbol is prefixed by two numbers: the first is the track number, the second the index point.

Wherever you see this symbol, you know that you will be able to hear the example played.

Most CD players are equipped to deal with index points, but it's not too much of a problem if yours is not. All you have to do is use the pause control on your CD player's remote control.

The last nine tracks on the CD are full-length versions of the backing tracks used throughout the book.

- You should be able to play some fairly demanding blues- and rock-based guitar solos.

- An understanding of scales and the way notes relate to one another that should give you the knowledge to improvise with a degree of confidence.

- You will understand the different types of amplifier and sound-processing effects that can be used to colour the sound of your playing.

THINK FOR YOURSELF
Unlike many types of teaching, this book is in no way didactic. We acknowledge that – to use a good old English expression – there's more than one way to skin a cat. There are, of course, plenty of "correct" techniques that you would be taught by a classical teacher – but if you want to do things differently, then who are we to say otherwise?

The true aim of *Total Electric Guitar* is to provide the basic ingredients to let you think, act, and play for yourself. After all, every one of you will have different needs, goals, dreams and musical aptitudes. Your reasons for wanting to play will be equally varied. For some, being able to strum the chords of a few songs will be more than enough; others may strive to play heavy-metal solos as fast as is earthly possible; some of you – like John Lennon was alleged to have done – may view it primarily as a way of impressing the opposite sex. That's cool, too.

But if there's a subtext to this book, it's to encourage you to get out there and do your thing with other like-minded people. With a bit of practice – and we'll inevitably talk more about that in a moment – BY THE END OF THIS CHAPTER you will be armed with as much knowledge as many of us had

when we first got together with a bunch of friends to form a band. No matter how satisfying it can undoubtedly be, our view is that playing the guitar is less an effective means in itself than one of the greatest musical tools for expressing and communicating your own creativity. If just one of you out there is sufficiently inspired to start writing his or her own songs, then (apart from selling several million copies) this book will have been a success.

THE DREADED "P" WORD
It wouldn't be fair to get through this little opener without uttering the word every novice dreads: as with any learning process, YOU WILL ONLY GET TO BE GOOD BY PRACTISING. The best musicians combine a mental facility – an understanding of WHAT they are trying to play – with the motor skills necessary to make their fingers carry out their "commands". The acquisition of the latter will only come about by repetition. THERE IS NO SHORT CUT HERE.

There will be times when this will be frustrating, and you'll want to hurl your guitar out of the nearest window. At times like these, relax and take a few steps back. Try to keep yourself mentally focused on your eventual aim. Work methodically through each chapter – they're geared in such a way that they become increasingly challenging – and don't move on until you have mastered the last one.

Whether you aspire to be a Jeff Beck, a Ritchie Blackmore, a Steve Vai or a Johnny Thunders or Kurt Cobain, remember this simple truth: EVERY ONE OF THEM HAD TO PASS THROUGH THE SAME LEARNING EXPERIENCE YOU'RE ABOUT TO GO THROUGH.

But keep a sense of perspective. Don't torture yourself. As the legendary Les Paul told me a few years ago: "You don't WORK the guitar, you PLAY it". What a wise man.

STRIKING THE RIGHT POSE

Besides the rather important issue of keeping your instrument in tune, it's critical that you feel relaxed and comfortable holding your guitar. There are no strict rules here but, generally speaking, most rock musicians perform in a standing position with the guitar supported by a shoulder strap. However, for practice, rehearsal and recording, those same guitarists often adopt a sitting position. It's a good idea to get yourself used to playing both ways.

STANDING POSTURE

If you want to play the guitar in the standing position you will need a shoulder strap. These come in many different forms, from cheap and nasty bits of plastic to those carved beautifully from leather. Almost any strap you see in a music store will do the job, although you should avoid those without reinforced strap holes – these will always snap at the most inopportune and embarrassing moments. Paying a little more money for a good-quality leather strap is usually a worthwhile investment, and with a bit of luck it should last you a lifetime.

If you are particularly paranoid about your instrument coming adrift from the shoulder strap – something you should strongly consider if you intend leaping around on the stage – you might invest in a set of strap locks. These are small metal fixtures which clamp onto the shoulder strap and can then be "clicked" into place on the body of the guitar. The strap lock is secured to the holes on either end of the strap by a simple nut, washer and bolt mechanism. Manufacturers usually supply their own strap buttons, which must be fitted to the guitar.

THE RIGHT ANGLE

Comfort and playability are your key words. The guitar should hang naturally against your body, leaving both arms free to move comfortably. For the best results, the neck of the guitar should be held at an angle of between 30° and 45° (*see below left*). It is also important that the strap is adjusted so that the guitar is held at the correct height. A good rule of thumb for a beginner is to ensure that the bridge of the guitar hangs at around about the same height as your waistband.

Standing position with guitar neck at 45° angle.

Sitting posture with the guitar resting on the right knee.

Johnny Ramone takes the low-slung posture to extremes. This position makes it tough for learning, but it does look very cool.

Of course, it is a common sight to see a rock musician playing on stage with an extremely low-slung instrument. While this may look cooler than the standard posture, it will make the initial learning process more difficult. The reasoning here is that the further away the guitar neck is held from the body, the more exaggerated the angle of the left hand has to become. You will quickly find yourself exercising hitherto unknown muscles in your wrist, which can be extremely painful. When you become more experienced you are certain to gravitate toward the height and neck angle that works best for you.

BE SEATED

There are two fundamentally different approaches to playing the guitar in the sitting position. The "classical" method demands that the waist of the guitar is placed between the legs,

We haven't forgotten all you left-handers out there. Most of the classic guitar models are available in mirror-image left-handed models, although some players find it easier to buy a standard model and re-string it in reverse. This is fine as far as the fingerboard goes, but you may well find that the cutaways in the body don't work too well for the balance of the instrument.

resting on the left thigh; the left foot is usually positioned on an adjustable footstool to bring the angle of the neck to about 45°. Holding the neck at this angle allows for the optimum positioning of the left hand for movement along the fingerboard, and the right hand above the strings.

INFORMAL POSTURE

To be honest, the only rock musicians who ever play this way are the few that had classical training. In practice, a far more informal posture is likely to be used. This is simply to rest the guitar on the right thigh, supporting the neck with the left hand so that it maintains a broadly horizontal angle (*see page 18, bottom right*). The body of the instrument is held in place by the inside of the right arm. This position is the one that most novices find the most natural for playing an acoustic instrument.

Playing a solid-body electric guitar when sitting can sometimes cause problems. Most of these instruments have been designed for playing in the standing position – their shape and balance can cause the instrument to tilt awkwardly. If this happens you can get additional support from a shoulder strap.

FINAL THOUGHTS

Give a bit of thought to the kind of clothing you wear when you play the guitar. A lot of the traditional staples of the rock stage, such as leather and chains, are not really the ideal clothes to be wearing when performing. Bulky jackets or tops can easily restrict the movement in the arms. Conversely, if your sleeves are too loose they can easily drag against the strings, muting the sound. Metal buttons, jewellery or zips are all liable to catch the body of the guitar at inopportune moments. As well as making an unpleasant noise, this can also scratch or damage the instrument.

When practising, bear in mind that not every seating surface is appropriate for playing the guitar. You should choose a sturdy stool or upright chair, and the floor on which the left-foot support is positioned also needs to be firm. Desk chairs are of little use since the arms will just get in the way. Nor is soft seating, such as a sofa or bed, ideal for learning – it's hard to hold the guitar in the correct position when lounging.

THE FRETTING FINGERS

Let's just state the obvious for a moment, since there might be someone somewhere who hasn't grasped this point: notes are played on a guitar when the fingers of the left hand force the strings down between the frets on the fingerboard. (If you are left-handed then the fingers of the right hand will do this job.) Achieving the correct fretting posture is crucial if you want to play any more than the simplest music. Pay careful attention now – if you adopt bad habits to begin with, they can be doubly hard to turn around or change later on.

THUMB POSITION

There are two very distinct approaches to left-hand and thumb positioning, making it a vexing subject for many guitar tutors. Standard classical guitar technique favours a left hand with the thumb held firmly against the centre of the back of the neck at all times (*see right, above*). This tension allows the neck to be gripped firmly, providing additional pressure when fretting notes along the fingerboard. This is important if you are to prevent strings buzzing or being muted. For correct classical posture the thumb must be kept perfectly straight. HOWEVER, MANY SELF-TAUGHT PLAYERS IGNORE (OR HAVE NEVER BEEN TAUGHT) THIS RULE. They can be seen sliding the left hand around the neck with the thumb resting along the edge of the fingerboard (*see right, below*). And what's more, they can play their chosen music on the guitar perfectly well.

This "alternative" thumb position is certainly an easy habit to acquire when learning, but it's positively frowned upon by classical teachers. So what's the problem? As far as we're concerned there isn't one. Some players find it considerably more comfortable. Furthermore, if you a have a wide enough fingerspan it can allow the thumb to fret notes on the 6th string (or even the 5th string in some cases), which can be useful when playing certain chords. There is no doubt, however, that if you use this method exclusively it can restrict agility on the fingerboard, in particular, your ability to change chords quickly.

So what's the verdict? Quite frankly, each system has its own virtues, so it's worth taking a serious look at both techniques.

FRETTING IT RIGHT

A good fretting technique is arguably the most important aspect of developing your left hand. The rule here is simple: THE TIP OF THE FINGER SHOULD FALL IMMEDIATELY BEHIND THE FRET. If it is held too far back from the fret the string is likely to buzz against the fret; if it is too close to the fret, the string will probably be muted.

Classical left-hand thumb position.

Alternative left-hand thumb position.

FINGER EXERCISES

Your biggest battle when first playing the guitar will be getting your fingers to obey your brain. You'll be calling on the services of muscles that you didn't even know you had – and they won't much like it.

In a single word, the solution to this problem is practice. However, that needn't always mean playing the guitar itself – although that's obviously the best real practice you can get. When you're away from your beloved (your guitar, that is) there are a number of simple finger exercises you can do while at your desk in school or the office, or while you're watching TV, that can help your playing.

The basic problem comes down to the strength of the fretting fingers. After all, if you're right-handed you use the left hand for fretting notes, and this is usually considerably weaker than your writing hand. To strengthen the fingers, press them down one at a time on a solid surface like the edge of a desk. Start by applying pressure with only the fourth finger for five seconds, then release the pressure and repeat with the third finger. Continue this with all of the fingers of your fretting hand. Repeat this exercise as many times as you wish. After a while you can speed it up – this will help to get each finger moving independently.

The angle of the fretting fingers is also critically important. To avoid accidentally muting the other strings, the fingers should be kept vertical – as close to 90° as possible – when held against the fretboard.

To be honest, this is one of the clearest benefits of using the classical left-hand technique – with the thumb applying pressure from the back, it's quite natural for the other fingers to form a "clamp". On the other hand, if your thumb is resting on the edge of the fingerboard, it can be extremely difficult to keep those fingers straight at all.

PAIN IS GOOD

Getting your left hand working can quite literally be a real pain. For a start you'll be working muscles in your fingers that you didn't even know you had. Pressing the strings down on to the fingerboard exerts a surprising degree of strain on the two smallest fingers. Their strength will have be built up if you are to play even the simplest guitar styles.

Also surprising is how frustrating it can be trying to get the third and fourth fingers to behave independently. But if you are to play chords or scales you will have to overcome this obstacle. To get an idea of how tricky this can be, try the Vulcan "Live long and prosper" hand greeting used by *Star Trek*'s Mr Spock. This entails creating a sort of "V" sign between the second and third fingers. (The thumb, first and second fingers pull together in one direction; the third and fourth fingers in the other.) Not many people can do this without practice – their fingers simply don't want to obey the brain.

SOFT SKIN SYNDROME

The most painful experience for most novices is the way the strings just love to "cut" into soft fingertips. With time

To prevent fret buzzing and string muting, the angle that the pad of the finger touches the fretboard at should be as close as reasonably possible to 90°.

the skin will harden, but if you over exert yourself at first you are likely to find yourself with some very unpleasant and painful blisters. The best advice is to stop playing as soon as your fingers get tired or start become painful. Remember, the pads at the tips of your fingers are rarely used for anything more demanding than holding a pen, so it will take a little time before they become hardened to the persistent pressure of metal strings.

Once they have hardened, try to avoid everyday tasks that will act to re-soften them. That means reaching for the rubber gloves if you have to do the washing up.

TIME TO TUNE

Whatever type of music you play – even if you're in thrashiest of noise bands – the first rule of the guitar is to make sure your instrument is in tune. One of the most difficult aspects of learning to play any instrument is the ability to hear tiny variations in pitch and recognise when the intonation is correct. You may not be gifted with a "musical ear", but tuning *is* something that can be learned just like any other skill. On these two pages you will be shown techniques for what is known as "standard tuning". This means the notes from top to bottom are E, B, G, D, A and E. As you will see later in the book, this is not the only way in which you can tune your guitar.

TUNING METHODS

The pitch of any musical note is determined by the frequency of sound waves travelling through the air. This frequency is dependent on three different factors: the length, thickness and tension of the string. Although guitar strings are the same length in relation to one another, each open string is of a different thickness. The fattest strings give the lowest notes and the thinnest strings the highest. The pitch of a string can be altered by turning the machine head. This increases or reduces the tension and thus allows you to alter the pitch of the notes played on that string.

To play with other musicians your guitar must be tuned to "standard concert pitch". The only way of accurately

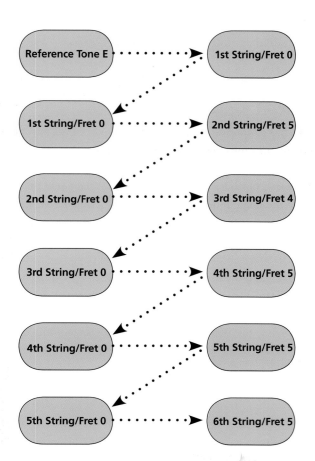

Guitar tuners come in many forms, even as mobile phone applications.

tuning your guitar is to use a reference tone, such as a guitar tune. An electronic keyboard will also do the trick nicely. All six tones can be heard on track 1/1 **1/1** of the CD.

TUNING TO A REFERENCE
The most common tuning methods revolve around tuning one string for use as a reference point for the other five strings:

● **1ST STRING (OPEN E)**   Play your reference tone. At the same time, play the top string. Turn the machine head until the notes ring together.

● **2ND STRING (OPEN B)**   Place your index finger on the 5th fret of the 2nd string. Play the note followed by the open 1st string. Adjust the 2nd string until the top two strings are in tune.

● **3RD STRING (OPEN G)**   Play the 4th fret of the 3rd string along with the open 2nd string. Adjust the 3rd string until in tune.

● **4TH STRING (OPEN D)**   Play the 5th fret of the 4th string with the open 3rd string. Adjust the 4th string until it is in tune.

● **5TH STRING (OPEN A)**   Play the 5th fret of the 5th string and the open 4th string. Adjust the 5th string until it is in tune.

● **6TH STRING (OPEN E)**   Play the 5th fret of the 6th string at the same time as the open 5th string. Adjust the machine head of the 6th string until the two strings are in tune.

FLOYD ROSE TUNING

Floyd Rose style locking tremolo units can make a guitar seem as if it's indestructible, but they do provide a number of problems for tuning. Here's how to do it correctly:

• Unlock the nut with an Allen key so that the strings can be altered using the machine heads.

• Tune the guitar in the standard way using the machine heads.

• When each string is just about in tune, lock the nut.

• All of the strings can be fine-tuned using the hand-adjustable screws found at the rear of the bridge mechanism.

Fine-tuning at the bridge end.

Locking and unlocking the nut.

OCTAVE INTERVALS

Here is another commonly used tuning method. This one compares the same notes played on different strings at intervals of a single OCTAVE.

An octave interval is the difference between one note and the same note of double the frequency. On a guitar fingerboard it is an interval of 12 frets between two notes on any string. Follow the diagram below, fretting the relevant notes and matching them to each of the open strings.

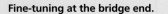

• **5TH STRING (OPEN A)**   Begin by tuning the 5th string (open A) to a reference tone.

• **1ST AND 6TH STRINGS (OPEN E)** Play the 7th fret of the 5th string (E) and use this to tune the 1st and 6th strings.

• **2ND STRING (OPEN B)** Play the 7th fret of the 1st string (B) and tune the open 2nd string to that note.

• **3RD STRING (OPEN G)**   Play the 8th fret of the 2nd string (G) and tune the open 3rd string to the same note.

• **4TH STRING (OPEN D)**   Play the 7th fret of the 3rd string (D) and tune the open 4th string to that note.

MIXED TUNING TECHNIQUE

You can also tune up using the top string and the lower frets:

• Tune the 1st string to a reference tone.
• Tune the 2nd string to the 7th fret of the 1st string.
• Tune the 3rd string to the 3rd fret of the 1st string.
• Tune the 4th string to the 3rd fret of the 2nd string.
• Tune the 5th string to the 2nd fret of the 3rd string.
• Tune the 6th string to the 2nd fret of the 4th string.

HARMONICS

If you place the tip of your finger gently on any of the strings directly over the 12th fret, and then pick the note, instead of hearing the fretted note you will hear a bell-like tone. This sound is a harmonic, which can also be generated by playing above other frets on the fingerboard.

You can also use harmonics to tune your guitar. First tune the 6th string to concert pitch. The other five strings can now be tuned by matching the harmonics as shown below.

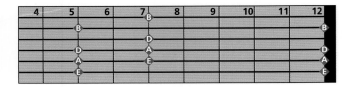

PICKS OR FINGERS?

If you want your guitar to make a noise, a string has to be struck by the right hand. This can be done either with the fingers (or fingernails) or with a pick. Whereas classical players, and other musicians who favour nylon-string guitars, invariably pluck the strings with the individual fingers, most rock musicians use a pick. This is a triangular-shaped object, usually made from plastic or tortoiseshell, which is held between the first finger and the thumb of the right hand. The two styles are by no means mutually exclusive: while it may be hard to execute a superfast solo with the fingers, arpeggios and other playing styles can be much more effectively executed by fingerpicking.

USING A PICK

Picks or plectrums (or even "plectra", if you prefer) come in many shapes and sizes. As innocent as these little bits of plastic may seem, the type you choose can have a significant effect on the tone of your playing: small, heavy-gauge picks, for example, are ideal for fast solo work; something thinner and more flexible is better suited for strumming. When starting out it's a good idea to get hold of as large a selection as possible. You'll almost certainly find yourself gravitating toward one particular type pretty quickly.

HOLDING THE PICK

Take the pick between the thumb and the top joint of the 1st finger. Hold it at an angle of 90° to the body of the guitar and parallel to the strings. The finger grip should be quite relaxed but tight enough so that it doesn't move around while you are playing. As you strike the string you should swivel the wrist and forearm, moving the joints of the thumb and fingers. It's important that this should be a gentle, flowing movement.

STROKES

There are two distinctly different ways to strike a string with a pick. They are commonly referred to as "downstrokes" and "upstrokes". A downstroke is made by taking the tip of the

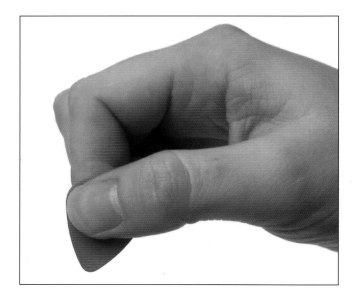

Hold the pick firmly between the thumb and the top joint of the first finger.

pick above the string and pushing down, leaving the string to vibrate. Unsurprisingly, the upstroke is the reverse – the tip is placed below the string and pulled upward.

When used independently, each stroke creates a unique type of sound. However, if you are truly to get to grips with this technique you must become well-acquainted with mixing

PICK MATTERS

Guitar picks fall into two broad categories: the "teardrop" variety (*see picture above*) and the triangular "wedge". The latter has one advantage in that when one of the corners wears down or is damaged there are two other usable ones remaining. These picks have plenty of surface to grip, so are less "fiddly" and harder to lose. They are also popular with bass guitarists. The smallest, hardest teardrop picks are sometimes also known as "jazz" picks. They are geared toward fast, precision playing.

Although plastic and (increasingly rarely) tortoiseshell are the most common materials for making picks, guitarists across the ages have found many alternatives. Queen's Brian May uses an old English "sixpenny bit" coin. One of the most unusual examples is the steel-tipped Dava Master Control pick, which actually alters its gauge depending on where it's held: focus toward the tip and you have a hard-gauge pick for lead work; gripping the flexible centre transforms it into a soft-gauge pick for rhythm playing.

When following instructions in written music, each stroke has its own symbol. This notation is usually found above the notes on the staff (although where that's inconvenient or difficult to interpret they can also be found below the notes on the staff).

⊓   V

DOWNSTROKE   **UPSTROKE**

strokes: this means making an upstroke after a downstroke in a single movement is the most effective way of playing. This is really the only way you can play fast lead passages.

When practising your picking technique, try to keep the speed at which you play the notes and the strength with which you hit the strings consistent.

USING THE FINGERS

Although there have been some notable exceptions, classical guitarists are trained to strike the strings with their fingernails rather than the pads of the fingers. But this is fairly uncommon outside of this field. The most commonly used alternative is the "clawhammer" style used by many steel-string players. This technique can also be used with an electric guitar.

The right hand positioning differs greatly from the classical method. Instead of resting the inside of the forearm at the upper

edge of the guitar's body, the clawhammer method rests the palm of the hand on the bridge.

When practising the clawhammer method make sure that you keep the thumb as straight as possible – the playing action should come from the thumb joint rather than the knuckle. Try to strike the notes evenly, playing through with a smooth, flowing motion.

When playing in this way, some musicians feel happier fitting special picks that slide over the fingers and thumb, creating what amounts to a set of long, false fingernails. These give a brighter tone and greater volume to this kind of playing.

HYBRID TECHNIQUE

An interesting hybrid originally devised by country musicians integrates playing with the fingers and a pick. It is both demanding and unorthodox in that it uses the "little" finger to play the top strings. To try out this method, the plectrum is held in the conventional way between the index finger and thumb – the remaining three fingers are then free to play each of the treble strings respectively. Once again, one of the most demanding aspects of this mode of playing is in getting the 3rd and 4th fingers of the right hand to operate independently.

Don't worry unduly about this technique for now. It's unquestionably quite difficult, and is best approached once you have become adept at playing both with the fingers and pick independently. It does illustrate, however (as you will realise the more you come into contact with different styles of music and playing), that hard-and-fast rules for playing the guitar are surprisingly thin on the ground.

The "clawhammer" picking technique.

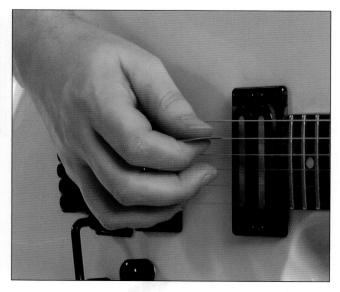

Fingerpicking with a pick (sometimes also called a plectrum).

NOTES AND THINGS

Any piece of music can be notated using a special language of lines and symbols. Most of the examples are shown throughout the book using standard music notation (five-line staves) accompanied by guitar tablature (six-line "tab"). If you are completely new to the idea of written music, the next few pages will give you a brief overview of what it's all about. This can seem a bit daunting when you first start, but don't worry – music works in an extremely logical way. If you learn to read music at the same time as learning to play an instrument, it will quickly become second nature – it's so much harder to learn when you have already become an accomplished (if notationally illiterate) musician.

NAMING THE NOTES

Before we start to look at written music we first need to clarify the most basic of principles: the nature of musical notes. Let's look at "When The Saints Go Marching In", a simple song that everyone knows. If you sing the first line of the tune – the one that goes: "OH, WHEN THE SAINTS…" – you will notice that it contains four different sounding notes. This is because each of these notes has a different PITCH. What's more, each of these notes can be scientifically defined in terms of the frequency of its soundwaves. This means that the pitch of any note is fixed.

OCTAVE INTERVALS

All traditional Western music uses the CHROMATIC system. This determines that music is made up of twelve different notes – that means twelve fixed pitches. These are best viewed as the notes of a piano keyboard (*see below*). Notes become higher in pitch as you move from left to right along the keyboard. The white notes on the keyboard are all named from A to G. Each

of the black notes can have two possible names, depending on their musical context, but we'll talk some more about those in a moment.

If you look at the way the notes are named on the diagram below, you can see that these sequences repeat themselves. When you get to G, the next white note along the keyboard is once again called A. Although this has the same name, it clearly has a higher pitch than the previous A in the sequence. If you play both notes, one after the other, you will hear that in spite of the different pitches, they have a similar quality – they are, in fact, the same note.

This special relationship is called an OCTAVE. The followers of Pythagoras (the same chap who conceived the theory about right-angled triangles) were the first to understand the basic mathematical principles that govern the way sound works. It was their work that taught us if you vibrate a string, by halving it's length you double the frequency of the oscillations. This creates the same note in the next cycle of named notes. If a vibrating string sounded the lowest-pitched "C" on the piano

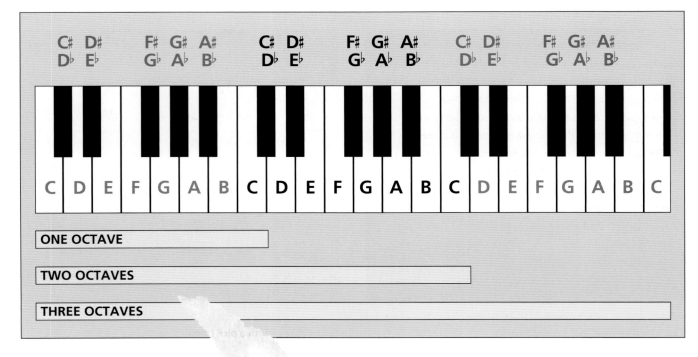

diagram across the page, then halving the length of that note (although obviously keeping the tension the same) would double its frequency, creating the same pitch as the next "C" along the keyboard.

SHARPS AND FLATS

The interval between any two adjacent notes is called a SEMITONE or HALF-STEP. This represents one-twelfth of an octave. In terms of the white keys, B and C are a semitone apart, as are E and F. However, the other white keys are two semitones apart. This is usually referred to as a TONE or STEP. If you move a semitone in either direction from these notes, you will play a black key. These can be given names relative to the notes on either side. For example, the black note between F and G can be called "F sharp" (which is written as F#) or G flat (notated as G♭). The term "sharp" means to raise the pitch of a note by a semitone, thus F# is the note F raised by a semitone. Similarly, the term flat means to lower a note by a semitone – so G♭ is the note G which has been lowered by a semitone.

Notes such as these, with two possible names, are referred to as being ENHARMONIC.

THE FINGERBOARD

The diagram on the right represents the fingerboard of a guitar and shows the notes on every string and fret up to and including the 14th fret. All guitars can go higher than this position – many can go right up to 24 frets. But once you get to the 12th fret – remember, there are twelve semitones that make up the octave – the cycle of notes repeats. To labour the point a little further, the 12th fret is exactly half way between the bridge and nut, which are the two extremities of each string.

The guitar differs fundamentally from the piano in one major respect: every note on the piano keyboard is of a different pitch; on a guitar the same pitches can be produced at different positions on the fingerboard. This is because of the nature of the guitar's six strings. Looking down from above on a standard guitar you will notice that the lowest strings (the ones to the left) are thicker than the higher-pitched strings on the right. This enables them to produce a different range of notes.

When standard E-A-D-G-B-E tuning is used, "Open E" on the 1st string (the top string), can also be played on the 5th fret of the 2nd string, the 9th fret of the 3rd string, the 14th fret of the 4th string, the 19th fret of the 5th string, and – if your guitar has sufficient range – the 24th fret of the 6th string. This opens up a great deal of choice to the guitarist when playing, and enables music of great harmonic complexity and sophistication to be played. There's no question: the guitar is a very cool instrument.

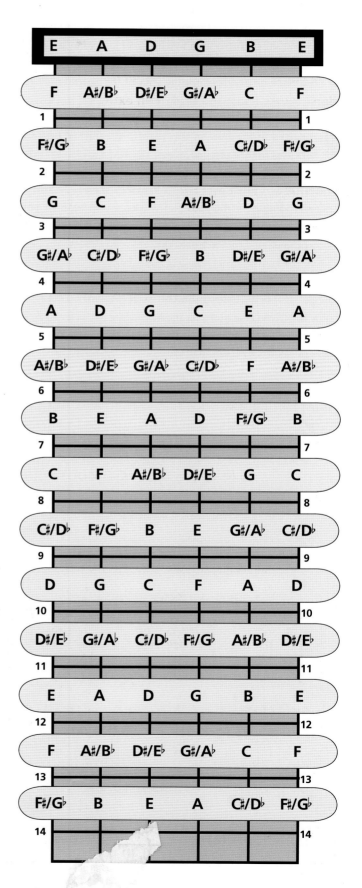

THE STAFF

Music is usually written on a five-line grid known as a STAFF (this becomes "staves" in the plural). A variety of symbols can be positioned on and between the lines of the staff to indicate the pitch and duration of a single note.

To make the pitch of the notes explicit, a CLEF symbol is positioned at the start of every staff. The TREBLE CLEF (𝄞) indicates higher pitched notes; the BASS CLEF (𝄢), the lower notes. Due to the range of the instrument, piano music is invariably written over two concurrent staves. Although understanding how the bass clef works is important if you want to arrange music for other instruments, guitar music can be accommodated on the treble clef.

FIXING THE PITCH

The clef defines the notes on and between each line on the staff. For a treble clef, the notes on the lines are fixed as E, G, B, D and F. The notes between the lines are F, A, C and E. Notes are represented by a circular symbol. By replacing the treble clef with a bass clef, the notes on the lines and spaces of that staff take on different names and pitches. By definition, the notes on the bass clef are lower in pitch than their treble counterparts. The lines are G-B-D-F-A; the spaces are A-C-E-G. The note E on the third space of the bass clef is exactly one octave below E on the first line of the treble clef.

LEARNING THE NAMES

Learning the note names on the lines and spaces of the staff is the most fundamental lesson in being able to read music. One of the most commonly used aids for memorising the notes on the lines and spaces of the treble clef is to use a mnemonic phrase. This is an easy-to-remember expression in which the first letter of each word (taken from bottom to top) represents the sequence of notes. For the notes on the line you can use the phrase "EAT GOOD BREAD DEAR FATHER"; for the spaces you can use the word "FACE". Similarly, on the bass clef try remembering the phrase "GOOD BOYS DESERVE FUN ALWAYS" to remember notes on the lines, and "A COW EATS GRASS" for the spaces.

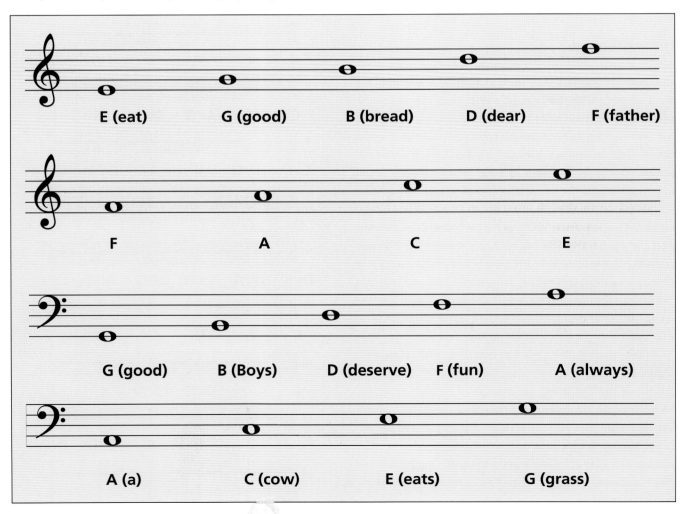

E (eat)   G (good)   B (bread)   D (dear)   F (father)

F   A   C   E

G (good)   B (Boys)   D (deserve)   F (fun)   A (always)

A (a)   C (cow)   E (eats)   G (grass)

LEDGER LINES

Each staff provides for a range of nine notes. That's not nearly enough to play most pieces of music. This range can be extended up or down using LEDGER LINES. Think of it as if extra staff lines have been drawn, but are only shown above, below or through the note itself.

In theory you can use as many ledger lines above or below a staff as necessary – three either side can accommodate every note up to the 12th fret on the top string.

The example below shows a range of nine notes, from G to A, played over both bass and treble staves. There is a crossover point where three of the notes – C, D and E – could be written on either staff.

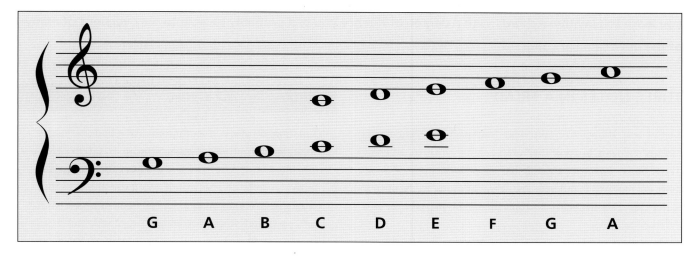

G A B C D E F G A

GUITAR TABLATURE

A complementary form of written music is the tablature system, which is often used for the guitar and other fretted instruments. Tablature (or "TAB" for short) is quite simply a six-line grid in which each line represents a string, from top to bottom. A number written on a line is an instruction to play a specific fret.

TAB has the advantage over conventional musical notation in that it provides very specific playing instructions. As you can see from the example below, the note E positioned on the top space of the staff can be played in the same register on every string of a

24-fret guitar. As you develop your playing skills you will quickly realise that notes don't always sound the same when played at different positions on the fingerboard.

The TAB we have used in this book is very simple indeed, merely representing the specific fretting instructions. In some printed forms of modern guitar music books, especially those produced in the USA, you may sometimes come across a hybrid form of TAB that adds the rhythm components of conventional notation to the TAB lines. An understanding of conventional notation makes this very easy to comprehend.

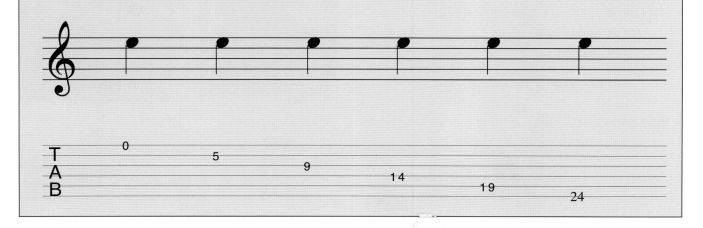

SIMPLE CHORDS

Chords are a central part of every type of music. A chord is the effect of three or more notes being played at the same time. The nine examples shown over the next four pages are the simplest and most commonly used chords in most forms of pop and rock music. They are referred to as OPEN-STRING CHORDS because they can be formed by fretting two or three notes close to the nut, meaning that at least three of the open strings – those that are not being fretted – are still in use. It's not too much of an exaggeration to say that if you learn to play these chords with a degree of fluency you will probably be able to play versions of many of the most familiar songs.

THREE NOTES IN A TRIAD

The chords shown over the next four pages are known as "triads". This is because they are made up of three different notes. Since, however, a guitar has six strings, some of those notes are repeated in different registers. For example, the open E major chord shown below features the note E played over two different octaves.

It is also possible to achieve a chordal effect by playing just two different notes, but this is technically an INTERVAL rather than a chord.

The note intervals used by every triad are always the same in relation to the chord's ROOT – the note by which the chord's key is identified. For a major triad, the sequence of intervals are named root, major 3rd and perfect 5th. For example, a C major triad uses the notes C (root), E (major 3rd) and G (perfect 5th).

E MAJOR

The E major chord is significant as the basic shape can be moved along the fingerboard to create a wide range of alternative chords. You can hear it played on track 1/2 of the CD.

● **5TH STRING**   Place the 2nd finger of your left hand behind the 2nd fret of the 5th string.

● **4TH STRING**   Place the 3rd finger of your left hand on the 2nd fret of the 4th string.

● **3RD STRING**   Place the 1st finger of your left hand on the 1st fret of the 3rd string.

● **STRUM**   Holding a pick in your right hand, bring it slowly across all six strings and let each one sustain until the chord fades.

CHORD DIAGRAMS

The chord diagrams used throughout the book are simple to understand. Think of each diagram as a if you were looking over the fretboard of a guitar. The dots placed between frets on the strings represent the positions where your fingers should go. The number on each dot tells you which finger you should use. Beside the chord chart you will find the note names of each string. If the note name is blank then the string should not be played.

1/2

E
B
G♯
E
B
E

0
0
1
2
2
0

THREE-CHORD TRICKS

The next two chords you will see are A major and D major. These chords are closely related to the E major you have just played. All three chords are related by the intervals of their root notes. Many of the best-known rock, pop, blues and country songs have comprised only this "three-chord trick". Such chord structures are also sometimes known as "one-four-fives", and are written down using Roman numerals (I-IV-V).

A MAJOR

When you play the A major chord, the 6th string is optional. The note is shown alongside the chord diagram in brackets. This "bottom E" is musically correct, but because it is lower in pitch than the chord's root note, in can create an imbalance in the overall sound. In some situations, playing this note simply makes the chord sound wrong.

- **4TH STRING**   Place the 1st finger behind the 2nd fret.

- **3RD STRING**   Place the 2nd finger on the 2nd fret.

- **2ND STRING**   Place the 3rd finger on the 2nd fret.

D MAJOR

There are several alternatives you can choose from when playing a D major chord. One approach is to ignore the bottom two strings, only playing the notes of the other four. More common, perhaps, is to include the 5th string – even though the note A is lower in pitch than the root D, the chord still generally sounds good played this way. These approaches can be difficult when strumming quickly in both directions with a pick. As a consequence, some players prefer to bring the thumb around the back of the neck to play the F♯ on the 2nd fret of the 1st string.

- **3RD STRING**   Place the 1st finger on the 2nd fret.

- **2ND STRING**   Place the 3rd finger on the 3rd fret.

- **1ST STRING**   Place the 2nd finger on the 2nd fret.

FLUENCY

The first stage of success for any guitarist is in getting the left hand to change chords without faltering. Try not to be discouraged at first: everyone from Segovia to the guy in the funny rubber mask in Slipknot has been here at some stage. And you can bet that they found it just as difficult.

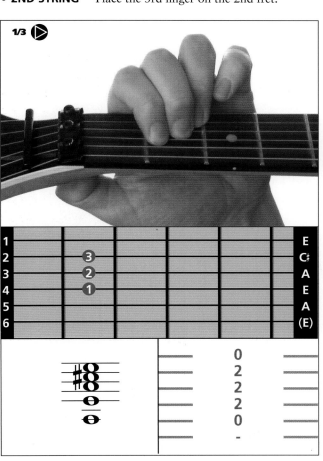

MORE MAJOR CHORDS

Now let's take a look at open-string major chords in the keys of G, C and F.

G MAJOR

There are two possibilities for playing a full six-string voicing for this chord. The most conventional one is shown in the chord diagram below (*left*):

- **6TH STRING**   Place the 2nd finger on the 3rd fret.

- **5TH STRING**   Place the 1st finger on the 2nd fret.

- **1ST STRING**   Place the 3rd finger on the 3rd fret.

- **STRUM**   Play all six strings.

A more demanding alternative requires the use of all four fingers. Instead of using the 3rd finger to play the 1st string, it moves across to play the 3RD FRET OF THE 2ND STRING; the 4th finger then plays the 3RD FRET OF THE 1ST STRING. The fingering on the 5th and 6th strings remains the same. This shape creates a chord that is better-balanced and fuller-sounding.   1/5 ▶

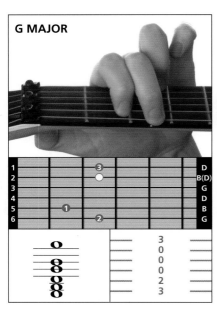

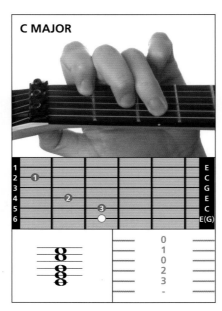

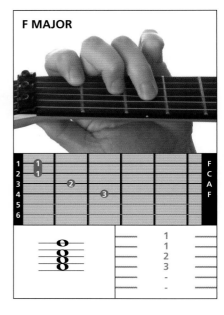

C MAJOR

The standard shape for C major is shown in the diagram above (*centre*):

- **5TH STRING**   Place the 3rd finger on the 3rd fret.

- **4TH STRING**   Place the 2nd finger on the 2nd fret.

- **2ND STRING**   Place the 1st finger on the 1st fret.

- **STRUM**   Play the first five strings.

A nice six-string alternative is to shift the 3rd finger across to the 3rd fret of the 6th string – use the 4th finger to play the 3rd fret of the 5th string.   1/6 ▶

F MAJOR

The diagram above (*right*) is slightly unsatisfactory – but nonetheless usable – version of the F major chord. It uses only the top four strings, and so can sound a little on the thin side:

- **1ST/2ND STRING** Place the tip of the 1st finger so that it covers the 1st fret of the 1st AND 2nd strings.

- **3RD STRING**   Place the 2nd finger on the 2nd fret.

- **4TH STRING**   Place the 3rd finger on the 3rd fret.

You'll learn a much better version of this chord later in the book.   1/7

As a guitarist, your fingers are your most basic tools, so you should take care of them.

When you start playing, you will quickly notice callouses appearing on the pads of your fingers. This is completely normal and all part of the transition your hand has to make. If these get too sore, stop playing for a while or they may well blister.

Once your finger tips are toughened up, treat them with a moisturising cream to prevent them flaking. You should also wear kitchen gloves when you wash up – you don't want those fingers going soft on you again.

MINOR CHORDS

The final three chords we'll introduce in this chapter are fundamentally different from the six that you have already seen. They are still triads, but they are MINOR TRIADS. A minor chord is created by "flattening" the third note of a major triad – that means reducing it by a semitone, or one fret on the fingerboard. For example, a C major triad consists of the notes C (root), E (3rd) and G (5th); to convert it to C minor, the E becomes E♭.

We'll look at some more of the theory behind chord building on page 88.

E MINOR

Fingering for the E minor chord is shown in the diagram below (*left*).

● **5TH STRING** Use the 2nd finger to hold down the 2nd fret.

● **4TH STRING** Use the 3rd finger on the 2nd fret.

You can also play E minor using just the 1st and 2nd fingers, but the advantage of using the voicing below is that by removing the 1st finger you can switch between E major and E minor chords. Try strumming this change a few times and you will quickly familiarise yourself with the minor sound. **1/8** ▶

A MINOR

Fingering for the A minor chord is shown in the diagram below (*centre*).

● **4TH STRING** The 2nd finger plays the 2nd fret.

● **3RD STRING** The 3rd finger plays the 2nd fret.

● **2ND STRING** The 1st finger plays the 1st fret. **1/9** ▶

D MINOR

Fingering for the D minor chord is shown in the diagram below (*right*).

● **3RD STRING** The 2nd finger plays the 2nd fret.

● **2ND STRING** The 3rd finger plays the 3rd fret. Take care that your finger doesn't mute the 1st string.

● **1ST STRING** The 1st finger plays the 1st fret.

EXERCISES

At this point, your fingers will probably be in some pain. Don't worry, it's just one of the many ways you'll suffer for your art.

The first thing you'll notice is muscular pain in your fretting fingers. To help get your fingers used to fretting chords, and to improve your general mobility, try this exercise. Stand up with the guitar strapped across your shoulder. Relax your arms so they hang down beside your hips. Now bring your left hand around the back of the neck and carefully fret an E major chord. Hold your left hand in place for 20 seconds or more, and then release your arm again. If you perform this exercise every few hours while you're learning, your fingers will soon begin to understand what's expected of them.

For a more advanced exercise, work through all the open-string chords you've so far played.

Only the top four or five strings should be played. **1/10** ▶

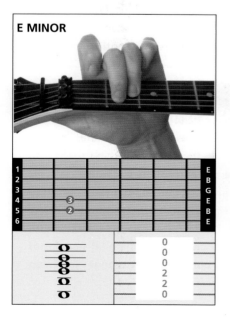

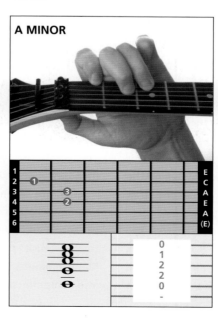

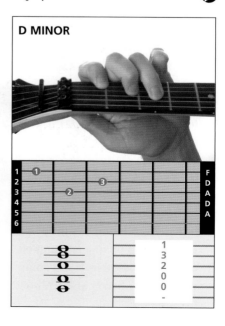

TIMING AND RHYTHM

Playing in time is a critical skill that every musician simply has to develop. But what does this actually mean? Keeping time is the ability to play a piece of music or accompany other musicians at the correct speed, without getting faster or slowing down. For most beginners it is the hardest skill to master, especially when most of the attention is focused on getting the fingers to behave properly. The fundamental problem is that whenever you play a note or chord, your right hand has to anticipate the exact moment that the pick or fingers will strike the string. Don't be put off if at first your playing sounds ragged or inconsistent. Eventually this skill becomes second nature – and will improve with practice.

TEMPO AND RHYTHM

TEMPO is one of two elements of timing; the other is RHYTHM. The tempo refers to the specific speed of a piece of music, which is usually measured in "beats per minute" (bpm). Printed guitar music often shows a tempo instruction at the top of the page above the staffs. The example below indicates that a piece of music should be played at a tempo of 120 beats per minute.

$$\quad = 120$$

Most classical music is specified only in terms of a general tempo, using Italian terms such as *Presto* (very fast), *Allegro* (fast) or *Adagio* (slow).

RHYTHM AND THE GUITAR

The term RHYTHM refers to the way in which notes are played or accented. It is the rhythm that creates the "feel" of a piece of music. The rhythm guitar has played a vital role in all forms of ensemble music since the early days of jazz and blues, and before amplification had given the guitar a voice "above" the music. It was only during the 1930s, when pioneering jazzmen such as Charlie Christian started experimenting with guitars fitted with electronic pickups, that the guitar joined the brass and woodwind instruments capable of having solo or "lead" parts that were audible in a large orchestra or band.

DEVELOPING TIMING SKILLS

There are many different ways in which you can develop your sense of timing, but one truth is certain: IT WILL ONLY COME WITH PRACTICE.

The time-honoured approach is to play along with records or CDs. However, your favourite music will not always be tuned to concert pitch, so you may have to re-tune the guitar. Alternatively, you can use a traditional metronome – a clockwork device which you can set to "click" at a specific tempo. A drum machine or computer sequencer can also fulfil the same kind of function.

To help you along the way, the CD that comes with this book contains nine specially recorded backing tracks in a variety of styles and tempos that you can use for practice.

STRICT TEMPO

If you perform with a group of musicians, unless you are playing to a mechanical rhythm – a drum machine or software sequencer, for example – the group will almost invariably create its own groove, pushing and pulling against the basic tempo at various times. (This is, of course, outside of an orchestral setting, where the tempos maintained by the conductor represent strict instruction.)

Far from being a sign of poor musicianship, the creation of a unique and unified "feel" is the hallmark of a good ensemble. If you doubt this in any way, listen to the house bands of the Motown or Stax labels, who backed some of the greatest soul singers of the 1960s, or James Brown's 1970s backing band, the JBs. If you tracked the beats per minute on a bar-by-bar basis, you may well find tempo variations of up to around 5%, and yet each band is playing so tightly as a unit that these time differences are not perceptible to the ear.

In an era when much of our popular music is based around computerised rhythm, it's interesting that many producers and manufacturers have gone to great length to "humanise" their sounds by using digital samples of real drummers, or by building slight changes in tempo into computer sequences.

ALL ABOUT NOTES

A note played on the guitar has three basic characteristics: PITCH, VOLUME and DURATION. The pitch is governed by the fret position; the volume by how hard the string has been struck; the duration by how long the note is allowed to sustain. In written music, the overall tempo is governed by how many BEATS are played every minute. An individual note obtains its value in relation to the length of that beat. The longest note value is a SEMIBREVE (or WHOLE NOTE, using US terminology) which is a note sustained for four beats. Subsequent notes may be halved in value until they reach the HEMI-DEMI-SEMIQUAVER, whose value is a sixteenth of a beat (although in practice this is rarely used in guitar music).

Each note type has its own unique symbol, all of which are shown on the table below. Each note below a CROTCHET (QUARTER NOTE) has a series of "flags" attached to the stem. When groups of these notes appear on the staff, the flag are replaced by "beams" which join the notes together.

UNDERSTANDING NOTE VALUES

A simple exercise to help you understand the breakdown of note values is to strum a chord and count out beats while the notes are still ringing. Continuously count in seconds from one to four, emphasising "one" – the first beat of the bar – each time. If you have a metronome or drum machine, this will be easier.

SEMIBREVE CHORD Strike the chord on "one" and let it sustain through "two", "three" and "four".

MINIM CHORDS Strike the chord on "one" and let it sustain through "two"; strike the chord again on "three" and let it sustain through "four".

CROTCHET CHORDS Strike the chord on "one", and again on "two", "three" and "four".

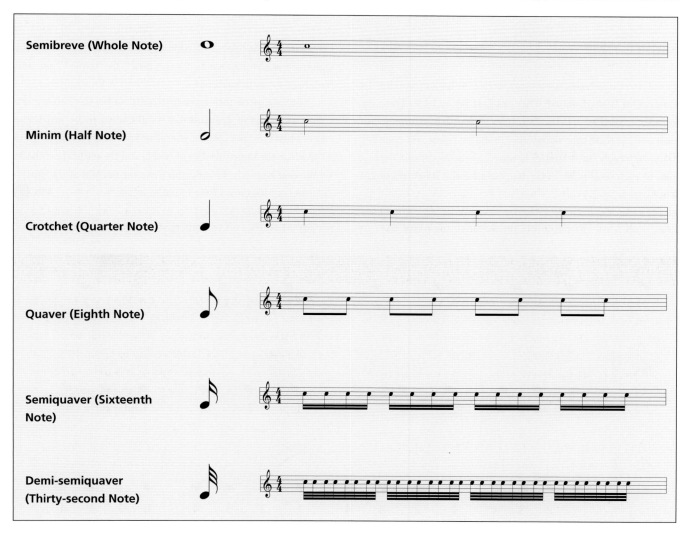

COMMON TIME

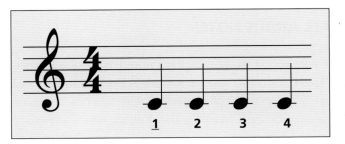

When notes are written down, they are grouped together in small blocks called BARS. These are represented as vertical lines that run from the top to the bottom of the staff.

Each bar contains a defined number of BEATS. It's easiest to explain this idea in terms of counting numbers out aloud. Slowly and evenly count out 1-2-3-4-2-2-3-4-3-2-3-4-4-2-3-4, emphasizing the underlined numbers. You have counted out four bars, with each single bar containing four beats.

You may have noticed that some of the written music you've seen on previous pages has begun with a pair of numbers, one sitting above the other on the staff to the left of the notes. These two numbers indicate the TIME SIGNATURE of the piece of music. The number at the top tells you how many beats there are in each bar, and the bottom number tells you the time value of each of those beats.

This can be a tricky notion for many beginners to grasp, so let's look at the example above. You will see four beats in the bar, each one with a value of a crotchet (quarter note), with a duration of a quarter of the bar. It does not mean that each bar has to consist only of four quarter notes, but simply that irrespective of how many notes are played in the bar, their total value must add up to the top figure, which in this case is four.

A piece of music like this, which has four beats in the bar is said to have a time signature of FOUR-FOUR. (This is usually written in text as "4/4".) Four-four time is far and away the most commonly used time signature in rock, pop and just about every other musical genre. Indeed, its use is so wide that it is also known as COMMON TIME and is sometimes abbreviated on the staff as the letter "C", or in its more stylised form, 𝄴.

SIMPLE TIME

There are three basic time signatures that accommodate the majority of Western music. They are 2/4, 3/4 and 4/4. These are known as SIMPLE TIME. Examples of four-bar groupings for each of these three time signatures are shown below. Try counting along with each line of music, as above, always accenting the first beat of each bar. In this way, the count for the four bars of 2/4 would go 1-2-1-2-1-2-1-2.

With its unique and unmistakable feel, the 3/4 time signature is also known as "waltz time" or "triple" time and has three beats in each bar.

You will probably have noticed that on the surface the time signatures in 2/4 and 4/4 would seem to be much the same. However, the former would require twice as many bars to produce the same number of notes, and the natural emphasis on the first beat would substantially alter the feel of the music. 2/4 time is often used for marching music.   **1/11** ▶

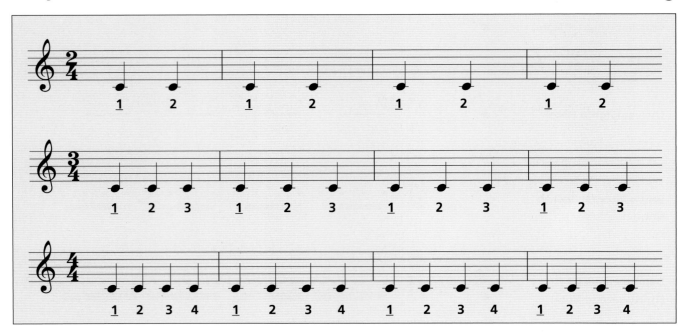

COMPOUND TIME

All of the simple time signatures (or METERS as they are also sometimes known) shown on the previous page can also be grouped into triplets – groups of three. This produces what is known as a COMPOUND time signature.

Looking at the first example below using 2/4 time, the two beats are played as two groups of three, which creates a bar made up of six beats. This is a time signature of 6/4, or 6/8 if semiquavers (eighth notes) are being used.

In a similar fashion, bars of triple time (3/4) can be played in groups of three, producing a compound time signature of 9/4 or 9/8, both of which have nine beats to the bar.

When bars of 4/4 time are grouped in the same way, a compound time signature of 12/4 or 12/8 is the result, with twelve beats in each bar. **1/12** ▶

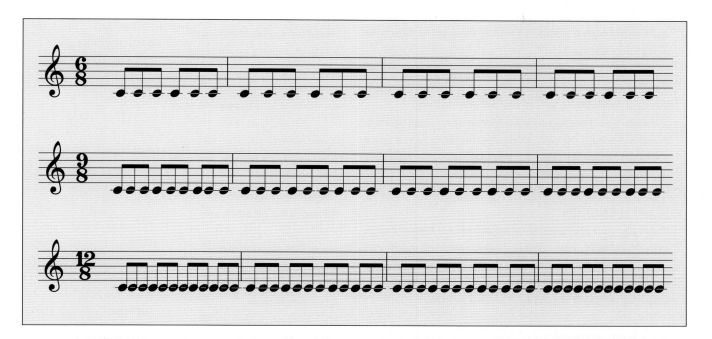

TEMPO AND TIME SIGNATURES IN PRACTICE

It's not always easy to get a feel for tempo and rhythm from reading a description. To put it in clearer context, here is a chart that lists the approximate tempos of some well-known pieces of music in terms of beats per minute.

With a little experience it will become possible to give a broad estimate of the tempo at which a piece of music is being played.

Here are few general rule-of-thumb examples: slow rock ballad (80-100 bpm); slow blues (90-100 bpm); classic disco (120 bpm); techno or garage (130-150 bpm); drum and bass (150-180 bpm); fast rocker (beyond 160 bpm); thrash metal/nu-metal (180 bpm and beyond).

Song/Artist	BPM
Bittersweet Symphony/The Verve	90
Blood And Thunder/Mastodon	185
Clint Eastwood/Gorillaz	85
Communication Breakdown/Led Zeppelin	170
Everybody Hurts/R.E.M.	80
How You Remind Me/Nickelback	130
I'm Waiting For The Man/Velvet Underground	125
In The End/Linkin Park	105
Jump/Van Halen	135
Layla/Derek and the Dominos	120
Novocaine For The Soul/Eels	85
Paranoid/Black Sabbath	165
Paranoid Android/Radiohead	85
People=Shit/Slipknot	240
Satisfaction/Rolling Stones	125
Smooth/Santana	115
Song 2/Blur	130

GUITAR RESOURCES ON THE INTERNET

The Internet is truly one of the great wonders of the modern age. And musicians were among the first to see its potential for both sharing information and selling their own products. Nowadays, of course, web presence is a basic necessity for any muso, whether using his or her own websites or social networking services such as MySpace and Facebook. Either route enables the musician to have direct contact with fellow artists or fans and followers anywhere across the world, keeping them up to date with news and their wares.

You won't be surprised to know that there is a vast resource of information on guitars, guitarists and the music business available to you at the tap of a button.

Below you'll see just a tiny selection of interesting sites. If you're looking for something specific, turn to the good old search engines – just type in your enquiry and wait for the pages to appear.

SEARCH ENGINES

These are your shortcuts to Internet heaven. Remember to experiment with your entries – using different words can yield very different results. And don't always use the same search engine: they all work in slightly different ways, and may give different results to the same enquiry.

www.aolsearch.com
www.ask.com
www.altavista.com
www.bing.com
www.excite.com
www.google.com
www.lycos.com
www.yahoo.com

SOCIAL NETWORKING

There are numerous social networking and blogging sites that may be invaluable to the musician.

www.myspace.com
www.facebook.com
www.youtube.com
www.linkedin.com
www.blogger.com
www.wordpress.com
www.typepad.com

THE GUITAR

www.a1guitar.com
On-line lessons on guitar technique and songwriting.

www.instructables.com/id/Build-Your-Own-Electric-Guitar!
How to build your own electric guitar.

www.crossroads-guitar.com
Video-streaming on-line courses.

www.datadragon.com/education/reading/
An introduction to reading music.

www.electric-guitar.co.uk
Downloadable lessons and tablature.

www.endprod.com/tab
All about guitar tablature.

www.farhatguitar.com
Video tutorials.

www.fender.com
The home of Fender guitars.

www.gibson.com
The history of the venerable Gibson company, along with their latest products.

www.guitar.about.com
Wide variety of general guitar resources.

www.guitarclassroom.com
Well-designed multimedia teaching site.

www.guitarforbeginners.com
One of the simplest and easiest to use tutorials on the web.

www.guitarist.com/classical
Classical guitar homepage.

www.guitarsite.com
An excellent place to look for information on playing the guitar in any style.

www.guitarsolos.com
General playing resource.

www.harmonycentral.com/community/guitars
The ultimate general store for the guitarist.

www.jazzguitar.com
This site is dedicated to jazz guitar.

www.looknohands.com/chordhouse
Chords galore, both simple and advanced.

www.martin.com
Home of the company started by the legendary C. F. Martin.

metalscript.homestead.com
Specialists in metal tabs.

www.music.indiana.edu/som/courses/rhythm/glossary.html
Music college website that teaches you the basics of rhythm and meter. Also features a useful glossary of terminology.

www.prsguitars.com
The homepage of Paul Reed Smith guitars.

www.tabspedia.com
Guitar chords and scale finder.

www.torvund.net/guitar
Chord progressions.

www.tuckandpatti.com/pick-finger_tech.html
Clear and detailed instructions on fingerpicking techniques.

www.worldguitar.com
Online lessons.

AMPLIFICATION AND EFFECTS

www.amptone.com
Reams of information on how to get the most useful amplifier sounds.

www.ampage.org
The ultimate site for gearheads.

www.buildyourownclone.com
Build your own guitar effects.

www.geofex.com
An introduction to the world of electronic effects.

www.instructables.com/id/Guitar-Tube-Amp
Build your own valve amplifier.

www.start-playing-guitar.com/guitar-amplifier.html
Useful novice guide to amplification.

www.zvex.com
Boutique effects manufacturer with plenty of other interesting information.

SOUND RECORDING

www.homerecording.about.com
Want to hear yourself on CD? This is the place to start.

www.recordingwebsite.com
Good general guide to home recording.

www.soundonsound.com/
Archives of equipment reviews from *Sound On Sound*, Europe's premier sound technology magazine.

www.soundwave.com
Website for sound engineering professionals.

THE BUSINESS

www.ascap.com
The American royalties organization

www.bmi.com
The thorny issue of musicians' royalties.

www.musicbusinesspage.com
Music industry links worldwide.

www.prsformusic.com
How to get paid when your music is played on TV or radio. Also covers mechanicals rights.

CHAPTER 2
ROCK BASICS

In this chapter we'll look at some of the fundamental elements that make up rock music. Like most of the other chapters throughout the book, lessons – if that's what you want to call them – are designed to be played as an accompaniment to a backing track found on the CD. This will allow you to put theoretical ideas in a practical context. The most important musical idea we'll be looking at here is the creation of rhythm. Initially, we'll concentrate on those that play directly on the beat, but more complex ideas are incorporated later on. We'll also take our first look at the important issue of sound: however it's produced, at the heart of most forms of rock music is some form of distortion. You'll see how these noises are created and how to make the best use of them.

WHAT IS "ROCK" AND WHERE DID IT COME FROM?

Nobody really knows who first coined the term "rock". The biggest claimant is US disc jockey legend Alan Freed. In 1951 he had a radio show called *The Moondog House Rock and Roll Party*. The music he played was almost entirely black rhythm and blues. The name of the show was likely to have been a joke at the expense of the conservative station owners who wouldn't have known that words like "rockin'", "rollin'" and "reelin'" were all black euphemisms for sex.

A young white man, Freed was one of the most important figures in taking rhythm and blues to white audiences. He was also a purist, refusing to play toned-down white cover versions of R&B hits. He soon achieved nationwide popularity, and became the major cultural influence over a generation.

By 1954, rock and roll became a known musical term. Bill Haley and the Comets took the world by storm with "Rock Around the Clock", and then, in 1956, Elvis Presley appeared. The classic rock and roll era petered out in around 1959, when hordes of dull and unprovocative light balladeers started to clog up the airwaves. It took the British "Beat Boom" – in particular the arrival of the Beatles – to breathe life into the charts again in 1964.

By this time, music was developing a split personality. Although lightweight "pop" guitar bands dominated the charts, there was a more serious-minded underground scene developing. The folk "protest" movement may have given lyrics a poignant edge for the first time. But it was the young, white, blues-oriented musicians that started to proclaim themselves as "rock" bands – almost as if to draw a line of distinction between themselves and their lightweight contemporaries.

IN THIS CHAPTER YOU'LL LEARN...

- About rock history
- How to use repeat symbols
- How to work out songs from a recording
- About plug-in effects pedals
- How to play to a backing track
- Minim (half note) rhythms
- Quaver (eighth note) rhythms
- Mixing note lengths
- Muting strings with the right hand
- Staccato
- Tied notes

- How to read chord charts
- Songwriting tips
- How to create distortion effects in an amplifier
- About multiple effects units
- Semibreve (whole note) rhythms
- Crotchet (quarter note) rhythms
- Semiquaver (sixteenth note) rhythms
- Muting strings with the left hand
- Rests
- Dotted notes
- Crescendo and diminuendo

THE ORIGINAL HEAVY ROCK BAND

In the early '60s, the British blues scene had been low profile, and centred largely on London. 1963, however, saw the explosion of the British Blues Boom, with small-time R&B cover bands like the Rolling Stones suddenly finding themselves pop sensations.

The Yardbirds, featuring Britain's best young blues guitarist Eric Clapton, looked set to follow in their footsteps. But after a disappointingly mainstream pop debut single hit the charts, Clapton became disillusioned and left the band. His was immediately taken under the wing of veteran blues crusader John Mayall. In his band, the Bluesbreakers, Clapton created a template for what would become the essential rock sound. With his Marshall stacks and a Gibson Les Paul guitar, he perfected the art of overdriving the valves to create a beautiful feedback-assisted sustain.

In 1966, Clapton left Mayall to form Cream (*below*). They were the original power trio. Their recipe for success? Driving guitar riffs played in unison with the bass guitar over thundering drums. The heavy rock sound was born.

CHORD CHARTS

Outside of the classical domain, where music is invariably notated, the player has a limited scope within which they can give their own interpretations of a piece of music. In other less formal fields, the most common way of working is to play from a chord chart. The backing tracks that form the basis of each lesson, and which can be heard on the CD that accompanies the book, are all described using a simple form of chord chart.

MAKING LIFE EASIER

Chord charts can take may different forms. Some can be little more than barely legible scraps of paper with basic chord names attached – and you might be surprised at how commonly this is the case. Others may be more sophisticated, written out on manuscript paper, and containing additional performance instructions, such as time signatures, rhythms, repetitions or suggested bass notes or bass lines. The form we'll use contains chord names and a limited degree of rhythm information and simple repeat instructions.

Repeats are used in what could be thought of as musical shorthand. They can save enormous amounts of time, not to mention cutting back on the otherwise inevitable writers' cramp. In formal music there is a vast array of repeat symbols available (*see box*). Some of these are so complex that they can take a good deal of time and experience to learn. But this approach is largely unnecessary in rock and pop music, which, by and large, revolve around a simple series of repeating sequences.

We will be using two symbols taken from this vocabulary. These will allow us to signify repeated chords from within a

Written music has many other repeat symbols. The DAL SEGNO sign (𝄌 D.S.) instructs the player to return to and repeat an earlier point in the music marked with SEGNO symbol (𝄋). The term DA CAPO (meaning "from the head" in Italian) tells the player to repeat from the beginning.

bar, and bars that are to be repeated. The first of these symbols is indicated by a "slash" character, the second by a standard "percentage" sign:

REPEAT PREVIOUS CHORD WITHIN BAR

REPEAT PREVIOUS BAR

Look at the box below for an explanation of how repeat symbols work in our chord charts.

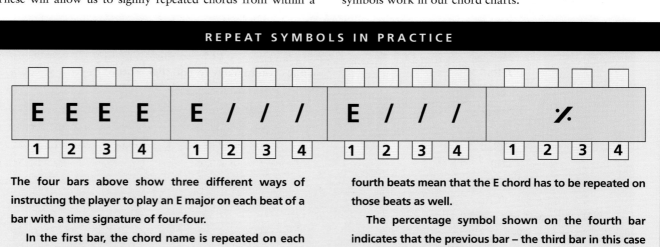

REPEAT SYMBOLS IN PRACTICE

The four bars above show three different ways of instructing the player to play an E major on each beat of a bar with a time signature of four-four.

In the first bar, the chord name is repeated on each beat of the bar.

The second bar shows the use of the first repeat symbol. An E chord is played on the first beat – that chord is written down. On the second beat you will see a slash symbol. This tells you that you have to play the chord that was last noted once again. The slash on the third and

fourth beats mean that the E chord has to be repeated on those beats as well.

The percentage symbol shown on the fourth bar indicates that the previous bar – the third bar in this case – has to be repeated in full.

Since this is an informal system there are no rules about how chords should be notated. In general, a letter on its own refers to the chord in its "major" form. Minor chords can be noted with the letter name followed by a small "m" (Em, for example).

WRITING A (SORT OF) SONG

The process of composing a song is one the great complexities of music. And the vast majority of pop and rock songs are not composed in any theoretical sense. Some of this is down to relative simplicity of most pop and rock song structures. The vast majority use a relatively narrow range of chord progressions.

As you work through the book you should gain something of an insight into the mechanics of harmony, melody and rhythm – the three main components. You will understand why certain chords sound better than others when they are played one after the other. And why, for example, when you strum a C major chord on your guitar, not all of the notes that could possibly be sung with it actually sound very nice.

For now, though, here are some very common chord sequences, the kind that have been used in numerous pop songs. Play each four-bar sequence over and over again. You'll notice how naturally they flow together.

Once you can play the chord sequence fluidly, try singing along. It doesn't matter what words you use – they can be any nonsense you make up as you go along – and it doesn't matter what tune you sing. You will quickly notice that some of the notes you are singing sound more pleasant than others, and you'll then start to gravitate toward the nice CONSONANT notes.

Here are the sequences:

A MAJOR	E MINOR	D MAJOR	A MAJOR
C MAJOR	G MAJOR	D MAJOR	G MAJOR
G MAJOR	E MINOR	C MAJOR	D MAJOR
E MAJOR	D MAJOR	A MAJOR	D MAJOR

ROUTINING A SONG

All conventional pop and rock songs have an identifiable structure. Understanding the way these structures work can be useful both in composing your own songs and working out existing songs so they can be arranged for other musicians. This process is sometimes known as "routining".

If you listen to your favourite songs you will be able to hear these component parts clearly. A typical rock or pop track may consist of something like this:

INTRODUCTION

(A)

VERSE

(B)

CHORUS

(C)

VERSE

(B)

CHORUS

(C)

MIDDLE "EIGHT"

(D)

SOLO

(THIS IS USUALLY A VERSE SEGMENT)

(B)

CHORUS

(C)

ENDING

(E)

ROUTINING EXERCISE

To try this idea out for yourself, take any popular song. For convenience choose one with a four-four beat. Start by playing along with the recording. If you don't know the chords, play the notes on a single string until you locate a root note.

Once you have worked out the chords that you need to use, you are ready to start working out the structure. If you find there are some "tricky" chords in the song that you can't work out immediately, don't let that slow you down: sticking with its root note will do for now. If you have trouble working out the simpler chords, refer to the key signature of the song (usually, but not always, the opening chord) and the chords built on the major scale. To be honest, in the case of many simple pop songs you're likely to find that most of the chords you need will be in there somewhere.

When you are familiar with the song itself, some patterns will emerge quickly. You will be able to isolate the verses and choruses. (By definition, a chorus is a repeating refrain.) Listen out for whenever something "different" happens, identify it and give it a unique letter. You should now be able to write down the structure of the song in terms of a sequence of letters.

If the occasion calls for it – if the music has to be played according to a set rhythm – you can add time values. The easiest way of doing this is to indicate the note stems above the chords.

| CROTCHET | QUAVER | SEMIQUAVER |

DISTORTION: THE SOUND OF ROCK

These days, rock music comes in many different guises, sporting many varied types of sound. One thing, however, that can be almost guaranteed is that somewhere in there you'll find a distorted guitar sound. There are two basic approaches to distortion: let your amplifier do the work; or use an external effect unit. Most modern guitarists use a combination of both.

DISTORTION IN AMPLIFIERS

Before discussing how to create amplifier distortion, let's take a look at the workings of a typical valve guitar amplifier.

POWER SUPPLY

All commercial guitar amps are fitted with high-quality power supply units. Electricity taken from the AC mains is transformed to a higher voltage and rectified to DC current through valve or semiconductor diodes. Circuitry smooths the direct current and provides different voltages to the various stages.

THE PREAMPLIFIER

Each of the input channels has its own preamplifier stage. This consists of valve circuitry to boost the initial guitar signal, a set of tone controls to alter the equalisation, a volume control governing the output, and second-stage valve circuitry to boost the loss of signal voltage resulting from the tone controls.

THE POWER AMPLIFIER

Bringing together the outputs from the preamplifier stage, the power amplifier, and its associated master volume control, governs the overall output signal that passes to the loudspeaker.

CREATING DISTORTION

Overdriving the preamplifier stage (boosting the volume) distorts the original signal. This can be modified by the tone controls, and the final level controlled by the master volume.

"Now here is an instrument that is capable of spewing forth true obscenity, you know? If ever there's an obscene noise to be made on an instrument, it's going to come out of a guitar... let's be realistic about this: the guitar can be the single most blasphemous device on the face of the earth. That's why I like it... the disgusting stink of a too-loud electric guitar: now that's my idea of a good time!"

Frank Zappa (1940-1993)

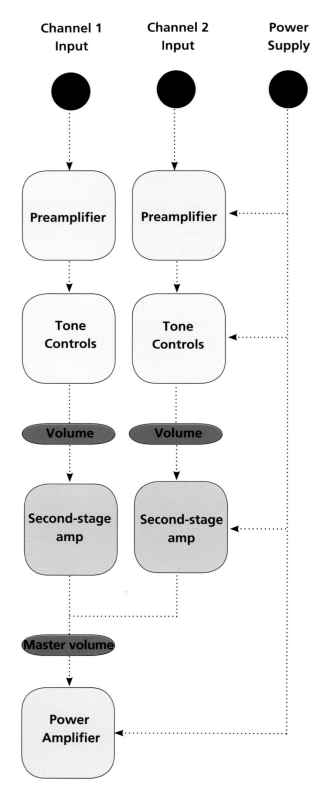

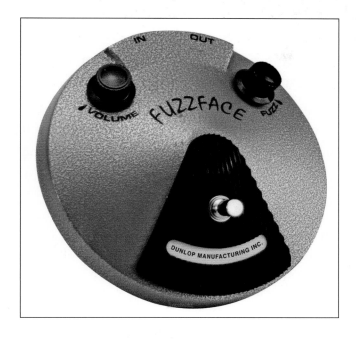

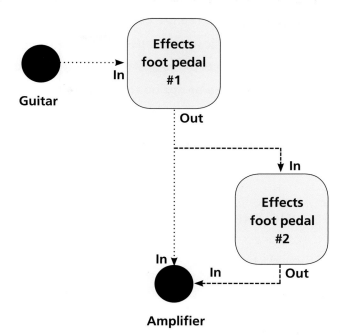

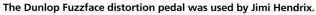

The Dunlop Fuzzface distortion pedal was used by Jimi Hendrix.

EXTERNAL EFFECTS

Electronic effects units – whether they are simple foot pedals or costly digital multi-effect units – enable the guitarist to produce a vastly greater range of sounds than could previously be achieved with just an amplifier and a guitar.

If you plug your guitar straight into an amplifier, by the time the signal emerges from the loudspeaker, it will already have gone through a wide range of tonal colouration in the preamplifier itself. Many players, however, prefer the convenience and versatility of altering their sound by plugging into an external effects unit.

The simplest and cheapest way of obtaining an electronic effect is to buy a plug-in foot pedal. These are usually referred to as distortion, overdrive or fuzz pedals. You can hear a range of these effects on track 2/1 of the CD. Most of the commonly heard effects, such as delay, chorus, phasing, flanging, can also be created using dedicated units.

Foot pedals are extremely straightforward to use. All you need is an additional guitar lead for every effect you want to use. The pedal is inserted between the guitar and amplifier, the guitar is plugged into the "In" socket on the effect, using one lead, and the second lead is connected between the "Out" socket on the effect and the amplifier. Effects pedals can also be linked together in a "daisychain" (*see above*). The output from one unit can be input directly into another. To all intents and purposes, any number of effects can be joined together in this way.

Your overall sound can alter radically, depending on the sequence in which you link the different units. Try to think logically about what is happening at each point along the chain. In the diagram above, if the first effect was a delay pedal, and the second was distortion, all of the delays would be distorted; if they were the other way round, a single distorted signal would be delayed, creating a cleaner and very different sound.

If you use a large number of effects pedals you can easily get into a muddle on stage. Some players like to attach all of their pedals to a board and connect them together using short patch cables. This not only makes it neater for stage use but helps to prevent them mysteriously "disappearing" into thieves' pockets after gigs.   **2/1** ▶

MULTIPLE EFFECTS UNITS

Effects pedals are a relatively cheap and efficient way of changing a basic guitar sound. However, their major drawback is that complex set-ups involving a large number of pedals can become unwieldy to operate. Additionally, many pedals have a large number of parameters that can be changed, making it difficult to store precise settings without recourse to written documentation. A modern solution to this quandary has come in the form of the multiple-effects module. Often specially designed with the guitarist in mind, these are usually high-quality, digital units capable of producing, at the very least, reverb, a full range of delays, distortions and compression effects at the same time. The greatest benefit is that all of the individual parameters can be stored and recalled either by a footswitch or rack-mounted and recalled by a MIDI foot pedal or sequencer.

UNDERSTANDING RHYTHM

So what is rhythm *really*? Let's ask for some help from that most venerable of tomes, *The Harvard Dictionary of Music* (every muso worth his or her salt should own a copy of this). So how about this for starters: "All aspects of musical movement as ordered in time." Or maybe this: "A patterned configuration of attacks that may or not be constrained overall by a meter or associated with a particular tempo." You may begin to get the idea that the concept of rhythm is a lot more difficult to explain in words that it is in actions. Over the next ten pages we'll try to put this idea into a practical context as you play along with the first of the CD's backing tracks.

FEELING THE PULSE

By now you should know a little about the names of the notes as they appear on a staff – even if you have to work out each one first. While this tells you the pitch of the note, what it fails to indicate is WHEN the note should be played, and HOW LONG it should be sustained. These are two critical aspects of rhythm.

If you listen to almost any piece of music you will experience a kind of "pulsing" effect. This is the BEAT. If you now clap or tap your foot along to the music, you will almost certainly find yourself naturally drawn to a consistent beat. Irrespective of the tempo of the music – how fast it is being played, that is – the time interval between each clap (or tap) will be the same value as all of the others.

The most common type of beat you will hear grouped together is four CROTCHETS (QUARTER NOTES). You will find that you can count along to most types of music by repeating the numbers one to four. In doing so, you will usually find that music naturally emphasises the first beat. This natural grouping of beats is known in written music as a bar. What we have here, then, is an example of a piece of music with four beats in the bar. It is, as you may recognise from page 36, a time signature of "four-four": the bottom "four" tells you the type of notes that make up the beat (four is a crotchet); the top "four" tells you how many of those note values there are in a bar.

What this time signature is definitely NOT telling you, though, is that the musical constructions must be made up of four crotchets – that would be dull in the extreme – but that the mixture of note values that make up that bar MUST add up to a total of four crotchets.

To help make more sense of this, listen to Backing Track #1 a few times through. Pay special attention to the pulsing effect – the beat – of the piece.   **2/2** ▶

BACKING TRACK #1

Let's just re-iterate how the chord charts throughout this book work one final time. Each of the two blocks below are divided into four bars. This means that Backing Track #1 is a simple repeating eight-bar sequence.

The first bar sees the chord E major being played on the first beat; it is then repeated on the other three beats. The second bar instructs the player to repeat the first bar in full.

Similarly, the chord D major is played on each beat of the third and fourth bars; A major is played on each beat of the fifth and sixth bars; E major is played on each beat of the seventh bar; and D major is played on each beat of the eighth bar.

You can hear a brief version of the track on CD Track 2/2, or the full length version on Track 11.

E / / /	⁒	D / / /	⁒
A / / /	**⁒**	**E / / / **	**D / / /**

SEMIBREVE (WHOLE NOTE) SUSTAIN

To get into the swing of practising rhythms, listen to the effect of a chord sustained over an entire bar.

Listen all the way through to Backing Track #1 before you start to play. Count along with it in cycles of one to four, each time emphasising the first beat. Don't make the mistake of counting along with the guitars on the recording since these are playing a chugging rhythm of quavers. This means that eight chords are struck in each bar, so there should be two chords for each beat you count out.

Ignore what the guitars on the recording are doing, and strike each chord on the first beat of each bar of the chord chart. If you're not sure of the chord shapes, take a quick look back at pages 30–33. The first two bars are shown below. Remember that the semibreves are the "no tails" – they appear on the written music as a series of circles. 2/3

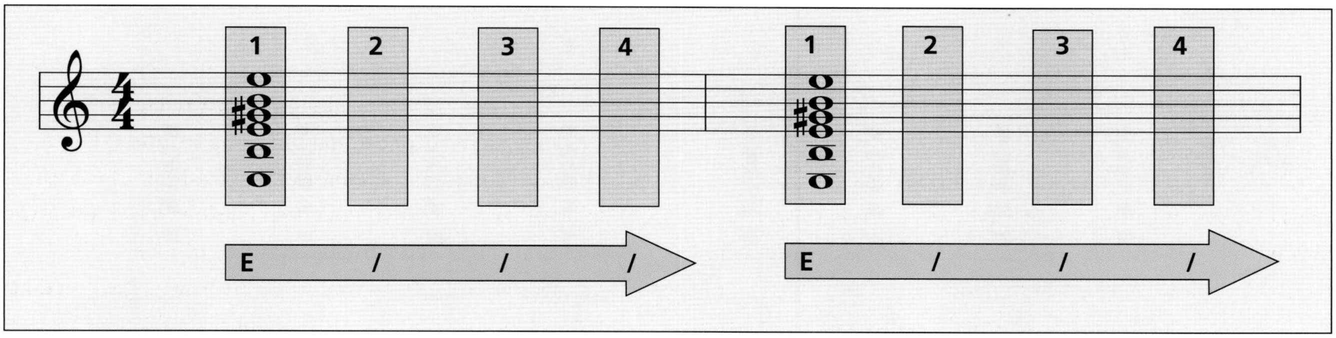

MINIM (HALF NOTE) SUSTAIN

Groups of notes that sustain for two beats are called MINIMS (or HALF NOTES, in US terminology). We'll now repeat the first exercise only this time playing the chords as minims.

- **FIRST BEAT** Play the E major chord.
- **SECOND BEAT** Sustain the chord.
- **THIRD BEAT** Play the E major chord.
- **FOURTH BEAT** Sustain the chord.

At this speed, you will probably find it easier to play these chords using a series of downstrokes of your pick. (You can check back to page 25 if you're not sure about aspects of using a pick.) 2/4

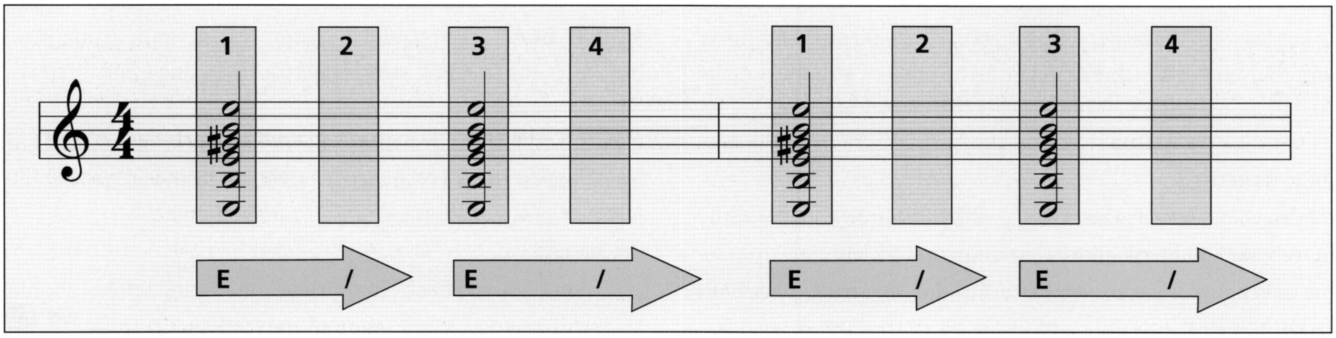

WATCHING OUR LANGUAGE

Although the key elements of written music are largely the same throughout the Western world, there are nonetheless a few critical exceptions.

In the United States, the note values are referred to as diminishing fractions, whereas those steeped in European musical training refer to such terms as CROTCHETS and QUAVERS. We have referred to both systems in this chapter, the European standard followed by the translation shown in brackets. Throughout the remainder of the book, we will use only the European names. (Both versions are tabulated on page 35.)

Similarly, intervals of one or two frets on the fingerboard, which are referred to as SEMITONES and TONES in Europe, are known simply as STEPS and HALF-STEPS in the US. Although we will use the European names, it's as well to be familiar with both systems.

CROTCHET (QUARTER NOTE) SUSTAIN

Let's take things up a level now. As before, we'll play along with Backing Track #1, only this time we'll be striking the chords on the beat.

- **FIRST BEAT**   Play E major.

- **SECOND BEAT** Play E major.

- **THIRD BEAT**   Play E major.

- **FOURTH BEAT** Play E major.

If your chord changing fluency isn't yet up to scratch, then you'll probably find a tendency on the last beats of bars 2, 4, 6 and 8 to cut off the sustain early to give yourself a little extra time to make the chord change. Watch out!   **2/5** ▶

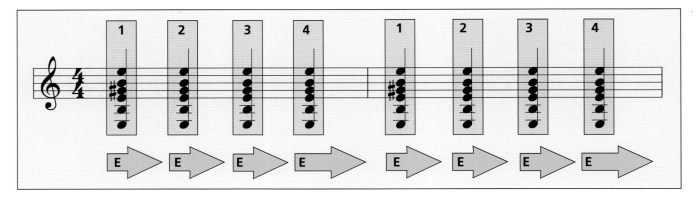

QUAVER (EIGHTH NOTE) SUSTAIN

This is the rhythm that the guitars on the backing track are actually playing. This time, as you'll notice from the music below, there are more chords being played than there are beats in the bar.

There are several different ways of counting out a rhythm where the notes are played faster then the beats. Some people prefer to double up the count so that instead of one to four, they count from one to eight, only twice as quickly. Others insert a count between the beats so that it goes: "one-and-two-and-three-and-four-and". Whichever method you choose, you must make sure that you strike a chord on every half-beat of the bar.

PICK STROKES

Playing at this speed poses a new problem: how do you physically move your hand back above the strings in sufficient time to strike the next chord? The answer lies in striking the strings with both DOWNSTROKES AND UPSTROKES. To be honest, with

practice, playing at the speed of Backing Track #1 – which has a tempo of 100 bpm – should be quite achievable.

If it's that characteristic chugging rock sound you're after, then using downstrokes is the only real way of managing it. But in terms of hand movement it's more economical to alternate downstrokes and upstrokes. The principle is simple – you play ON the beat with a downstroke, and OFF the beat with an upstroke.

- **FIRST BEAT**   Fret the E major chord and bring your picking hand DOWN, striking across the strings.

- **FIRST OFF BEAT ("AND")** Leaving the picking hand where it completed the previous stroke (below the strings), bring the pick UP across the strings.

For maximum effectiveness, these alternating strokes should be performed as a single, smooth movement.   **2/6** ▶

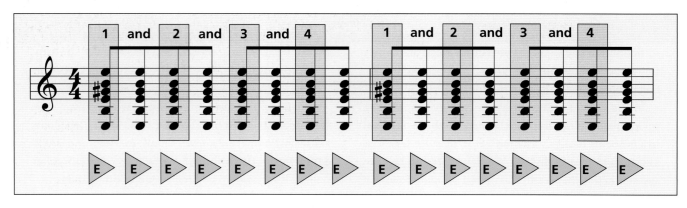

SEMIQUAVER (SIXTEENTH NOTE) SUSTAIN

This final example plays four chords for every beat. Each chord consists of a series of SEMIQUAVERS. (Using American terminology they are known as SIXTEENTH NOTES, since each note represents one sixteenth of a bar.)

To be able to play at this speed really does require using alternating pick strokes. In fact, playing this way could almost be described as STRUMMING.

Playing such rhythms can be tricky for the novice, so try this idea for the count: "<u>one</u>-and-one-and-<u>two</u>-and-two-and-<u>three</u>-and-three-and-<u>four</u>-and-four-and".

If you haven't quite got the idea, start off by counting on the beat ("one-two-three-four"). Then – keeping the tempo steady – double up the count, inserting "and" between each of the beats. Finally, double up the count once more, making insertions between the off beats. **2/7** ▶

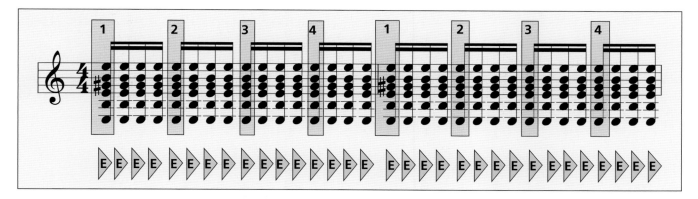

STRUMMING

Strumming is the most commonly heard way of accompanying a vocalist on a guitar. Although it is usually performed with a pick, for most players it is quite different from the standard picking technique. To play single notes or tight, chugging rhythms with any accuracy you need to retain a firm grip on your pick; strumming can be a much more relaxed business.

For best results, use a flimsier light-gauge pick, one which is flexible enough to bend back as it plays across the strings – small hard picks just won't work as well for this.

Let's try an alternative approach to the exercise above. Start by altering your sound. If you have distortion switched on, get rid of it. We're after a clean tone here. You can also experiment by switching between your pickups. The BACK PICKUP (the one nearest the bridge) gives a biting treble sound, whereas the FRONT PICKUP (the one nearest the fingerboard) gives a bassier mellow sound better suited to rhythm.

Play the same part shown above, only this time strum the strings gently in a more relaxed fashion. As before, every odd numbered semiquaver (sixteenth note) is played on a downstroke; the even notes are played as upstrokes.

This is also a good moment to experiment with the sound of your strings. Try varying the point at which you strike the strings. You'll find that the further from the bridge your pick hits the strings, the less treble you will hear.

DEMI-SEMIQUAVERS

In a slow piece of music you may come across note values with three "tails". These are called DEMI-SEMIQUAVERS (or THIRTY-SECOND NOTES). Each is worth one eighth of a beat.

The next division is a HEMI-DEMI-SEMIQUAVER (or SIXTY-FOURTH NOTE). Since there are sixteen of these to a single beat you are unlikely to come across them in guitar music.

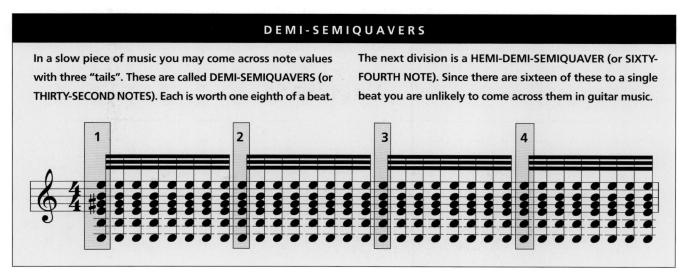

CREATING "REAL" RHYTHMS

The examples on the previous three pages have all been based around using notes of the same value. Consequently, although they are extremely common in most forms of modern music, they are simple and – let's be honest – a bit dull. To create something more sophisticated we must mix together different note lengths. The examples leading up to the end of the lesson use the simplicity of Backing Track #1 to build up a variety of more interesting rhythm sounds.

MIXING NOTE LENGTHS

The examples below show how you can create "movement" by using notes of different lengths within a bar. Each time, to make life a little easier, the count is written above the staff.

In the first example, play on "one", "two" and "three", letting the final chord sustain through "four"; in the second bar, play on "one", let the chord sustain through "two", and then play on "three" and "four".

The final staff is a tough one for you to work out: remember that the combined value of the first pair of quavers is one beat, as is the combined value of the four semiquavers.   **2/8** ▶

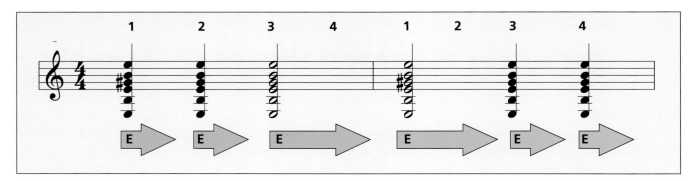

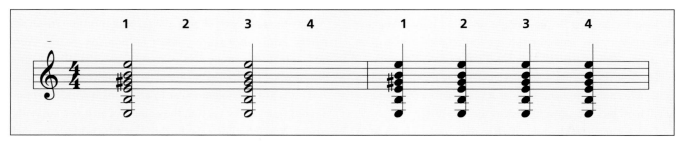

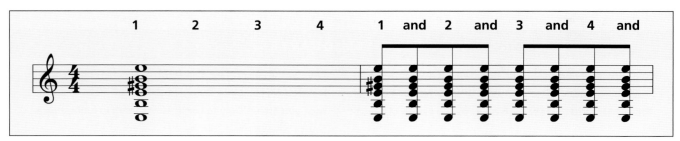

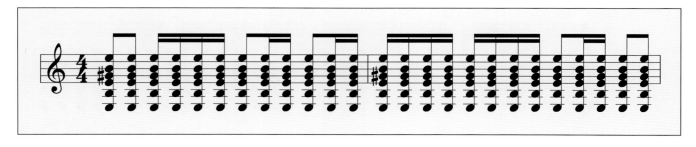

MUTING AND ACCENTING

By altering the volume of a chord or note within a bar you can dramatically alter the tone, rhythm and "emotion" of a piece of music. Such effects can be created either by striking the strings harder with the right hand or by MUTING them.

There are two common methods you can use to mute (or dampen) the strings. For an abrupt cut-off of sound, the tension of the fingers on the left hand can be released as soon as the notes have been played. For a more consistent effect you can bring the edge of your right hand gently to rest on the strings above the bridge (*see right*). Notes can still be picked while the strings are being dampened. In fact, this can be an extremely effective technique, especially when the signal is being fed through a delay effect.

Who can hear the impact of muted and accented notes in the examples below. The upward-pointing arrows indicate the chords that should be played louder. Although the note values are all the same, the accents create three very different effects. **2/9** ▶

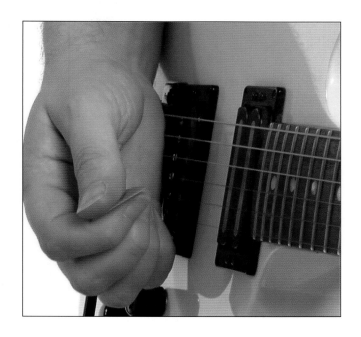

The right hand can be used to deaden the strings at the bridge.

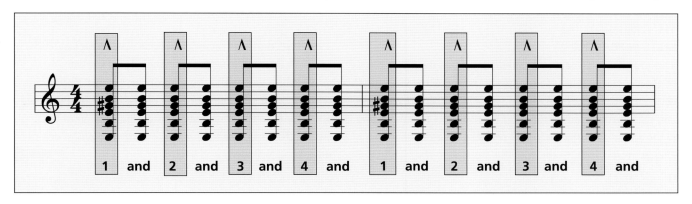

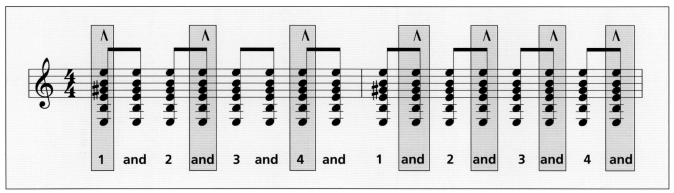

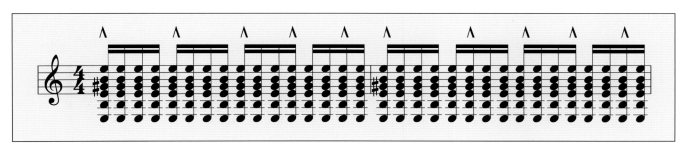

RESTS

If music consisted wholly of a continuous stream of notes played one after the other, it would soon become relentlessly dull for both performer and listener. It may sound strange at first, but for guitarists, or any other musician for that matter, choosing when NOT to play is every bit as important as the notes he or she does play. These critical silences are known as RESTS.

Like all music, the use of rests is quite logical: when written in a piece of music, the rest instructs the player NOT to play for a specified time. For this to work, each of the different note types have a uniquely identifiable associated rest symbol.

If a bar of four-four music contains a semibreve rest (*see below, top left*), the musician would not play during that bar. Rests can also be combined – to indicate a three-beat silence, a minim rest and a crotchet rest can be shown together.

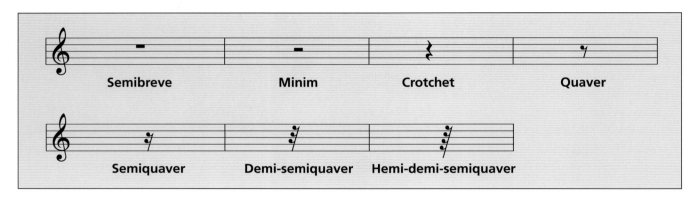

RESTS IN PRACTICE

A rest may have an extremely subtle impact on the way a piece of music is played. The first example below shows the distinction between two similar bars when a rest is introduced. In the first bar, the chord played on the third beat sustains for two beats; in the second bar, that minim is replaced by a crotchet and a crotchet rest. Listen to the way this sounds on the CD: in the

second bar, the chord on the third beats sustains for just one beat, and then there is silence for the remainder of the bar.

The third example is the kind of rhythm usually associated with reggae or ska. The chords are played on the off-beat, but to allow for the alternating quaver rests, the sustain must be cut off swiftly. (Releasing the tension of the fretting fingers as described on page 51 will work well here.)   **2/10** ▶

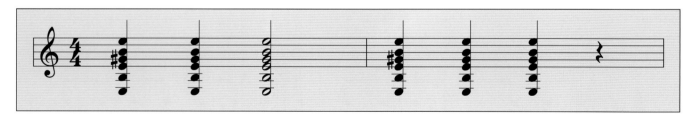

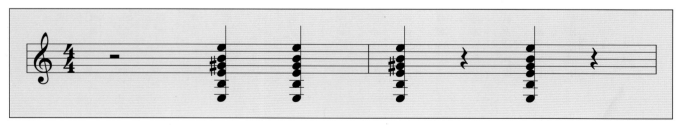

CUTTING NOTES SHORT

In certain situations, we can avoid the use of rests in written music by using the STACCATO symbol. An Italian word, *staccato* literally means "short and sharp". It is an instruction for a note to be played for half its value, but keeping to the overall rhythm. It is shown on the staff with a dot either above or below the note.

As the example beneath illustrates, it is effectively a shorthand instruction for showing a note (or chord) followed by a rest of the same value: the four crotchets when played staccato (first bar) sound identical to four quavers each followed by a quaver rest (second bar). **2/11** ▶

STACCATO – NOT STACCATISSIMO!

When interpreting a staccato symbol in written music, the key is in judging exactly by how much to reduce the length of the note. Although this is unequivocal – the instruction is to halve the note value – in practice this may not be so easy to recognise. A mistake many players make is to shorten the length of the note as much as possible. This is incorrect: such an effect is called STACCATISSIMO. Although the difference may be slight when applied to low note values on a piece of music with a fast tempo, practising by counting out the beat will give you a clearer feel for the difference.

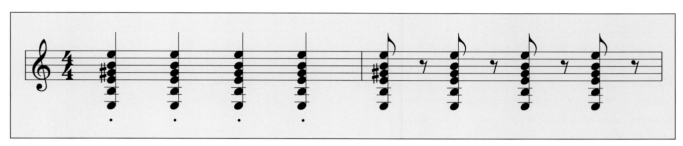

STACCATO IN PRACTICE

In the first example, a bar of straight quavers is followed by a bar of quavers played staccato. Performing in this way requires considerable discipline in knowing when, and how best, to dampen the strings.

There are different problems associated with both types of muting. When playing single notes, releasing tension in the fretting fingers is probably how most guitarists would approach playing staccato – in the first example, the tense/release action is also a naturally rhythmic movement, which makes the process easier. However, since we're playing open-string chords, we can only dampen three of the strings using the left hand – the 1st, 2nd and 6th strings will carry on ringing whatever we do with our left hand. Using the right hand to dampen and release with any speed is more difficult. Since the action comes from the wrist, delicate movements can't be made too swiftly.

In the lower example, you could play the staccato notes using right-hand damping, and release the hand to play non-staccato notes. The key, however, is to maintain a uniform volume between the notes. **2/12** ▶

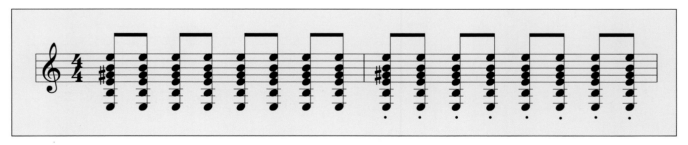

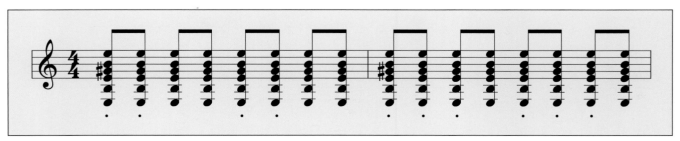

DOTS

The notes we have already seen – from the four-beat semibreve to the sixteenth-of-a-beat hemi-demi-semiquaver – can be thought of as our basic units of musical currency. However, these values are all based on cumulatively dividing the bar in half. What happens if we want a note to last for three beats, for example? Or one-and-a-half beats? We can alter a note's core value by adding a DOT or linking it to another note using a bracket known as a TIE.

Any note followed by a dot has the effect of lengthening that note by half its value. Thus a crotchet with a dot – known as a DOTTED CROTCHET – has a value of one-and-a-half beats. Play the staff below to hear the effect it creates. The panel underneath the staff shows the note values of dotted minims, quavers and semiquavers.

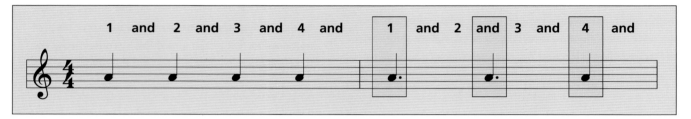

TIES

Another way of lengthening a note is by linking it to another note using a tie bracket. This has the effect of giving the first note the value of the two notes combined. THE SECOND NOTE IS NEVER PLAYED IN ITS OWN RIGHT. In the first staff below, you will see that the first two crotchets are tied. This means that the first note is effectively a minim. This is a rather artificial example just to make the point – you are unlikely to come across a tie used in this way.

CROSSING BARS

The time signature of a piece of music indicates how many beats there are in a bar. Thus, a piece of music written in 4/4 tells you

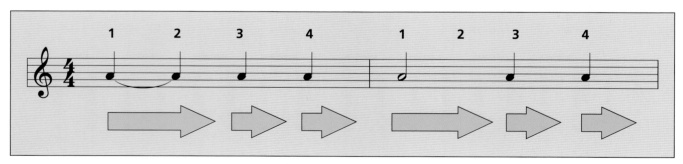

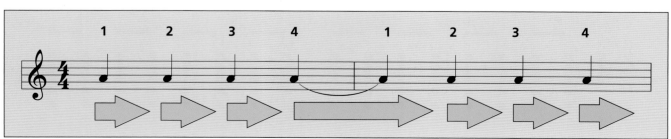

GETTING LOUDER OR SOFTER

Gradual changes in volume can be used to create dynamic effects. CRESCENDO describes a sound that gradually increases in volume; DIMINUENDO is the reverse – a sound that gets quieter over time. They can be indicated in written music using the "hairpin" symbols positioned above the staff to indicate the range of notes (beneath) which are affected.

Bar one shows a crescendo symbol covering four notes, which should be played increasingly loud; bar three shows an example of a diminuendo.

CRESCENDO   DIMINUENDO

that whatever combination of note lengths exists within that bar, they MUST total up to four beats. However, it is often necessary for a note to be sustained across a bar line. In the second example, at the foot if page 54, the crotchet on the fourth beat of the first bar is tied to the first crotchet of the second bar. This means that the note is struck on the fourth beat of the bar and must be sustained until the second beat of the second bar.

Returning to Backing Track #1, let's hear the effect of dotting notes and sustaining chords across bar lines in practice. In the first example below, take the following steps:

- Play E major on "one" and count through "and-two".

- Play E major on "and" and count through "three-and".

- Play E major on "four" and count through "and-one-and".

- Play E major on "two" and count through "and-three".

- Play E major on "and", counting through "four-and".

2/13

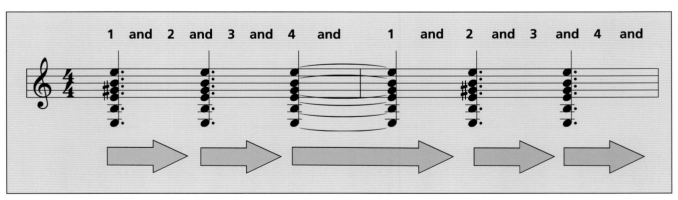

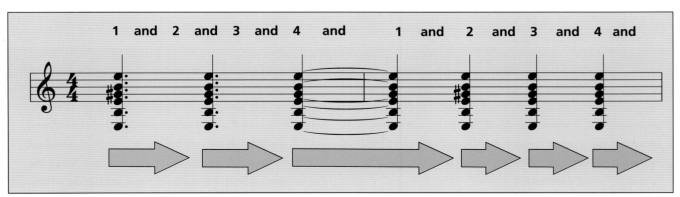

ADVANCED RHYTHMS

Here are three exercise to play along with Backing Track #1. They mix various note values, as well as notes that are tied or dotted. You can hear all three played on Track 2/14 of the CD.

EXERCISE 1

The tricky part here is in the crossover between the two bars. Count "one-and-two-and" etc through the first bar. The crotchet played on the fourth beat sustains through to "one-and-two" in the second bar.

2/14 ▶

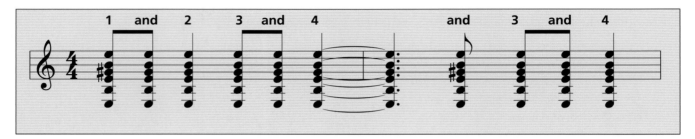

EXERCISE 2

This exercise features some nicely played semiquavers set among higher note values. As you may have discovered, such fast note sequences can be fairly simple if you're playing them one after the other – for example, an entire bar of semiquavers. Your hand gets into the rhythm and, after a while, it becomes automatic. But when note values are mixed (as in the example below), it takes discipline to keep in time.

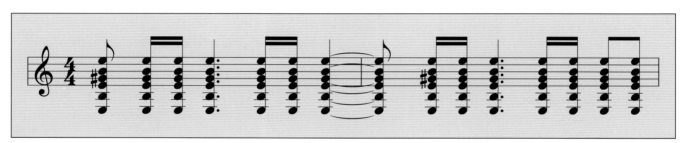

EXERCISE 3

Working out a rhythm from written music can be quite tricky at first, especially when dealing with very small note values. The key to mastering this skill is in simple recognition. You might not yet recognise the way the grouping of a dotted quaver and a semiquaver sounds, but what you can tell is that since each of these groups has a combined value of one beat, then the rhythmic emphasis remains ON rather than OFF the beat.

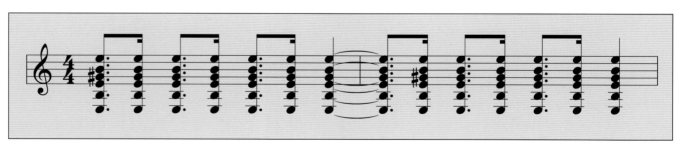

LOOKING FOR PATTERNS

Music of pretty well any genre you can think of has a strong basis in repetition. After all, it's how we manage to assimilate our favourite tunes so easily. Imagine what it would be like if every verse of every song had a completely different melody and rhythm. It would certainly make for a very different experience.

If you are learning to play a piece of written music, start by looking for patterns. This can include both rhythmic patterns – where the note values perform similar functions, even if the pitches are not the same – or pitch patterns. Understanding this fundamental principle can make the idea of reading and playing from music far less daunting.

KEY SIGNATURES

By now you may just about be getting used to the idea of reading pitch and rhythm values on the staff. So now is as good a time as any to throw a spanner or two in the works by discussing KEY SIGNATURES.

Just as the root note of a chord provides it with its KEY, a piece of music can be identified in the same way. If, for example, a melody comprises notes from the G major scale (don't worry about these terms for the moment – we'll meet those in the next chapter), it is said to be "in" G major. What this means is that it has a KEY SIGNATURE of G major.

As you have already seen, the notes as they appear on the lines of a treble staff are E-G-B-D-F; the notes that sit between the spaces are F-A-C-E. This is all well and good if a piece of music is written in the key of C major, which has no flats or sharps.

Unfortunately life – and music theory – is not that simple: all of the other major keys contain at least one sharp or flat. If you look back at the chord chart for Backing Track #1 (*see page 46*) you can see that it begins with an E major and RESOLVES back to an E major. Indeed, Backing Track #1 could be said to be "in" the key of E major.

Now if you look at an E major chord shown in any of the previous exercises, you will notice that it uses the note G♯. Every time that E major chord is shown, you will see a sharp next to note G. It would be possible to indicate sharp and flat symbols alongside each note as they occur, but if you came across a piece written in F♯ (whose scale includes six sharps), the music would appear to be an illegible blur of sharp symbols: even the most careful eye would have trouble reading it. Instead, the practice is to show an instruction at the beginning of the staff that any occurrence of a specific note should be sharpened or flattened, unless specifically shown otherwise. Therefore, the key signature of a piece of written music can always be identified by the number of sharps and flats appearing after the clef at the beginning of a piece of music. Had we "correctly" notated the music for the key of E, the staff would have appeared with four sharps after the clef. Then, when the E major chord was shown, the note G would no longer have required a sharp symbol. This is because the key signature tells us that all of the notes on the "G" line must be played as G♯.

When shown on a staff with a key signature of E, the sharp "disappears" from the notes within the music. This is because the KEY SIGNATURE tells us that all Gs are to be played as G♯.

THE "FLAT" KEYS	THE "SHARP" KEYS
F MAJOR	G MAJOR
F MAJOR	D MAJOR
B♭ MAJOR	A MAJOR
E♭ MAJOR	E MAJOR
A♭ MAJOR	B MAJOR
G♭ MAJOR	F♯ MAJOR
C♭ MAJOR	C♯ MAJOR

CHAPTER 3
MELODIC MATTERS

What is melody? A detached definition would doubtless describe it as something like a coherent sequence of pitches. By "pitches" we mean specific notes; by "coherent" we mean that they have been deliberately arranged according to some kind of musical principle. But let's cut to basics. What we're really talking about here is a good old TUNE. All musical cultures – even those most alien to Western ears – are grounded in some concept of melody. It is one of the three components of which music as whole is often informally divided: the other two are HARMONY and RHYTHM.

MELODY AND SCALES

The concept of melody is underpinned by one of the most important ideas in music: the SCALE. It comes from the Latin world *scala*, which literally mens "ladder" – and that's not a bad way of thinking of the way scales work. A scale is a set of related notes that progress from a root to the same note one octave higher. Scales come in many different forms, but any one scale can be distinguished from any other by a single factor – the semitone intervals between the root and the octave form a uniquely identifying pattern.

WHAT USE ARE SCALES?
The most important scales in Western music are called DIATONIC. Each one has seven different pitches. There are four diatonic scales: the MAJOR and THREE MINORS. As you will see over the coming pages, each one has a unique set of intervals. If you play all four scales from the same root note

THEY WILL ALL SOUND DIFFERENT. The sets of intervals between each of the seven pitches are not the same. Each one has a unique sound and character. If you play a major scale from a root note of C, and then play another major scale from a root note of G, you will hear that they both have what could be described as a "major" quality about them. This is because although they use a different set of notes, the semitone intervals between each step – or DEGREE, to give it's correct term – remain the same.

Scales are so significant because they are at the heart of all melody. The way notes work relative to one another – the pitch intervals before and after each successive note – all but defines the nature of any tune.

There are many other types of scale that exist in Western music. PENTATONIC scales, as the name suggests, are built from five different pitches. We'll come across those later in the book. Others include DIMINISHED and WHOLE-TONE scales – both widely used by jazz musicians.

IN THIS CHAPTER YOU'LL LEARN...

- About the nature of melody
- The names of the scale degrees
- The intervals that make up a major scale
- 6th-string major scale finger patterns
- The intervals that make up a natural minor scale
- The intervals that make up a harmonic minor scale
- The intervals that make up a melodic minor scale
- Relative major scales
- Playing scales over a backing track
- Transposition
- Speed-picking exercises

- The importance of scales
- The major scale
- 5th-string major scale finger patterns
- The minor scales
- 6th-string natural minor scale finger patterns
- 6th-string harmonic minor scale finger patterns
- 6th-string melodic minor scale finger patterns
- Relative minor scales
- Ascending and descending scale exercises
- Practising broken scales
- Turning scales into tunes

MELODIC MASTERS

All too often, guitarists are celebrated for the technical proficiency of their soloing skills. Whilst watching the fingers of a master musician weaving their way effortlessly all over the fingerboard can be a sight to behold (catch a video or DVD of Jimi Hendrix at full tilt and you'll get the idea), this is but one facet of the electric guitar.

Take, for instance, a player like Peter Buck (*see right*) of R.E.M. You rarely (if ever) hear him let loose with a rip-roaring, high-speed solo. His playing could broadly be described as melodic embellishment. His mastery is in understanding what is appropriate for the song he's playing. For a band like R.E.M., the song and synergy of the band sound as a whole is far more important than any of the individual components – however expertly crafted they may be. He is most definitely a master of understatement.

In a very different vein, Jeff Beck is another guitarist who can always be guaranteed to show impeccable taste in his playing. Of course, from his early days replacing Eric Clapton in the Yardbirds, he has long been established as a very fine soloist. And yet in spite of the nimble virtuosity of his playing, his style has never seemed pointlessly flashy. His views on soloing are forthright:

"I've got no particular desire to play ten-minute solos. Those were never valid in my book – never. It was a cheap way of building up tension in the audience... A solo should do something – it shouldn't just be there as cosmetic. It should have some aim, take the tune somewhere."

(AGAIN) WHAT USE ARE SCALES?

Almost since the birth of formal education, students have yawned in unison at the very thought of having to learn their scales. While our view is that a good deal of classical-style teaching has little or no relevance to the rock musician, scales are a different matter altogether.

There is some dogged reluctance among some self-taught people to engage in this area. This may be because a lot of modern music uses such a small area of the possible musical palette that many people with a reasonable "ear" can assimilate naturally what works and what doesn't work, simply because they have been exposed to so much music throughout their lives. As you will see on the next page, even if we don't know

what a major scale is, most us know what one sounds like: it's almost ingrained in the Western collective subconscious.

Well, here are four very good reasons why all but the very least ambitious of guitarists should embrace their scales:

1. It's easily the best way to get to know the names of the notes on the fingerboard.

2. Practice will improve your fluency and speed.

3. Learning and practising scales is the best training you can give to your ears.

4. They will help you to understand chord theory.

SCALES

A scale is a series of related notes. Each type of scale follows a pattern of intervals played in sequence from a specified note to the octave of that note. The first note of the scale is always the ROOT. This indicates the "key" of the scale. The most commonly used scales are the major and the three minors.

INTERVALS AND THE MAJOR SCALE

Almost everyone knows a major scale – even if they don't know they know it. Anyone who has ever seen the film *The Sound Of Music* will have heard the song that begins: "Doe, a deer, a female deer…". If you sing the entire sequence of notes "do-re-me-fa-sol-la-ti-do", you have just sung a major scale.

As we've already discussed, an INTERVAL is the distance in pitch between any two notes. The pattern of intervals that define the scale is made up either of TONES – a distance of two frets on the fingerboard (which are referred to as "STEPS" in the US), or SEMITONES, which are a distance of one fret apart (called HALF-STEPS in the US). Every major scale progresses in the following way from the root to the octave:

TONE (STEP)

TONE (STEP)

SEMITONE (HALF-STEP)

TONE (STEP)

TONE (STEP)

TONE (STEP)

SEMITONE (HALF-STEP)

In the key of C, the notes are C, D, E, F, G, A, B and C – the white notes on a piano keyboard.

Once a key has been defined – meaning that the root is known – every note (or DEGREE) of that scale can be named both on its own and in terms of the interval between itself and the root. The diagram on the right shows how the notes of a C major scale are named in terms of the guitar fingerboard.

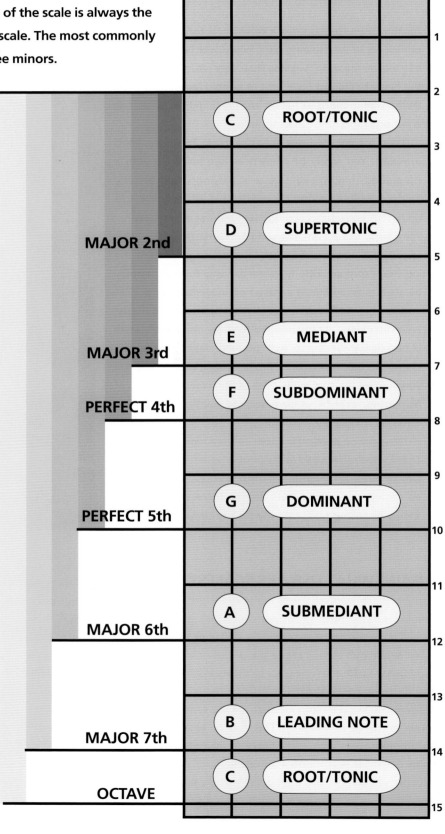

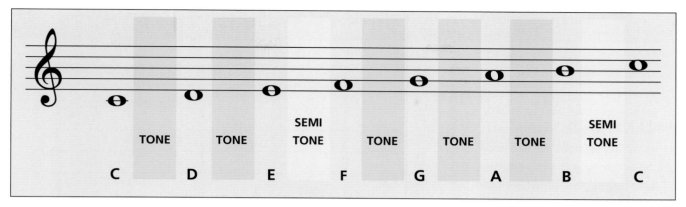

	TONE	TONE	SEMI TONE	TONE	TONE	TONE	SEMI TONE	
C		D		E	F	G	A	B	C

FINGERING

By adopting the correct fingering you should find yourself able to play all of the notes of the major scale without having to move your left-hand position. Try this with a C major scale. The range of notes you need are all found within the 2nd to 5th frets on the fingerboard. Irrespective of which strings are being used, the notes played on the 2nd, 3rd, 4th and 5th frets are ONLY held in position by the 1st, 2nd, 3rd and 4th fingers respectively. You are likely to find this exercise challenging, since it makes heavy use of the 4th finger. **3/1**

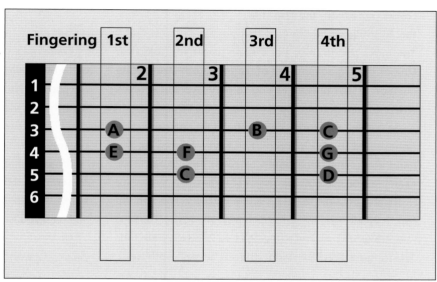

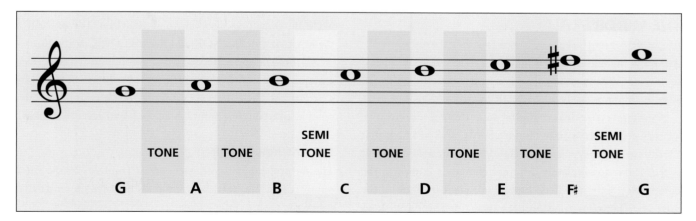

	TONE	TONE	SEMI TONE	TONE	TONE	TONE	SEMI TONE	
G		A		B	C	D	E	F♯	G

CHANGING KEYS

Once your fingers become used to their positions, playing a scale in a different key becomes a matter of finding a new root note along the same string. By moving your hand so that the fingers begin the same pattern of intervals played from the 10th fret, you can play a major scale in G. **3/2**

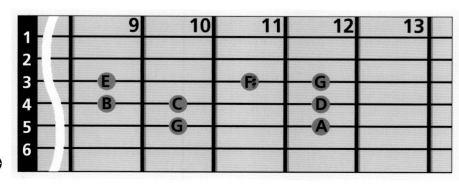

ALTERNATIVE MAJOR SCALE POSITIONS

There are many different ways in which you can play a major scale. One of the most commonly used and versatile alternatives is shown on the right, starting from the 6th string. As before, you can adopt the one-finger-per-fret rule: in this case the 1st finger covers notes on the 7th fret; the 2nd finger, the 8th fret; the

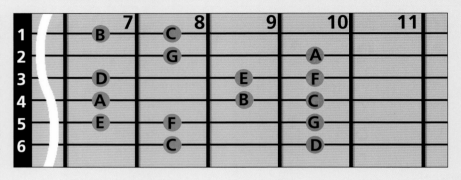

3rd finger, the 9th fret; and the 4th finger, the 10th fret. One of the big advantages of using the 6th-string scale position is that it enables you to play two full octaves straight through from the 1st string to the 6th string.

As before, this scale can be moved up and down the fingerboard to play in alternative keys – by moving the hand along the fingerboard to cover frets 2 to 5, for example, you can play the major scale in G.

It's also possible to play a single-octave version on the top three strings: 3rd string/5th fret; 3rd string/7th fret; 2nd string/5th fret; 2nd string/6th fret; 2nd string/8th fret; 1st string/5th fret; 1st string/7th fret; 1st string/8th fret.

There is also a possible major scale pattern that starts on the 4th string. However, because the interval between the 2nd and 3rd strings differs from the intervals between the others, it would require a range of five frets, meaning that one of the fingers of the left hand would have to cover two frets, which is unnecessarily awkward.

It's extremely worthwhile mastering these various fingering patterns, both ascending and descending the scales. The ability to use them with a degree of fluidity will help you to develop your skills as a lead player.

On the right, every degree of every major scale is shown. Again, it's worth taking time to learn this information.

THE MINOR SCALE

Although the major scale is much the most common type of scale used in Western music, it is by no means the only one. Also in common use is the MINOR SCALE.

So what exactly does minor mean in this context? You've already come across some minor chords, and so know that the difference between a major chord and its minor equivalent is that it has a completely different character. Although the comparison may be a little superficial, you can think of the difference between music written in major and minor keys as being rather like the difference between a sound that is happy and one that is sad. Generally speaking, music with a melancholy flavour will have been written in a minor key: a good symbolic example of this difference can be heard in the contrast between the joyful "Wedding March" (major key) and the mournful "Funeral March" (minor key).

Unlike the major scale, in which the pattern of intervals always remains the same, there are three different types of minor scale, each of which has its own subtly different characteristics. The three minor scales are the NATURAL

MINOR (sometimes also known as the RELATIVE MINOR), the HARMONIC MINOR and the MELODIC MINOR.

All three minor scales have one common difference from a major scale in that the third degree is always flattened by a semitone. The differences among the three minor scales revolve around movements of the sixth and seventh degrees.

THE NATURAL MINOR
The natural minor scale is the most common of the three minor scales. The pattern of intervals between the notes that define the natural minor scale are:

TONE
SEMITONE
TONE
TONE
SEMITONE
TONE
TONE

In the key of C, the notes in the natural minor scale are C, D, E♭, F, G, A♭, B♭ and C. This set of notes and intervals can be seen on the staff across the page.

I	II	III	IV	V	VI	VII	I
A	B	C♯	D	E	F♯	G♯	A
B♭	C	D	E♭	F	G	A	B♭
B	C♯	D♯	E	F♯	G♯	A♯	B
C	D	E	F	G	A	B	C
C♯	D♯	F	F♯	G♯	A♯	C	C♯
D	E	F♯	G	A	B	F♯	D
E♭	F	G	A♭	B♭	C	D	E♭
E	F♯	G♯	A	B	C♯	D♯	E
F	G	A	B♭	C	D	E	F
F♯	G♯	A♯	B	C♯	D♯	F	F♯
G	A	B	C	D	E	F♯	G
A♭	B♭	C	D♭	E♭	F	G	A♭

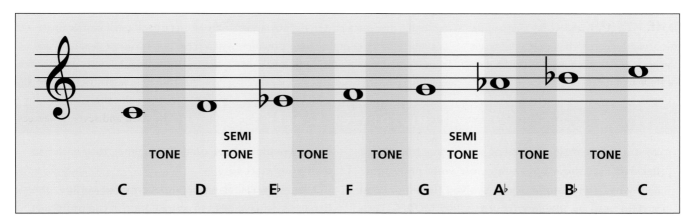

THE NATURAL MINOR POSITION

The diagram on the right shows the finger positions for a natural minor scale in C played from the 6th string. There is also a 5th-string alternative: 5th string/3rd fret; 5th string/5th fret; 5th string/6th fret; 4th string/3rd fret; 4th string/5th fret; 4th string/6th fret; 3rd string/3rd fret; 3rd string/5th fret.

3/3

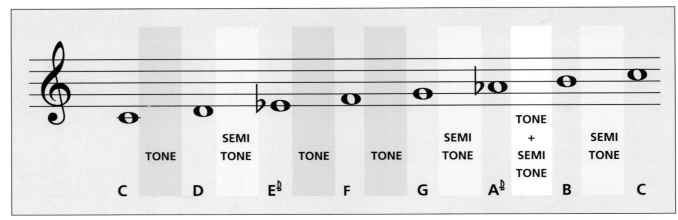

HARMONIC MINOR SCALE

The HARMONIC MINOR scale differs from the natural minor in that the sixth degree is SHARPENED. This means that it's raised by a semitone. The pattern of intervals required to create the scale are:

TONE

SEMITONE

TONE

TONE

SEMITONE

TONE + SEMITONE

SEMITONE

In the key of C the notes used are C, D, E♭, F, G, A♮, B and C. By sharpening the seventh degree, the interval between the sixth and seventh degrees is now one of three semitones.

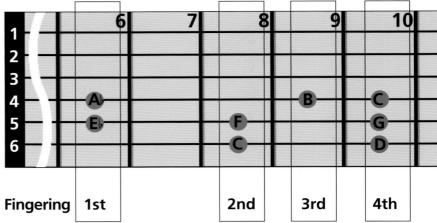

If you look at the fretboard diagram above, you will see that playing a harmonic minor scale from the 6th string is slightly more complex than previous scales in that you are forced to break the one-finger-per-fret rule. In instances such as these, the most effective alternative is to allow the 1st finger – which is likely to be the strongest and most mobile finger – to cover the first two frets (6 and 7), and use the 2nd, 3rd and 4th fingers with the 8th, 9th and 10th frets respectively.   **3/4** ▶

HISTORY OF SCALES

Where did the major and minor scales come from? Who decided that these note sequences were important? And why? The diatonic scales evolved from a musical system used by the early church called MODES. Each of these modes was a sequences of notes each with a specific pitch value. They were used in music written for plainsong, such as Gregorian chant. By the middle ages, notated melodies were listed in liturgical songbooks according to the modes they used.

The most significant difference between the "church modes" and the modern idea of scales is that modes were fixed in pitch. Although each mode had a unique set of intervals between the root and the octave (such

terms would not have used at this time), they each had a different start note.

Like many other aspects of European culture, the Renaissance gave birth to an evolution in compositional thinking. Two new modes were introduced; the Aeolian (the notes A to A) and Ionian (C to C). The use of these modes became widespread, composers gradually taking the idea of strict intervals but applying them freely to other notes. The Ionian and Aeolian modes became known as the Major and Minor scales respectively and, during the late 17th century, were at the centre of the birth of so-called "tonal" music. This system dominated the composition of European music thereafter.

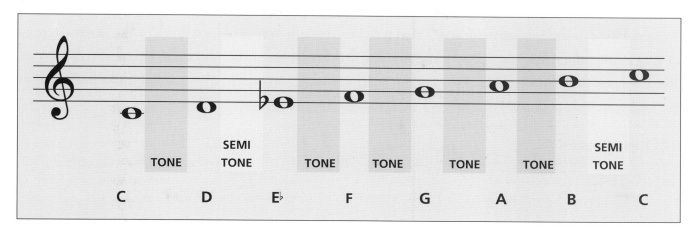

	TONE	SEMI TONE		TONE	TONE	TONE	TONE	SEMI TONE
C		D	E♭	F	G	A	B	C

MELODIC MINOR SCALE

One of the problems faced when working with the harmonic minor scale is in the "difficult" pitch interval of three semitones between the sixth and seventh degrees. To make this more musically palatable, the submediant (the sixth degree) can be raised by a semitone to create what is called a MELODIC MINOR scale.

The pattern of intervals that defines a melodic minor scale are shown on the staff above. The notes you need to play

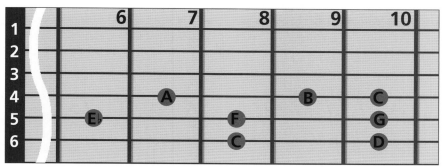

in the key of C are: C, D, E♭, F, G, A, B and C. Once again, you cannot use one finger per fret, so the 1st finger alone must cover the 6th and 7th frets.

The melodic minor is unique among the diatonic scales in that it can only

be played when ascending the scale. When descending, the sharpened sixth and seventh degrees can sound awkward, so to resolve such a problem we revert to the notes of the natural minor scale. **3/5** ▶

MAJOR/MINOR SCALE RELATIONSHIPS

If you play a C major scale followed by its natural minor counterpart, it will be self-evident that the two scales are different. This is because the pattern of intervals used by a major and natural minor scale are not the same. However, an interesting relationship between these two types of scale can be heard when you build a natural minor scale from the sixth degree of a major scale. The C major scale and the A natural minor scale actually use the same set of notes, even though they start from different roots. But if you play the two scales one after the other you will hear that they have very different characteristics.

This significant relationship between the C major scale and the A natural minor scale can be described in two different ways. The A minor scale could be called the RELATIVE MINOR of the C major scale. Equally, the C major scale can be referred to as the RELATIVE MAJOR of A minor.

The relationships between these two scales can be useful to understand. Since both scales are played without sharps or flats, the key signatures appear to be exactly the same. You've already seen that it's possible to tell the key of a piece of music by counting the number of sharps and flats between the clef and the time signature (*see page 57*). The relationship between the major and natural minor scales means that the

same observations can also be made for music written in a minor key.

Below you can see a list of the most commonly used major key signatures along with their relative minors.

C MAJOR	=	A MINOR
G MAJOR	=	E MINOR (1 sharp)
D MAJOR	=	B MINOR (2 sharps)
A MAJOR	=	F♯ MINOR (3 sharps)
E MAJOR	=	C♯ MINOR (4 sharps)
B MAJOR	=	G♯ MINOR (5 sharps)
F♯ MAJOR	=	D♯ MINOR (6 sharps)
F MAJOR	=	D MINOR (1 flat)
B♭ MAJOR	=	G MINOR (2 flats)
E♭ MAJOR	=	C MINOR (3 flats)
A♭ MAJOR	=	F MINOR (4 flats)
D♭ MAJOR	=	B♭ MINOR (5 flats)
G♭ MAJOR	=	E♭ MINOR (6 flats)

SCALES IN CONTEXT

The trouble with learning about scales is that it can be difficult at first to understand what use they really are. By putting them in a practical rock context, you should be able to see how scales of one sort or another form the very basis of all melody, being at the heart of pretty well every tune and lead guitar break you're ever likely to hear or perform.

BACKING TRACK #2

Here is the second backing track. This has a slow tempo, and sounds like the kind of thing often heard played by "jangly" indie bands who have roots in classic '60s pop and rock. The chords are all of the simple open-string variety that

should not pose too much of a problem for you.

Listen to the backing a few times on its own (on Track 3/6 of the CD), and when you're familiar with it, begin by simply strumming along.

The rhythm has deliberately been kept simple to aid the exercises, but there's no

reason why you can't liven things up on your own by using some of the rhythms we looked at during the latter stages of the last chapter.

Simple backing tracks such as this one should serve you well into the future as a tool for practising scales and other lead guitar exercises.   **3/6** ▶

A / / /	⁒	G / / /	⁒
C / / /	⁒	D / / /	⁒
A / / /	⁒	G / / /	⁒
C / / /	⁒	D / / /	⁒
Em / / /	⁒	C / / /	⁒
D / / /	⁒	G / / /	⁒
Em / / /	⁒	C / / /	⁒
D / / /	⁒	⁒	⁒

UP AND DOWN

Backing Track #2 has two distinct segments. Think of them, if you will, as a cycle of verses and choruses.

The verse section is made up of the first 16 bars. Since these are all major chords, then major scales played in the same key as each chord will naturally sound harmonious.

The staves below show the "verse" section played as a series of scales. Beneath each staff you can see the appropriate chord name. To make life a little simpler, the TAB lines are also shown. Just to refresh your memory, these indicate the fret positions and strings that should be used – the first note indicates that A on the 12th fret of the 5th string should be used (as

opposed to the 17th fret of the 6th string, the 7th fret of the 4th string, or the 2nd fret of the 3rd string – all of which have the same pitch).

The first eight bars are ascending sets of crotchets – since the tempo is quite slow these shouldn't be too tricky for you to master. For the final eight bars, the same set of scales are played in reverse sequence. **3/7** ▶

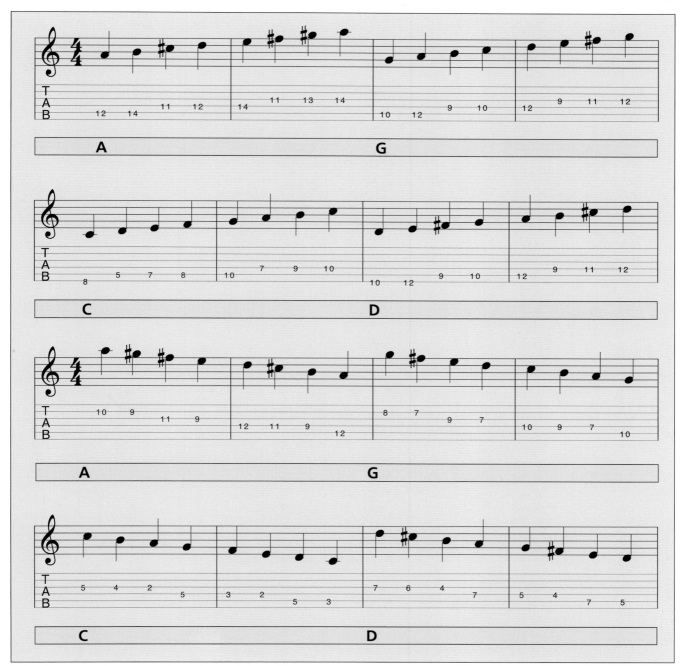

THE "CHORUS" SECTION

Let's now repeat that exercise for the second part of the song. Once again this uses the major scales in C, D and G. This time, however, there is also an E minor chord present, so for these bars we will play ascending and descending scales in the key of E natural minor.

Now try to play the whole verse and chorus cycle through in one go. **3/8**

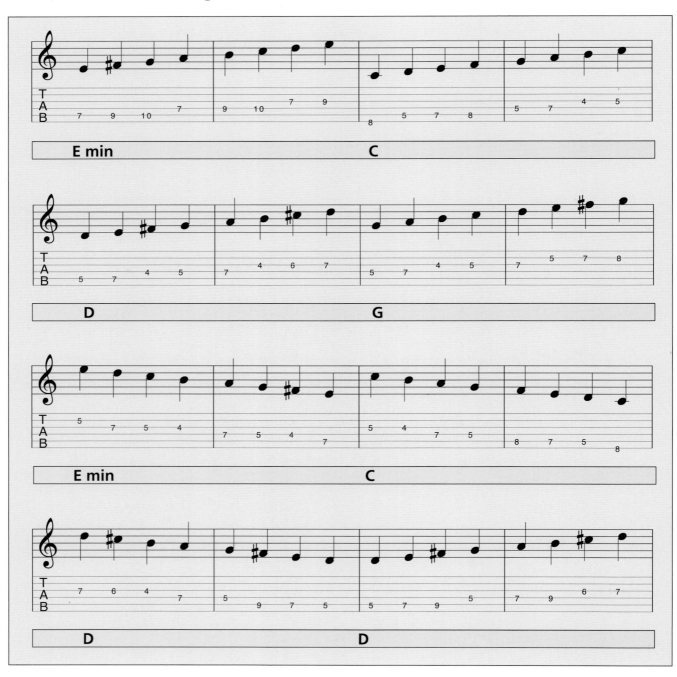

CHANGING KEYS

Life would be much easier if all music was written in one key. So why do we bother with different keys? For a start, different instruments have different tonal qualities depending on which notes are used. But there are also a number of practical reasons for choosing to play a piece of music in one key over another.

In a rock context, the most common reason for changing key is to accommodate the range of a vocalist. Even the best singers have specific note ranges with which they are happiest working, or with which they feel they can give the best performance. You may also want to change keys to fit in when playing with other musicians: some instruments – especially reed and brass – are much harder to play in certain keys or registers.

At the start of this chapter, you took the pattern of intervals that made up a C major scale and repeated them with a different

root note. In this way, the C major scale became a G major scale. This process is called TRANSPOSITION. Any sequence of notes can be moved in this way. By applying that rule consistently, the intervals between the notes always remain exactly the same – the only difference is that they are in a different key.

The diagram below will help you make your own transpositions. Backing Track #2 is in the key of A major. Let's now convert it to D major. The chords in the original track are A, G, C, D and E minor. We already know that the A chord becomes D (that's the key change). To see what G becomes, look for the note G in the row marked "A". Now follow the notes down until you reach the equivalent note on the row headed "D" – you'll see that the note is C. This means that every time you would've played a G chord in the original key (A major), you instead play a C major chord. The transposed chords are: D (formerly A), C (G), F (C), G (D) and A minor (E minor).

I		II		III		IV		V		VI		VII		I
A	A#	B	C	C#		D	D#	E	F	F#	G	G#		A
B♭	B	C	D♭	D		E♭	E	F	G♭	G	A♭	A		B♭
B	C	C#	D	D#		E	F	F#	G	G#	A	A#		B
C	C#	D	D#	E		F	F#	G	G#	A	A#	B		C
C#	D	D#	E	F		F#	G	G#	A	A#	B	C		C#
D	D#	E	F	F#		G	G#	A	A#	B	C	F#		D
E♭	E	F	G♭	G		A♭	A	B♭	B	C	D♭	D		E♭
E	F	F#	G	G#		A	A#	B	C	C#	D	D#		E
F	G♭	G	A♭	A		B♭	B	C	D♭	D	E♭	E		F
F#	G	G#	A	A#		B	C	C#	D	D#	E	F		F#
G	G#	A	A#	B		C	C#	D	D#	E	F	F#		G
A♭	A	B♭	B	C		D♭	D	E♭	E	F	G♭	G		A♭

BROKEN SCALES

Let's return to the "verse" section of the track. Now we're going to play an alternative version of the four major scales. These are called BROKEN SCALES, because they play the notes of the scale but not in a strict chromatic sequence. Look at the first two bars: the first note is the key-defining root (A); the second note, however, is the third degree of the scale (C♯); we then jump back to B, the second degree of the scale, and so on.

These are not complete broken scales since we don't actually play all of the notes – that would take four bars to do, and Backing Track #2 changes chords after two bars. Remember, you are playing A major over the first two bars; G major over bars 3 and 4, C major over bars 5 and 6, and D major over the last pair.

Not only is this useful in that you become acquainted with the idea of scales, it is also an excellent way of improving your picking skills.   **3/9** ▶

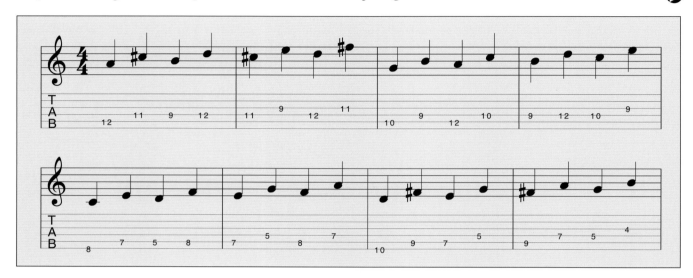

OCTAVE LEAPS

For this exercise you play only the first three notes of every scale. However, after each note, you play the same note an octave higher. This is especially demanding as it calls for you to pick strings that are not immediately next to one another. The first note (A) is played on the 12th fret of the 5th string; the second note (A) is played on the 14th fret of the 3rd string. As you work your way through the piece, make sure that you don't accidentally hit the 5th string with your pick.

To save on space, some of these exercise are only shown accompanying the verse segment. You should find them easy enough to adapt for the chorus sections as well.   **3/10** ▶

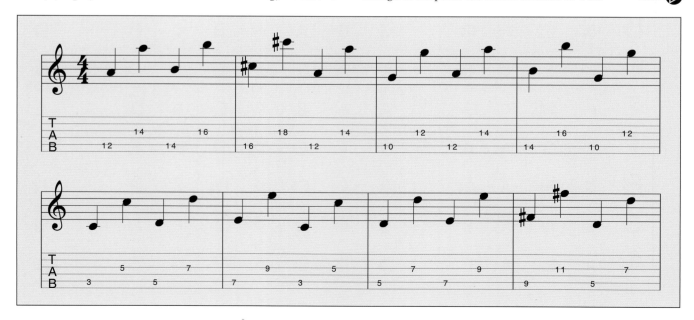

SPEED PICKING

Let's speed things up a little. This piece is essentially the same as your very first scale exercise, the only difference being that instead of picking single crotchets, you play pairs of quavers – the left-hand movement should be unchanged.

The most effective picking technique to use here – and for any other high-speed single note playing – is to alternate a downstroke with an upstroke. Play the sequence through unaccompanied as slowly as you like before trying it with the backing track. If it helps, remember the quaver count: "one-and-two-and-three-and-four-and".   **3/11** ▶

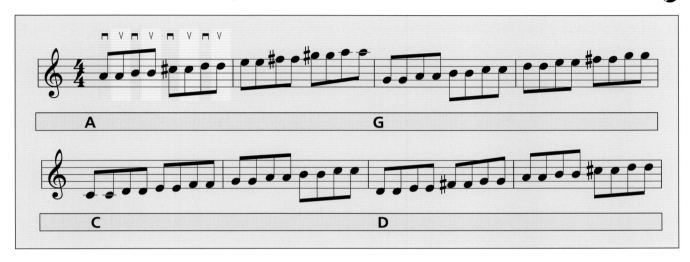

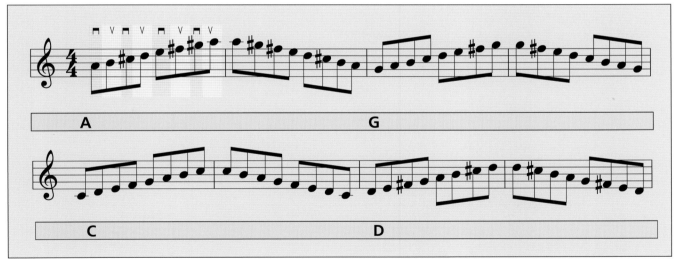

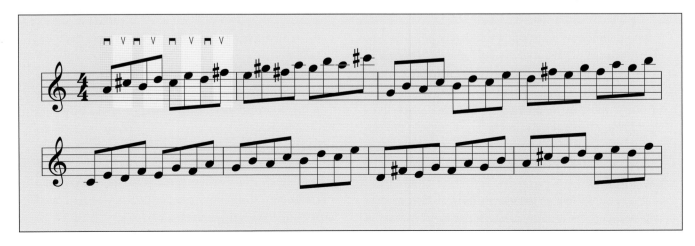

SAME SCALE, NEW RHYTHMS

Here we are going to take the basic major scale and stretch it out rhythmically: you're still going to play the notes of the scale, but this time the individual values of the notes are varied.

Start by working out the time values of each note. To give yourself an idea of the rhythm, tap out the notes with your finger while counting out the time signature. Once you've worked out the notes themselves, play the riffs unaccompanied until you have them off pat.

You will notice that in this example there are two different sets of TAB for you to try out. Although the notes are exactly the same, the top line is based around the use of open strings; the lower line uses more conventional scale pattern fingering. As you play each example listen out for the subtle differences between the way each one sounds.   **3/12** ▶

LEARNING TO IMPROVISE

It would be foolish to imagine that every guitarist who steps forward to take a solo views what is about to be played as a blank canvas, and that the resulting sound is a manifestation of pure inspiration. In fact, in the hands of many musicians improvisation can mean little more than linking together a series of stock musical phrases which, although they might not be identical from one performance to another, amount to minor variations on the same theme.

It may sound like an oxymoron, but you CAN practise improvisation. The facility you develop to improvise will, as much as anything, be down to attitude as much technical capability. The very act of improvisation IS practice for future improvisation, and the more you do, the better you become at it.

In fact, the discipline of improvising within a very tight musical framework teaches you how to draw out as much as possible from very little. You can integrate this approach with your everyday practice of scales. The exercises above are essentially scales with rhythms attached. You can take this approach further by creating your own versions of ascending, descending and broken scales.

TURNING SCALES INTO TUNES

Here are two more rhythms for you to try. This time, we won't be playing scales, but little melodies constructed from those scales. As you play them you'll hear that they still have the essential "majorness" that you get from playing a major scale, but they also have a melodic identity of their own.

The first example shows a practical use of a tie within a single bar. Here we have a note that must sustain for two and a half beats. There isn't a satisfactory way of indicating such a single note, so the minim is tied to the first of the group of quavers. Don't forget, as with all tied notes, the second of the tied notes is never played.

If you're worried about what to play over the chorus section when the E minor chord plays, it's easy enough to convert both sets of riffs so that they work. Let's begin by transposing the riff in the first two bars from A down to E. Look at the transposition chart on page 69 to get the notes. The first six degrees of the major scale are being used. This means that the notes A, B, C♯, D, E, F♯ become E, F♯, G♯ A, B and C♯. However, if we play that riff using those notes over the E minor chord it will sound terrible. This is because the riff is still in E major. To correct this, remember the differences between a major scale and a natural minor scale: both the third and sixth degrees must be flattened – lowered by a semitone. So if we play the riff using the notes E, F♯, G, A, B and C everything will work just fine.   **3/13** ▶

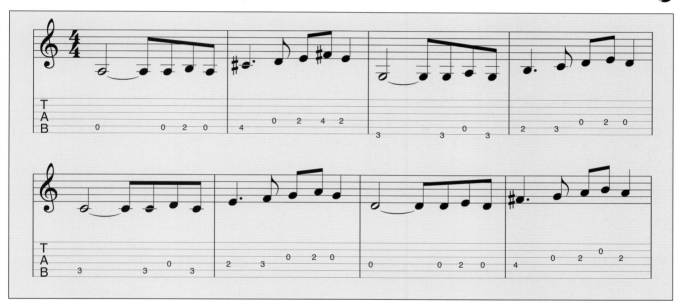

SINGLE-NOTE RHYTHMS

Rhythm guitar is usually more readily associated with strumming chords. However, by picking out repeating sets of single notes in quick succession it becomes possible to create an effective rhythm guitar part. This can be even more effective if you are prepared to experiment with different amplifier settings and effects.

The rhythm below has a rather off-centre feel to it. This is because the root note is played only on the off beat – the natural accents are on the first and third beats. To fret the notes, just use standard open-string chord shapes. You can also transpose this to play over E minor in the chorus, but don't forget to flatten the third note (that means playing C and not C♯). As an alternative, try playing the rhythm with the strings slightly muted by the right hand, giving a staccato effect.   **3/14** ▶

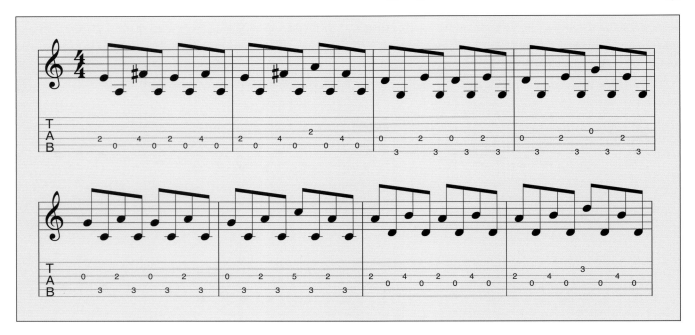

ALMOST A BOOGIE

This exercise uses the first four notes of the major scale. The rhythm is made up from a single crotchet followed by grouped quavers – the first quaver begins on the count of "2".

By now you should be getting used to the fingering patterns, so no TAB has been shown. It's very easy at this stage to ignore options, going for the fingering that feels easiest. Try to avoid this trap. Learning your scales (major and natural minor at the very least) from all possible starting points on the fingerboard is the basic key to developing versatile skills as a lead guitarist.

With that in mind, try these four fingering variations on the exercise below:

- A (6th string/5th fret); C♯ (5th string/4th fret); D (5th string/5th fret); E (5th string/7th fret).
- A (open 5th string); C♯ (5th string/4th fret); D (5th string/5th fret); E (5th string/7th fret).
- A (open 5th string); C♯ (5th string/4th fret); D (open 4th string); E (4th string/2nd fret).
- A (open 5th string); C♯ (5th string/4th fret); D (5th string/5th fret); E (4th string/2nd fret).   **3/15**

MORE SINGLE-NOTE RHYTHMS

This final exercise is a variation on the previous two. This time, the emphatic first beat of the second bar has been pulled a half a beat back into the first bar. This is one of the most commonly heard rhythmic devices in rock music. It can be really effective in giving the impression of "driving" or pushing the beat ahead of itself.

Let's also give a final check to your left-hand fingering. The first bar below indicates which fingers of the left hand should be used to fret each note. If you're following the one-finger-per-fret rule then you will already be doing this.

FOOTNOTE

Backing Track #2 is written in the key of A major. Although we have covered key signatures on page 57, to make things more straightforward (and to get you used to the idea of seeing sharps and flats used on the staff), the music in this chapter has been shown without one. To present the music correctly in A major, three sharp symbols (on C, F and G) would appear directly before the time signature (4/4). Were that the case below, the sharp symbol shown against the note C in the music would no longer be needed since C♯ would be the default value of that line. HOWEVER, since the third bar uses an unsharpened C, that note would have to be indicated with a NATURAL symbol (♮).

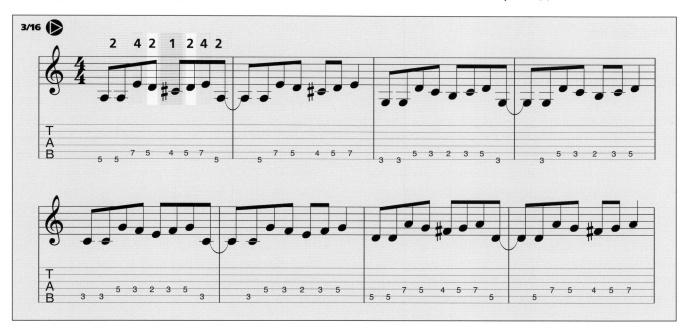

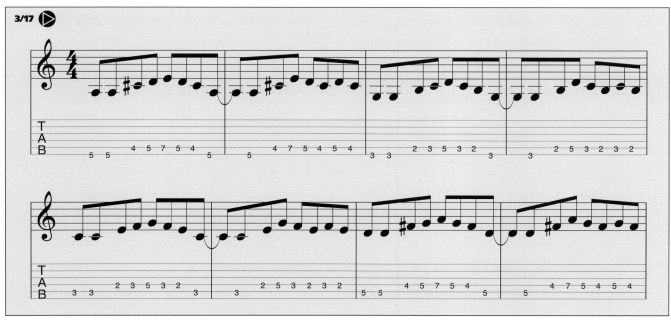

CHAPTER 4
GETTING HEAVY

In this chapter we're going to look at some of the basic techniques used in heavy rock rhythm guitar. Foremost among these is the BARRE CHORD. This type of chord gives you a huge amount of flexibility. With just two basic shapes, you can play powerful chords in any key. There will also be a little more music theory in the shape of INVERSION – juggling around the order of the notes of a chord. We also have Backing Track #3 for you – a speedy rocker with perhaps a slight nod toward British rock legends Black Sabbath.

ROCK GETS HEAVY

With their launch in 1967, the "power trio" Cream, lead by Eric Clapton, spearheaded the first wave of heavy rock. They broke up in 1969, with Clapton pursuing an unexpectedly low-key career thereafter – drug problems and a desire to lose the "guitar hero" tag kept him out of the limelight for most of the 1970s.

The ground laid by Clapton and Jimi Hendrix was taken further by a new breed of "heavy" rock sound, less obviously schooled in the blues tradition. In the US, bands such as the infamously loud Vanilla Fudge, Iron Butterfly and Grand Funk Railroad filled stadiums across the country. But it was the UK that provided the three brand leaders of the period: Led Zeppelin (*see across the page*), Deep Purple and Black Sabbath. Their three respective guitarists – Jimmy Page, Ritchie Blackmore and Tony Iommi – made a major impression on

young musicians growing up in the 1970s. All three bands followed a broadly similar pattern in that most – although by no means all – of their music comprised powerful driving riffs played at a fast tempo and high-volume, high-speed soloing (plus, one might also add, lyrics of a highly dubious nature).

Although Zeppelin were the most musically interesting of this group, special mention should be made of the unusual range of influences that Ritchie Blackmore brought to the Deep Purple sound. Although his riffs for rock classics such as "Smoke on the Water" and "Black Night" have become "air guitar" standards, his playing owes as much to the classical tradition as the blues, especially his use of arpeggiation on tracks such as "Mandrake Root". Purple would later go on to record the *Concerto for Group and Orchestra* with the Royal Philharmonic Orchestra, conducted by Sir Malcolm Arnold, although this was driven by the band's classically trained keyboard player Jon Lord.

IN THIS CHAPTER YOU'LL LEARN...

- A brief history of heavy rock
- The E-shaped alternative "thumb" technique
- C-shaped barre chords
- Playing barre chords over a rock backing track
- Chord slides
- Inverting triads
- Playing 5th "power" chords
- Feedback

- E-shaped barre chords
- A-shaped barre chords
- G-shaped barre chords
- Finger slides
- Inversion theory
- Interval inversions
- All about valve amplifiers

LED ZEPPELIN: MASTERS OF ROCK

Of the many British guitar heroes who emerged out of the blues boom – such as Eric Clapton, Jeff Beck, Peter Green – it is ultimately Jimmy Page (*see right*) whose work has displayed the most variety and enduring appeal. And the influence of his band, Led Zeppelin, can still be heard in many of the bands that have emerged during the 1990s.

By his late teens, Page was already finding regular work playing on the London session scene, gaining a reputation as one of the most versatile and hard-working guitarists around. Often playing three or four different sessions in a day, among the earliest beneficiaries of his playing were Them's "Baby Please Don't Go" and Tom Jones's "It's Not Unusual".

In 1964, his reputation was such that he was offered the job of replacing Eric Clapton in the Yardbirds. He turned it down – a measure, perhaps, of the lucrative nature of his session work. Two years later he was asked again, and this time he accepted. By then, the Yardbirds starred Jeff Beck in the leading role, so it was perhaps inevitable that there would be friction between the two players. When the volatile Beck walked out in early 1968, the band disintegrated, leaving Page on his own with the rights to the Yardbirds' name and a contracted tour of Sweden to fulfil. With Peter Grant as a manager, Page went about forming the New Yardbirds for the tour. The musicians they found were session bass star John Paul Jones, drummer John Bonham and singer Robert Plant. The band completed the Scandinavian tour as the New Yardbirds, but returned to England with a new identity – Led Zeppelin. The name was alleged to have been the idea of Who drummer Keith Moon – he suggested that it was how their music would go down with audiences.

Moon couldn't have been more wrong. Their 1969 debut album was a revelation. The sound was an awesome "heavy" blues, each musician giving virtuoso performances. It sold by the bucketload on both sides of the Atlantic and almost overnight established the band as number one in their field.

At the heart of the Zeppelin sound lay the intricate guitar work and production skills of Jimmy Page. His brilliance on the acoustic guitar can be heard on his altered-tuning version of the folky "Black Mountain Side". However, it is his electric playing that has enthralled (and influenced) so many – the power-charged riffing and,

let's not forget, the gently picked arpeggios of Zeppelin's "theme tune", "Stairway To Heaven".

In 1980, after a decade of unsurpassed success, the band broke up following the death of John Bonham. Although Page has remained active, it is with the eleven Led Zeppelin albums that his reputation will always rest. With an extraordinary body of work behind them, Led Zeppelin set a new benchmark for technical excellence in rock without ever seeming to be dull, self-important or over-indulgent. It is a benchmark that no other heavy rock band has really come close to reaching.

THE POWER OF THE BARRE CHORD

The chords you have played so far have been formed around the open strings of the guitar. However, restricting yourself to using only these chords gives you little access to playing in many of the sharp or flat keys. The solution to this problem comes in the form of the barre chord. While a lot of music that falls under the broad category of rock can be played using only open-string chords, ignoring the full range of possibilities is rather like a painter not using colours. One solution is to use BARRE CHORDS.

CHORDS ON THE MOVE

Barre chords are essentially open-string chord shapes that can be formed at different positions along the fingerboard. To form a barre chord, the 1st finger is stretched across the width of the fingerboard, and the remaining three fingers are used to form the chord shape. In effect, the 1st finger acts like the nut or zero fret. The great thing about barre chords is that they allow open-string chord shapes to be played in any key.

The most commonly used barre chords are variations on the E- and A-shaped open-string chords. Less common are those formed around the open C and G chords – they are possible, but much trickier. Barre chord are also sometimes known as "slash" chords.

FORM E MAJOR WITH THE 2ND, 3RD AND 4TH FINGERS.

MOVE THE HAND ALONG THE FINGERBOARD.

POSITION THE 1ST FINGER ON THE 5TH FRET.

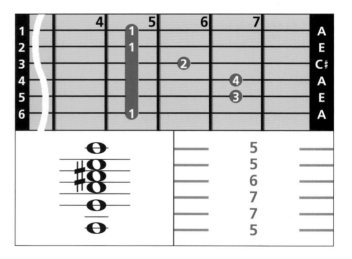

MOBILE NUTS

Barre chords work because the 1st finger acts as a repositioned nut from which open-string shapes can be built. In practice this is more complex since you no longer have a 1st finger with which to fret individual notes.

Some guitarists like the way in which open-string chords sound; others appreciate the ease with which chord changes can be made. Therefore, instead of using the 1st finger to create a barre, some choose to fit a mechanical device called a CAPO instead.

The capo fits over the strings on the fingerboard and fastens at the back of the neck. It clamps the strings down acting exactly like a 1st finger barre.

If a capo were to be fitted to the 5th fret, a standard open E major shape could be strummed – the resulting chord would be A major chord.

USING THE THUMB

The left-hand fingering for the E-shaped barre shown across the page is designed to provide you with maximum flexibility to switch between playing chords and single notes. This is because the thumb is maintained firmly against the back of the neck. However, not everyone follows this rule: some guitarists can be seen using the 1st finger to barre just the top two strings – the thumb is then stretched around the back of the neck to hold down the 6th string.

Most formal tutors would consider this to be (at the very least) quite unorthodox. But is this such a bad thing? On the one hand it may make changing chord shapes a little more difficult, but it does also allow for the alteration or muting of notes on the 6th string. Those with a particularly wide fingerspan may also be able to reach over to fret the 5th string. This theoretically enables you to play rhythm with integrated moving bass parts over all six strings at the same time.

Which one is best? Frankly, both have useful advantages. A good compromise is to learn the formal positioning (which will probably be the most versatile and useful in the long-run) and then, when you're feeling particularly experimental, try out the alternative technique to see whether it has any potential uses for your own playing. There's no single, all-encompassing set of rules by which the guitar should be played – anyone claiming otherwise is likely to be an extremely inflexible, old-fashioned music teacher.

This is not intended to sound like some sort of inverted snobbery. Although the classical system can provide everything you need to become a good guitarist, you may well find other approaches or have other ideas that may be more appropriate to your own music – when that happens you should at least give them a go.

E-SHAPED BARRE

Look at the photographs across the page to see how to form a barre chord based around the open E shape:

• Begin by forming a regular open-string E major chord. This time, however, use the 3rd, 4th and 2nd fingers to fret the 5th, 4th, and 3rd strings respectively.

• Slide your left hand five frets along the fingerboard, so that the 3rd and 4th fingers are on the 7th fret.

• Place the 1st finger firmly behind the 5th fret. Now play across all six strings of the chord. This is an A major played using an E-shaped barre on the 5th fret.

Making effective use of an E-shaped barre relies totally on a good knowledge of the notes on the 6th string. If, for example, you need to play a C♯ major chord, then you can play an E-shaped barre with the 1st finger covering the 9th fret – so long as you already know that the 9th fret of the 6th string is C♯. Here are the root notes on the 6th string:

Open string	E major
1st fret	F major
2nd fret	F♯/G♭ major
3rd fret	G major
4th fret	G♯/A♭ major
5th fret	A major
6th fret	A♯/B♭ major
7th fret	B major
8th fret	C major
9th fret	C♯/D♭ major
10th fret	D major
11th fret	D♯/E♭ major
12th fret	E major

A-SHAPED BARRE

Here is how you can create barre chords using the basic open A major shape:

- Form a regular open-string A major chord. This time, however, use the 2nd, 3rd and 4th fingers to fret the 4th, 3rd and 2nd strings respectively.

- Slide your hand seven frets along the fingerboard, so that the 2nd, 3rd and 4th fingers are on the 9th fret.

- Place the 1st finger behind the 7th fret. Now play across the first five strings of the chord. This is an E major played using an E-shaped barre on the 7th fret.

As with open A major chords, playing the 6th string is optional. The root will always be on the 5th string – the note played on the 6th string is the perfect 5th below the root. When playing barre chords with distortion the 6th string can add to the general effect of the sound without ruining the tonal balance.

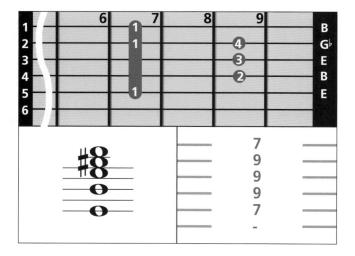

FORM A MAJOR WITH THE 2ND, 3RD AND 4TH FINGERS.

MOVE THE HAND ALONG THE FINGERBOARD.

POSITION THE 1ST FINGER ON THE 7TH FRET.

BARRE TIPS

Before you can play barre chords with any fluidity you need to build up strength in your fingers. Here are some tips that might help you ease the pain.

Concentrate only on the strings you HAVE to push down for the chord. In an E-shaped barre, because you have three other fingers at work you only need to worry about the 1st finger covering the 1st, 2nd and 6th strings. So keep your barre finger as close to the fret as possible, but you can bring a slight curve to it if it makes life a little more comfortable. Also, try gently pulling the neck toward you with your fretting hand. This may make keeping the fretting fingers in place a little easier.

You should also consider your guitar. If the action is poor – the strings are too far from the fingerboard – and you are using heavy-gauge strings then you're going to have your work cut out playing barre chords at all.

Efficient practice is a must, though. Strumming along with barre-chorded versions of your favourite music will certainly help: you'll get the best results if you find a way to make it fun.

SLASHING MADE SIMPLE

Many modern styles of rock require chords to be executed at high speed. Consequently, a lot of rock players find it more convenient to play the A-shaped barre as a kind of double-barre. To do this, the 1st finger acts as the nut. This time, however, the 3rd finger is used to cover the 2nd, 3rd and 4th strings.

As with any A-shape chord, because it's lower in pitch than the root note, playing the 6th string is optional. At the top end, ensure that the tip of 3rd finger is bent back so that the 1st string is not accidentally muted. Or just don't play the string all.

This way of playing an A-shaped chord is exceptionally good for sequences that make fast shifts between E-shaped and A-shaped barre chords. One reason for this is based on the familiar I-IV-V pattern of chords (the "Three-Chord Trick" we saw on page 31). With the barre on any fret, a progression from the

THE 1ST FINGER FORMS THE BARRE

THE 3RD FINGER FORMS A PARTIAL BARRE

THE 4TH FINGER IS HELD CLEAR OF THE STRINGS

E shape to the A shape is a "I-IV" movement. This means that probably the most common chord change in pop and rock can be made easily and in any key without even having to move the 1st finger.

In a similar way, the movement between an A-shape and an E-shape barre on the same fret is a "I-V" progression – this time the root chord playing down to a second chord which is lower in pitch.

OTHER BARRES

Barre chords based around the open E major and A major shapes are also sometimes referred to as 6TH-STRING and 5TH-STRING BARRES. Although they are far and away the most common types of barre chord, it is possible to build other open-string shaped barre chords.

C-SHAPED BARRE

Here's a way you can turn an open C major shape into an E major chord.

- Form a C major shape with the 2nd, 3rd and 4th fingers playing the 2nd, 4th and 5th strings respectively.

- Now slide the fingers four frets along the fingerboard. Place the 1st finger behind the 4th fret.

- Strum the top five strings – an E major chord.

The C-shaped barre places considerable strain on the little finger. Not only does it require a sizeable stretch, but it also has to fret one of the bass notes, which, being of a higher gauge, requires more pressure to hold it down against the fret. As such, practicing the C-shaped barre has the added advantage of strengthening the little finger considerably.

G-SHAPED BARRE

Less common is the G-shaped barre. Because of what would be an unfeasible stretch between the 2nd, 3rd and 4th fingers, it is not possible to play a complete six-string open-G chord on the barre. Therefore, the 1st string is not used.

- Form a partial open-G major chord using the 3rd and 4th fingers to fret the 5th and 6th strings.

- Slide your hand five frets along with the index finger behind the 5th fret. This creates a C major chord.

PETE TOWNSHEND: RHYTHM MASTER

Having established themselves in the mid-'60s, the Who – led by songwriter and guitarist Pete Townshend – carved out a reputation as one of the greatest live acts of the 1970s.

Townshend's greatest asset was his ability to produce awesome power without resorting to the excessive soloing which was so common in much rock music of the time. A testimony to his playing can be heard on the band's classic *Live At Leeds* album – arguably the greatest rock concert album ever produced. Indeed, by the end of the decade, Townshend was one of an "old school" elite that was able to claim the respect of the punk generation.

Like Keith Richards of the Rolling Stones, Townshend has always defined himself as a rhythm player. And, like Richards, he is likely to be remembered for the sheer power of his playing and the ability to pen some of the most memorable intro riffs of the past 30 years – the "sus4" chords which herald the opening of "Pinball Wizard", for example.

BACKING TRACK # 3

The third backing track in our series is an update on the style of early heavy rock bands from the first half of the 1970s, such as Deep Purple or Black Sabbath. The track consists of two alternating sections – each one plays through twice before changing.

The "A" segment is a straightforward driving riff in the key of A. Like a lot of rock music of this type, it is the bass line which is really driving the riff – the guitar simply vamps along with the chords.

However, something strange happens in the "B" segment; the song transforms itself into a completely different key: B♭.

Such a key change within a song is known as a MODULATION. The interval between the two roots makes for a jarring but powerfully dramatic chord change as part "A" crosses into part "B". (Contrary to common misconception, modulation and transposition are not interchangeable terms: modulation describes a tonal movement within a piece of music; transposition describes a piece of music being changed from one key to another.)

SOUND

To play music in this style really requires distortion, and plenty of it. This can be in the form of natural amplifier overdrive, or that provided by an external effect *(see pages 44–45)*. Furthermore, the addition of a compression pedal will make the sound even greater since it reduces the DYNAMIC RANGE – the volume between the loudest and softest notes – creating a tighter and generally more powerful sound.

PLAYING TIPS

Backing Track #3 calls for the use of a well-developed right-hand damping technique. The entirety of part "A" is, in fact, played with dampened strings. By releasing the muting effect for the "B" section, the dramatic impact of the unusual chord change can is further heightened.

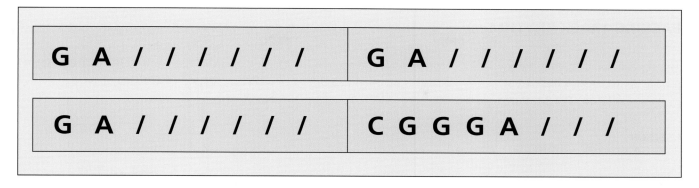

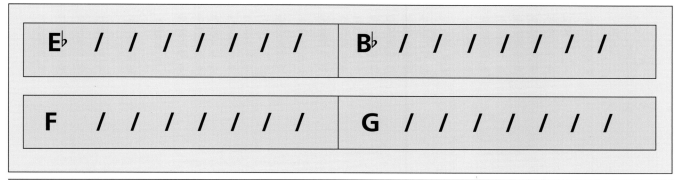

BARRE CHORDS IN PRACTICE

Backing Track #3 can be played just by using barre chords.   4/1 ▶

E-SHAPE

To play G major, create an E-shaped barre with the 1st finger on the 3rd fret. To make the change to A major, simply move the hand two frets along so that the 1st finger is on the 5th fret.

A-SHAPE

Things get a little trickier for the C major chord. Because of the nature of

the rhythm, and the speed of the chord change between bars three and four, it simply becomes impossible to move the whole shape up the fingerboard to the 8th fret (C), and then back down to the 3rd fret (G) in sufficient time. To get over this problem we can play an A-shaped barre chord on the 3rd fret – this means that the position of the hand along the neck barely has to change.

There is one further speed-related problem with this C major chord. even the best guitarists around would be hard-pressed to move from an E-shape to a full four-fingered A-shape and back

at such speed. This is an ideal instance to bring out the double-barred chord – the 1st finger is positioned over the 3rd fret and the 3rd finger is positioned over the top four strings of the 5th fret.

PART B

The principles are exactly the same for the "B" section of the track:

- **E♭ major is an A-shape with the 1st finger on the 6th fret.**
- **B♭ major is an E-shape with the 1st finger on the 6th fret.**
- **F major is an E-shape with the 1st finger on the 1st fret.**

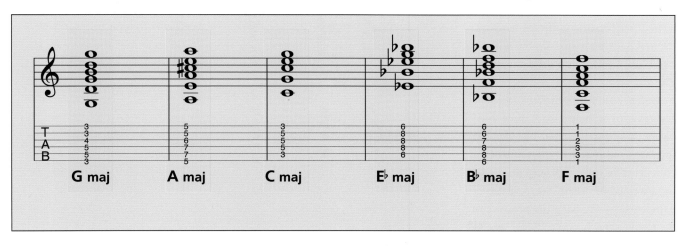

BACKING TRACK RHYTHM

The rhythm used by both the guitars playing on the backing track are shown on the staves below. The first three bars of the first part are very simple groups of quavers. The rhythm changes for the first two beats of the fourth bar. The first quaver is followed by a dotted crotchet – notes of a half beat and one-and-a-half beats respectively. If you're counting, play on the emphasised half-beats: "ONE-AND-two-and-THREE-AND-FOUR-AND". (There should be slightly less emphasis on the final three quavers.)

A SECTION

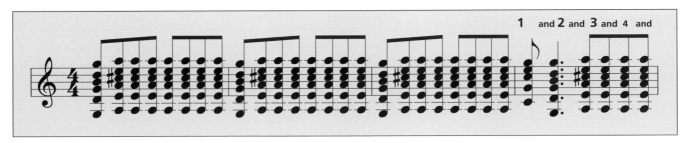

B SECTION

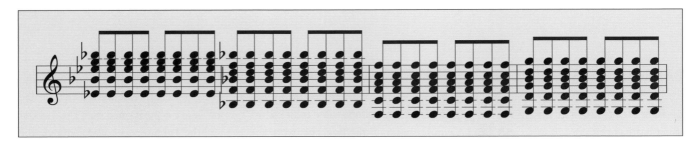

A NEW ENDING

Let's now look at some alternative ways of dealing with the fourth bar of the first section. The three quavers at the end of the bar are really superfluous in marking out the rhythmic device used. But would it sound just as powerful if they were replaced by a sustained note?

The three bars shown on the right have three slightly different endings; the first bar simply sustains the note for two beats – this feels a little unnatural. The second bar ends on a crotchet and a crotchet rest. This means that the note sustains for a count of "three-and" before it stops. The final bar uses the staccato symbol to half the value of the crotchet. This time, the chord must only be sustained for a half beat – it can be dampened by releasing the pressure of the barring finger. **4/2** ▶

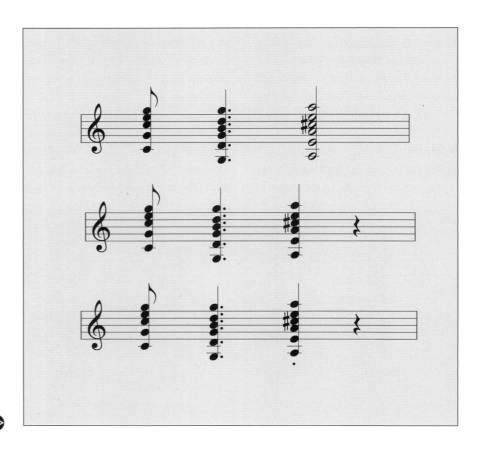

FINGER SLIDES

A SLIDE refers to the effect of running one or more of the fingers of the left hand along the string between notes. There are a number of different types of commonly used slide, all of which produce their own distinct effects.

SLIDING BETWEEN NOTES

The most common type of slide plays one note, then slides the finger along the string – while it is still vibrating – to a new note. Try the example on the right for yourself.

- **Poise the 1st finger above the nut on the 1st string.**
- **Play the open 1st string (E).**
- **While the string vibrates, drag the 1st finger along the string until you reach the 12th fret.**
- **Hold your finger in position and let the note on the 12th fret ring.**

Make sure that you keep the pressure consistent throughout – if you release the pressure from the string while you move your hand it will dampen the sound.

This slide is notated with the two notes linked by both a curve and a line. If you remove the curve, then the second note has to be struck in its own right. **4/3**

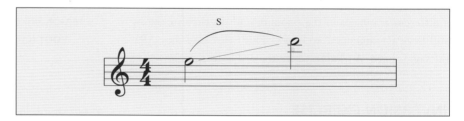

Instead of making the first chord change two independently struck quavers, use a slide: strike the chord on the first beat, and then slide the left hand up from the G position to the A position on the half beat.

In the second example, the line after the final minim indicates that the chord should end with an indeterminate downward slide that gradually fades away, but not on any particular note.

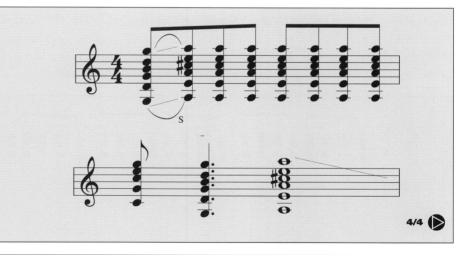

4/4

SLIDE EXERCISES

These exercises will help you get to grips with the various slide techniques. Begin by playing a simple C major scale on the 5th string:

- **Play C (3rd fret) with the 1st finger; with the note still ringing, slide the finger up to D (5th fret).**

- **Play E (7th fret); with the note still ringing, slide the finger up to F (8th fret).**

- **Play G (10th fret); slide the finger up to the 12th fret.**

- **Play B (14th fret); with the note still ringing, slide the finger up to C (15th fret).**

Now repeat the exercise, this time sliding to a struck note:

- **Play C (3rd fret) with the 1st finger; with the note still ringing, slide the finger up TOWARD D (5th fret). As the 1st finger is about to reach the 5th fret, strike a clean D with your pick.**

INVERTING CHORDS

When looking at an open-string A major chord, we've already discussed the pros and cons of playing the 6th string: although the note is E, which is part of the A major triad, because it is lower in pitch than the 5th string root note (A), in some cases it can create an unbalanced sound. Where chords like this are played – with the notes out of ascending pitch sequence – this is called INVERSION.

Look at the three triads on the right. The first chord is C major, using the notes C (root), E (major 3rd) and G (perfect 5th). But what happens if you move the root note (C) ABOVE the 3rd and the 5th notes, as shown in the middle chord below? If you work out the notes from the bottom up, you can see that the lowest note is now E. So does this make it a chord in the key of E? Before answering, play the two triads, one after the other. You will hear that they clearly have a different emphasis in their sound, and yet they somehow still have a "sameness" to them. This is because they ARE the same chord. A triad in which the 3rd note is the lowest in

pitch is called a FIRST INVERSION. That same triad can be further rearranged so that the 5th is the lowest in pitch. This is known as a SECOND INVERSION.

COMPARING INVERSIONS

You can compare the sounds created by the original C major triad (ROOT POSITION), and the first and second inversions by playing them as shown below.   **4/5** ▶

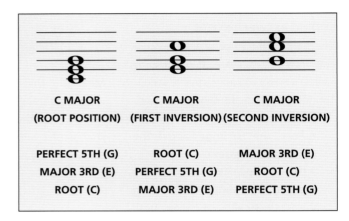

C MAJOR (ROOT POSITION)	C MAJOR (FIRST INVERSION)	C MAJOR (SECOND INVERSION)
PERFECT 5TH (G)	ROOT (C)	MAJOR 3RD (E)
MAJOR 3RD (E)	PERFECT 5TH (G)	ROOT (C)
ROOT (C)	MAJOR 3RD (E)	PERFECT 5TH (G)

INVERSION EXERCISE

If you place a 1st-finger barre on any fret and only play the 2nd, 3rd and 4th strings, you will always be playing a second inversion of a major chord. In a rock context with heavy distortion, this will make a simple and effective substitute for

a root chord; in more delicate surroundings the limitation of this approach will be heard.

The "B" section at the foot of the page uses the same technique. This time, however, the first beat of the second, third and fourth bars has been "pulled" into the previous bar. Try both sets of staves along with Backing Track #3.

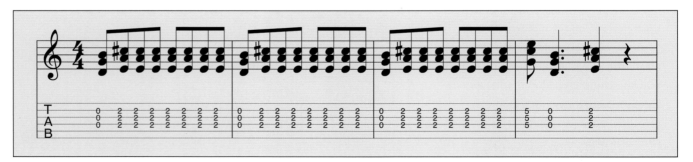

A SECTION

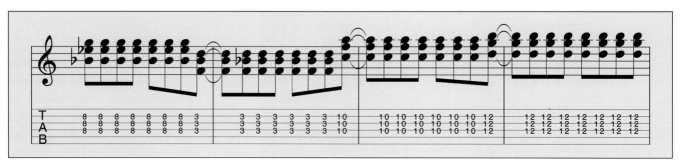

B SECTION

FURTHER INVERSIONS

Let's now extend the idea of the barred 2nd, 3rd and 4th strings. The two chord diagrams on the right both represent major triads. If the bar were on the 7th fret, the upper diagram would be a second inversion of D major. By adding the 2nd and 3rd fingers to that barre (as shown in the lower diagram) you are creating a new major chord – in this case, a first inversion of G major.

If you use these chord shapes to play the staves shown below, you will hear that the movement between the two is an extremely familiar one, used by rock bands in every sphere since the 1960s. To work out the rhythm, count like this, emphasizing the half beats in capital letters: "ONE-AND-TWO-and-THREE-AND-four-AND-one-and-TWO-and-THREE-AND-four-and".   4/6 ▶

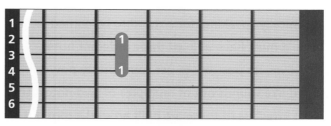

D MAJOR (SECOND INVERSION) WHEN BARRED ON 7TH FRET.

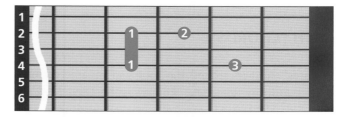

G MAJOR (FIRST INVERSION) WHEN BARRED ON 7TH FRET.

A SECTION

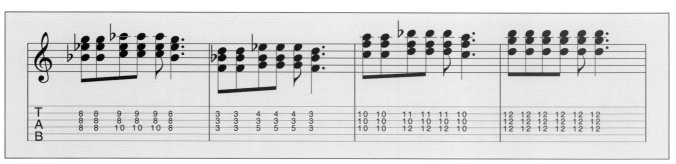

B SECTION

INTERVAL INVERSIONS

When triads are inverted their sound and function alter. The same can be applied to any two-note intervals. In the key of C major, the interval between the first degree (C) and the fourth degree (F) is a perfect 4th. If you invert that interval so that the F is now lower in pitch than C, the interval changes. Counting DOWN the scale degrees, it becomes a perfect 5th. This may substantially alter the musical uses of this interval.

There is a consistent link between inverted intervals.

Rather like the opposite sides of a dice adding up to seven, the intervals above or below add up to nine: a 4th becomes a 5th; a 3rd becomes a 6th; and a 2nd becomes a 7th.

Let's go back to one of our earlier examples, "Oh, when the saints go marching in". We all know this tune, but how would it sound if instead of the first four notes rising in pitch, the second note of the melody dropped below the first? The notes would be the same, but the intervals would be different. In practice, the tune is altered substantially.

POWER CHORDS

Technically speaking, for a chord to be named as such, it must have at least three different notes. However, it's possible to get some pretty powerful chord-like sounds out of multiples of two notes. The most effective of these are built around a root note and a perfect fifth.

FIFTH "CHORDS"

"Chords" formed around the root and an interval of a perfect fifth are sometimes known as FIFTHS, FIVES or POWER CHORDS. Harmonically speaking, they are tonally ambiguous, which makes them all the more versatile. The reason for this lies in the characteristics of a major and minor triad. The only difference between the two is in the second note: the presence of a major 2nd or a minor 2nd WHOLLY defines the chord either as being a major or a minor. The "five" chord, on the other hand, has only the first and third notes of the triad. This means that both major and minor scales in the same key could be played over that chord. Or in a group setting, the major or minor notes could be played on different instruments, thereby creating the full triadic effect.

This type of chord is particularly popular in metal and rock because of its simplicity. When played with heavy distortion, "five" chords tend to retain their character and emphasise the harmonious nature of the two closely related notes.

BRIGHTENING UP 5THS

Additions can be made to 5th chords that can create a more interesting effect without detracting from the basic sound. The most common variation is to bring in an ADDED 2ND. This is the second degree of the major scale in a given key. In the key of C, that means adding a D; in G that means adding A.

To get a feel for how a 5 ADD 2 sounds, fret a regular open-string A major chord and then remove your finger from the 2nd string so that it plays an open B. If you strum the top five strings the notes are (from bottom to top) A (I), E (V), A (I), B (II), E (V).

Because some 5th chords are only made up from playing three strings, they are often combined with melodic phrases – crossing the boundaries of lead and rhythm guitar.

PLAYING THE FIVES

Five chords are extremely easy to play, the simplest examples being based around the E- and A-shaped barre forms.

In the first example shown below, the fingering is taken from a standard E-major barre chord shape. In this instance you only need to play the bottom three strings. Although there are three notes being played in each case, the highest-pitched note is an octave doubling of the root – so it still isn't a real chord. Take care to mute the other strings or else you are likely to saddle yourself with unwanted noise.

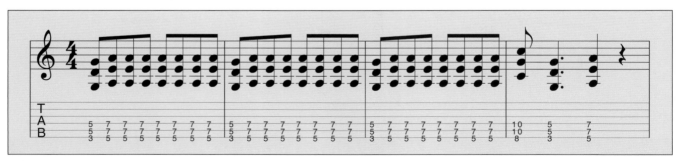

A SECTION

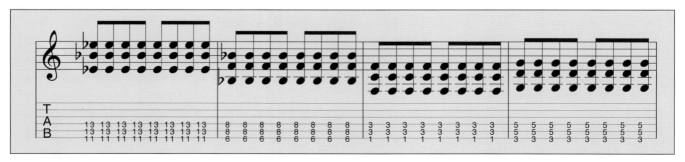

B SECTION

FULL-BODIED FIVES

It's also possible to create fuller versions of these chords. On the right you can see a chord diagram and hand photograph of a five-string fifth chord in the key of A. (In fact, you could play the bottom E string as well if you felt that way inclined.)

The top four strings of this chord can also be used in a mobile fashion, the root always being the notes played on the 1st and 3rd strings. Try this out over the top of section "B" of the backing track. To play E♭, the 1st finger barre is placed on the 11th fret; G♭ is on the 4th fret; F on the 1st fret; and G is on the 3rd fret.

FIFTH IN E

The chord diagram beneath shows a full six-string voicing for a fifth chord in E. This can be used to create a particularly powerful or droning sound since it features the root (E) played over three octaves, and the perfect fifth (B) played over two.

Note that by playing B on the 4th fret of the 3rd string and open B on the 2nd string you are doubling up the same note. If you find the sound this creates attractive, you will probably also find the pages on alternative tunings (pages 164–165) of further interest. You may also find it satisfying to experiment with 12-string guitars.

You can also create interesting effects by using a droning PEDAL TONE, moving the basic chord shape to different points on the fingerboard but still playing the open bottom E.

FIFTH "CHORD" IN A.

FINGER POSITION FOR A FIFTH IN THE KEY OF A.

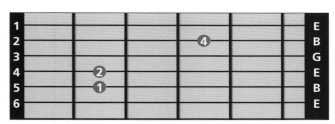

FIFTH "CHORD" IN E.

BARRE CHORD FINDER

This chart provides a reference for playing the different barre chord shapes. The numbers represent the fret on which the 1st finger creates the barre. Each column header indicates the chord shape played on the barre. Each cells tells you the key that will result from chords played on different frets. For example, if you wanted a C-shaped barre chord in F, look down the third column until you see F – if you look at that row number on the left you'll see that the barre must be placed on the 5th fret.

With knowledge of the notes on the fingerboard, the positioning of the barre for E and A shapes will become second nature because they simply follow the notes of the 6th and 5th strings.

FRET	E-SHAPE	A-SHAPE	C-SHAPE	G-SHAPE
0	E	A	C	G
1	F	A♯/B♭	C♯/D♭	G♯/A♭
2	F♯/G♭	B	D	A
3	G	C	D♯/E♭	A♯/B♭
4	G♯/A♭	C♯/D♭	E	B
5	A	D	F	C
6	A♯/B♭	D♯/E♭	F♯/G♭	C♯/D♭
7	B	E	G	D
8	C	F	G♯/A♭	D♯/E♭
9	C♯/D♭	F♯/G♭	A	E
10	D	G	A♯/B♭	F
11	D♯/E♭	G♯/A♭	B	F♯/G♭
12	E	A	C	G

FEEDBACK EFFECTS

The sound of feedback is heard in many types of rock music. When played under the right conditions, a single sustained note or chord can be made to "morph" into a pure, high-pitched overtone. Although there are a number of artificial ways of creating this effect, it is, in fact, a natural acoustic phenomenon: indeed, it was one that the pioneers of electric guitar design worked hard to eliminate.

WHAT IS FEEDBACK?

Feedback is caused by an amplified sound being played back loud enough for it to affect the source signal. We've all heard the unpleasant squeal of a microphone being positioned too close to a connected amplifier and speaker. What happens is that the microphone picks up the sound that it has just generated coming from the loudspeaker. It is effectively a continuously building loop of sound that continues to "feed back" on itself until either the microphone or speaker is unplugged, or the volume of the amplifier is reduced to a level where the microphone will be unable to pick it.

In the realm of the guitar, feedback first became an issue during the 1930s – when the first electric guitars appeared they were little more than acoustic models with magnetic pickups fitted beneath the strings. Players found that if the amplifier volume was too great, the sound coming from the loudspeaker would cause the body of the guitar (and hence the strings) to vibrate, generating unwanted sounds.

Players found that they could begin to overcome the problem of feedback by repositioning themselves in relation to their amplification. A better solution, however, was to redesign the idea of the electric guitar so that the body would be less prone to vibration. This was achieved by increasing the mass – by making it out of a solid block of wood, rather than fitting the hollow sound chamber used on traditional acoustic guitars.

THE PIONEERS

Although jazz pioneer Charlie Christian was reputed to have attempted to integrate feedback into his playing during the 1940s, the power of this sound was harnessed effectively by the first generation of Chicago electric blues players, especially Muddy Waters. It was through their influence that the stars of the 1960s "Blues Boom" made feedback a central part of the rock sound.

Over the years, while many of the thrashier rock styles have used feedback as a "noise" effect, some guitarists have been able to create more conventionally "musical" sounds. Among the finest exponents is British guitarist Jeff Beck – much of the lead playing on his 1970s solo albums makes extensive use of feedback. One particularly effective technique is to play a single note, let it sustain, and as the feedback overtone fades in, put a gentle touch of vibrato on the string.   **4/7** ▶

VALVES AND FEEDBACK

Although solid-state transistor amplification continues to find its own followers, most rock guitarists favour the classic valve amplifier sound. Unlike the sharp, clean and brittle tones of a "trannie" amp, valves produce a characteristic warmth and smoothness of tone. Valve amplifiers are also noted for producing a pleasant tonal distortion as the volume increases. Different types of valves are capable of producing different tones, so some guitarists have been known to experiment endlessly with various combinations.

As far as feedback is concerned, a valve amplifier is an absolute necessity for creating natural, usably "musical" sounds. To be honest, attempting to do this with most solid-state models usually creates a deeply unpleasant squeal which is more akin to microphone feedback.

SETTINGS FOR FEEDBACK

To get usable feedback it's critical that you have your amp set up properly. As we've already seen, a valve amplifier is a necessity for natural feedback, but some form of distortion is also needed. Here is an amplifier setting that should get things going for you.

A high input volume causes the preamplifier to distort. Set the treble high to generate a cutting sound. The output control governs the overall volume – the higher it is, the more likely you are to get feedback.

Since the treble control is essentially a volume control for the treble frequencies, if it is too high, feedback may become uncontrollable. Some guitarists control this using the tone dial on their guitars.

If you are a sold-state user it's possible to get artificial feedback from effects pedals, although they won't sound anything like as good. Some guitar manufacturers have also experimented with building in feedback and sustain effects – the early 1990s Kramer American had an "infinite sustain" switch that gave a good approximation of feedback when played with distortion.

INPUT   BASS   MIDDLE   TREBLE   OUTPUT

POSITIONAL ISSUES

Since feedback is a natural acoustic phenomenon, the position of the guitar in relation to the amplifier and loudspeaker, and the surroundings in which you are playing, will have an important impact on the way feedback behaves.

The diagram below shows that by positioning yourself directly in front of the speaker, feedback is most likely to occur, although here it may be difficult for you to control. The two bands either side of the "hot area" are more likely to yield usable results. In these areas you should be able control the sound more effectively – indeed, you will probably find that a small movement in the angle of the guitar in relation to the speaker can give very different results. With that in mind, it's no surprise to find that some guitarists spend a good deal of time during the soundcheck before a concert finding their own hot spots and making chalk marks on the stage.

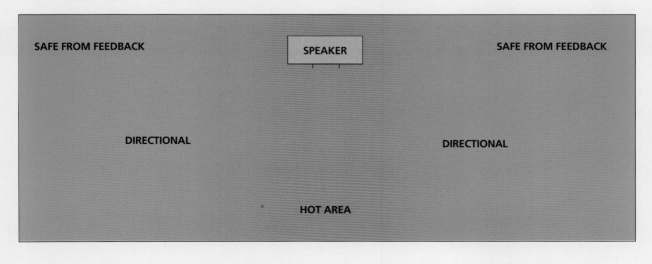

SAFE FROM FEEDBACK   SPEAKER   SAFE FROM FEEDBACK

DIRECTIONAL   DIRECTIONAL

HOT AREA

CHAPTER 5
A CASE OF THE BLUES

Blues music is absolutely fundamental to the history and development of most forms of popular music over the past century. The musical form evolved out of the experience of Black Americans, whose ancestors were transported from their homes in Africa to work as slave labour in America's Deep South. Combining with other folk forms brought to the continent by European migrants – especially religious music – by the early 20th century it had become a uniquely American folk form.

ALL ABOUT THE BLUES

In 1912, bandleader W.C. Handy published his composition "Memphis Blues". It is noteworthy in that it's the earliest record we have of the word "blues" being used in a musical context. But the blues were being sung long before this time, by the slave labourers on the cotton and tobacco plantations of Mississippi, Tennessee and Virginia.

Handy had moved to Clarksdale, Mississippi in 1903 to take a job as musical director of a black band. It was while travelling around the South that he was exposed to a variety of indigenous folk musics which we now know as blues: a lone guitarist scraping a knife across a battered guitar and singing the familiar three-line blues verse; the ramshackle jug bands; the informal gospel choirs.

Because of the prevailing attitudes to race at the time – remember, it was barely 50 years earlier that the issue of slavery had thrown America into civil war – traditional blues first became popularised by white entertainers, in musical hall variety "minstrel" shows, before the first generation of popular black entertainers emerged. By 1920, for example, blues belter Ma Rainey was one of America's biggest top-of-the-bill concert attractions. Others followed in her wake – Mamie Smith, Ethel Walters and, maybe the greatest of them all, Bessie Smith.

But however popular, the concept of a blues singer – a vocalist performing nothing but the blues – was not "authentic". It was a product of the entertainment and fledgling recording industries. The first genuine blues artist to be discovered in obscurity "doing his own thing", and then be brought to the attention of a wider audience, was guitarist and singer Blind Lemon Jefferson. His 1926 recording "I Got The Blues" created a market for what would soon be known as "Race Music".

By the end of the decade, convoys of New York recording technicians were making their way to the Deep South in search of a new sound and a fast buck. (A tragically predictable postscript to the Blind Lemon Jefferson story is that between

IN THIS CHAPTER YOU WILL LEARN...

- Blues history
- Shuffle rhythms
- Triplets and tuple time
- Diminished and augmented triads
- Minor seventh chords
- Diminished seventh chords
- Ninth chords
- Minor pentatonic finger positions
- Pulling-off
- String gauges and how they affect bending

- The twelve-bar system
- Playing over a blues backing track
- Extending chords
- Dominant seventh chords
- Major seventh chords
- Extending barre chords
- The minor pentatonic scale
- Hammering-on
- String bending
- Vibrato

MUDDY WATERS: ELECTRIC BLUES PIONEER

Muddy Waters brought the music of the Mississippi Delta into the modern world, becoming the first great electric blues guitarist in the process. He was largely responsible for introducing the blues to white audiences, and in doing so laid the foundations for much of the rock music of the 1960s.

His first records were cut for archivist Alan Lomax – a man who re-discovered many of the great blues artists of the 1920s and 1930s. Lomax had been scouring the state looking for the legendary Robert Johnson. Before discovering that Johnson had died three years earlier, Lomax was told that there was a local man who played like him, and pointed him toward the Stovall Plantation where Waters was employed.

Taken under the wing of blues ambassador Big Bill Broonzy, in 1943 Waters moved to Chicago, where he bought his first electric guitar. In 1950 he was one of the first artists to sign to the Chess label, home of his great recordings of the decade that followed. Many of these songs were covered in the early 1960s by the young white British and American "Blues Boomers" such as the Rolling Stones.

1926 and his death three years later, although he sold hundreds of thousands of records, he was paid virtually nothing: the first genuine black blues star was buried in a pauper's grave.)

The 1930s saw blues music in the doldrums. With the Depression, many of the specialist labels went out of business, and blues fell from fashion, replaced by big band jazz and the new white-oriented "country" sound. This period also saw the brief emergence of one of the legendary figures of blues

guitar – Robert Johnson. He seemingly appeared out of nowhere, cut 29 tunes between 1936 and 1937, and then died in mysterious circumstances. His playing would later inspire many of the young white rock players of the 1960s.

From the 1940s, blues had a new home: Chicago. Here, a new generation of singer-guitarists emerged, including such legendary names as Muddy Waters, Howlin' Wolf, Buddy Guy, Otis Rush, Freddie King. These players were the pioneers of a new electric blues, and

by now the electric guitar was the instrument most likely to be used by blues musicians.

While the rhythm and blues dance bands of the early '50s had a crossover appeal that effectively led to the birth of rock and roll, the Chicago blues players played to largely black audiences. It wasn't until the 1960s that they found wider appeal under the patronage of a generation of young white musicians, such as Eric Clapton, the Rolling Stones, Paul Butterfield and Canned Heat.

THE TWELVE-BAR SYSTEM

Most blues music – or music derived from blues forms – fits into a fairly standardised chord pattern – the famous "twelve-bar" sequence. Also sometimes called a "I – IV – V", the chords used are built around the first, fourth and fifth degrees of the major scale. A blues in the key of C will use the chords C, F and G. As you will see, however, there is still plenty of room for variation.

BACKING TRACK #4

Before we go any further, let's take a look at the backing track you'll be using for this lesson. This is a blues boogie in the key of G – since it's a "I-IV-V" sequence, the chords used in this key are G, C and D. In this case they are all major chords.

This basic format is good for playing pretty well any type of blues. **5/1** ▶

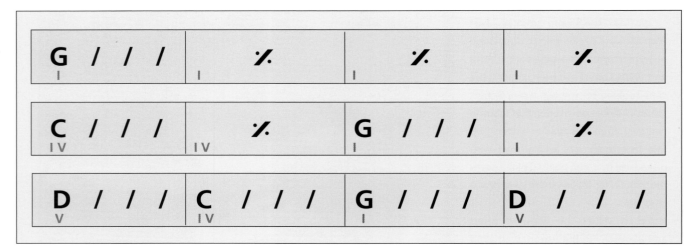

THE SHUFFLE RHYTHM

The basic boogie or shuffle rhythm is based wholly on what is called TUPLE TIME. This is the division of a note into three equal values. In regard to quavers, each note (or group of notes) is shown with the number "3" above or below the head of the notes. This indicates that there are three TUPLE QUAVERS to each beat.

To illustrate this idea more clearly, try this triplet count, always emphasising the first beat each time: "ONE-two-three–TWO-two-three-THREE-two-three-FOUR-two-three".

Now let's take this a step further: repeat the count only this time also emphasising the third note of each group: "ONE-two-THREE–TWO-two-THREE-THREE-two-THREE-FOUR-two-THREE". That's a shuffle rhythm.

DOES ANYBODY REALLY KNOW WHAT TIME IT IS?

Since we're effectively counting out blocks of 12 quavers, why – you may ask – is the backing track in four-four time. Wouldn't it be more accurate to describe it as twelve-eight?

Both are correct. Twelve-eight is more logical in that the note values are quavers (hence the number eight) and the number of them in the bar is twelve. Nevertheless, showing them in four-four time is much more common.

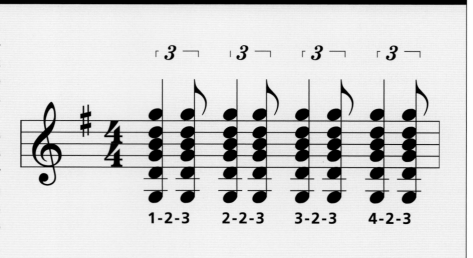

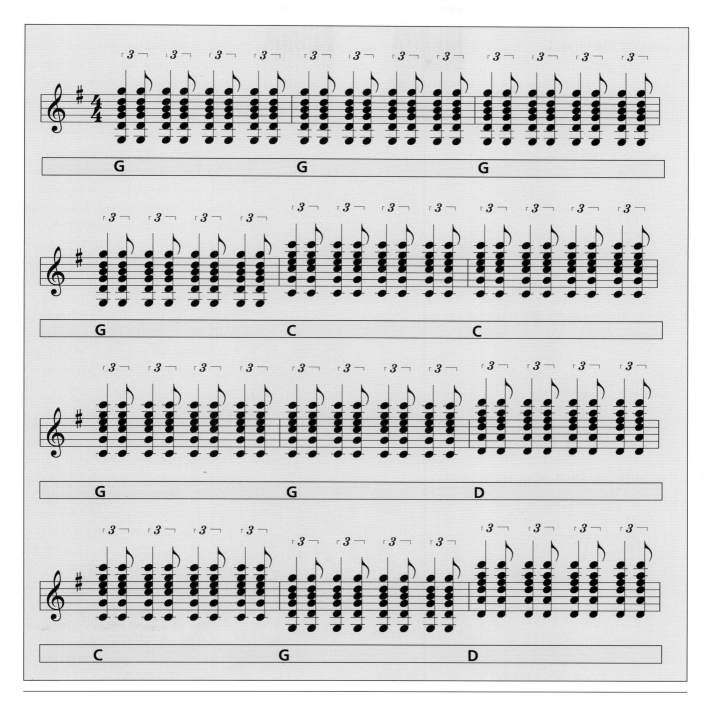

THE COMPLETE BOOGIE

The music above shows Backing Track #4 played as a series of E-shaped barre chords on G major, C major and D major. The chord names are written beneath each staff.

You may notice that although the D major triad contains the note F♯, no sharps can be seen alongside the note. The reason for this is that this time around we have correctly identified the key signature at the start of each staff.

The sharp symbol on the top line of the staff before the music begins tells us two important things. Firstly, if you've learned your key signatures (*see page 57*), you will be able to tell immediately that the music is in the key of "one sharp", or G major. From that, you can ascertain that whenever a note appears as F in the music, it has to be played as F♯. If an F were required, it would have to be shown as a NATURAL (♮).

One final thing you should remember about the enharmonic symbols (sharps, flats and naturals) is that when they are used within bars of the music (ie, not the symbols that show the key signature) they ONLY CHANGE THE VALUE OF A NOTE WITHIN THAT BAR. Once the barline has been crossed, the note reverts to the value indicated by the key signature.

BLUES VARIATIONS

Here are some simple accompaniments that you can play over Backing Track #4. Only one bar is shown in each case – in the key of G. These can be played from the E-shaped barre position with the root on the 3rd fret of the 6th string. To play them in C and D, move the root up to the 8th and 10th frets respectively.

G FIVE WITH THREE NOTES

This example reintroduces the idea of the tonally ambiguous "power chord". To play this part for a standard E-shaped barre chord and strike only the bottom three strings. Muting them at the same time with the right hand will sound even more effective.

G FIVE WITH TWO NOTES

This is the same as the first example, only the octave has been removed. To play this, you don't necessarily need to retain the full barre chord. A more orthodox approach would be to fret the root note on the 6th string with the 1st finger, and the perfect 5th on the 5th string with the 2nd finger.

Because there is no note defining whether the chord is a major or a minor, both of the first two riffs could be played over a major-key or minor-key blues.

CLASSIC BOOGIE

The final two examples on this page are classic blues boogie riffs. The first one alternates between an interval of root/perfect 5th and root/major 6th. To play the new interval, fret the note E on the 7th fret of the 5th string using the 4th finger.

The bottom example adds a further interval of root/minor 7th. This requires the 4th finger to reach to the 8th fret of the 5th string. There's no doubting that at first you may find that stretch to be just too long and painful. With practice it will come, though – that's a promise.

BOOGIE VARIATIONS

Across the page you will find four further exercises all based around the same set of notes. The first two examples break the classic boogie riff into single notes. Experiment with pick direction to see which works best for you. (Tip: try starting the first exercise with an upstroke.)

The third exercise alters the basic rhythm. All the crotchets apart from the first are tied, so the count is: "ONE-two-THREE-two-two-THREE-three-to-THREE-four-two-THREE".

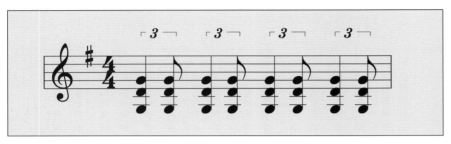

1. G FIVE WITH THREE NOTES (ROOT, PERFECT 5TH AND OCTAVE).

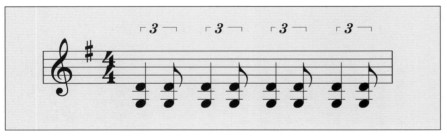

2. G FIVE WITH TWO NOTES (ROOT, PERFECT 5TH).

3. THREE–NOTE BOOGIE (ROOT, PERFECT 5TH AND MAJOR 6TH).

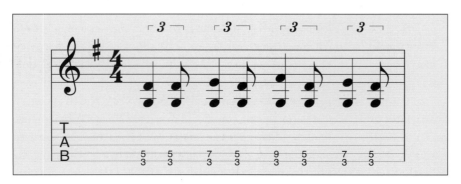

4. FOUR–NOTE CLASSIC BOOGIE RIFF. THE THREE INTERVALS USED ARE ROOT/PERFECT 5TH; ROOT/MAJOR 6TH; AND ROOT/MINOR 7TH.

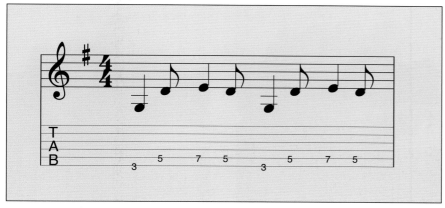

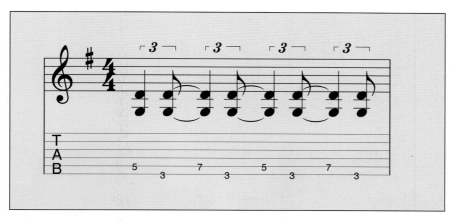

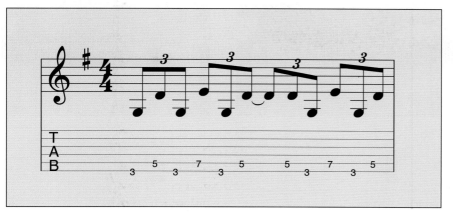

SEVENTHS AND NINTHS

All of the chords you have played so far have been based around major and minor triads. Although these are the most commonly used chord types, there are many other possibilities. For example, the blues boogie exercises on page 96 included intervals between the root and the major 6th, and the root and the minor 7th – neither of these feature in standard major or minor chords.

THE TRIAD SET

To understand the way in which these new chord types work, there are two further forms of triad that you really need to know about: AUGMENTED and DIMINISHED triads. The augmented triad differs from the major triad in that the 5th note is raised by a semitone; the diminished triad has both 3rd and 5th notes lowered by a semitone.

By taking the four triads (*see right, above*) and the notes related to the root, it is possible to create a rich variety of alternative chord types. Each of these new chords can be described in terms of the original triad with added intervals.

5/3

SEVENTHS

The most common family of chord extensions is the SEVENTH. There are many possible types of 7th chord (most of them can be found in the Chord Finder on pages 174–179). They are formed by adding either a diminished 7th, a minor 7th or a major 7th to one of the four types of triad.

The four 7th chords which are most commonly used in modern music are the DOMINANT 7TH, MINOR 7TH, MAJOR 7TH and the DIMINISHED 7TH.

DOMINANT SEVENTH
Usually referred to simply as a SEVEN (or 7th) chord, the dominant 7th is formed by adding a minor 7th to a major triad. In the key of C, the notes used are C (root), E (major 3rd) and G (perfect 5th), with an added B♭ (minor 7th). Its common abbreviation is C7.

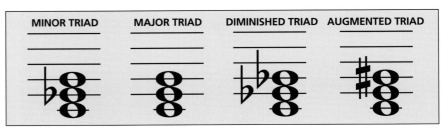

MINOR TRIAD	MAJOR TRIAD	DIMINISHED TRIAD	AUGMENTED TRIAD

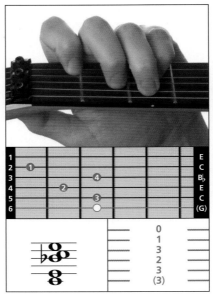

DOMINANT SEVENTH

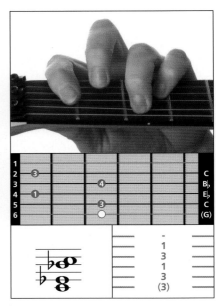

MINOR SEVENTH

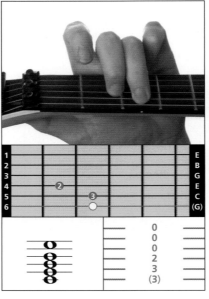

MAJOR SEVENTH

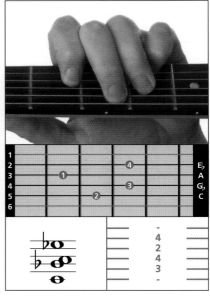

DIMINISHED SEVENTH

NON-MAJOR BARRE CHORDS

Barre chords really come into their own when playing minor, seventh and other chord types. It can be extremely difficult to play minor and seventh chords in some of the most common open-string keys – in others, only barely adequate three- or four-string voicings may be possible.

The three chord diagrams on the right show how minor, dominant seventh and minor seventh chords can be played from a 6th-string root. As you should be able to see, they are all simple variations on the standard barre formed around the open E major chord.

MINOR

SEVENTH

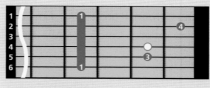

MINOR SEVENTH

The minor chord is simple to play: you just take away the 2nd finger. Things are more challenging for the sevenths. The difficulty is the stretch required between the 3rd finger (which is fretting the 5th string) and the 4th finger (which is covering the 2nd string). It's quite likely that you've never before been required to do anything with your left hand that requires such an unnatural stretch. The only way to overcome this is to practise. One good exercise is to continually move your left hand between the major and dominant seventh chord positions

MINOR SEVENTH

Minor 7th chords are formed by adding a minor 7th note to a minor triad. In the key of C, this chord uses the notes C (root), E♭ (minor 3rd) and G (perfect 5th), with an added B♭ (minor 7th). Its abbreviation is Cm7.

MAJOR SEVENTH

Major 7th chords are formed by adding a major 7th note to a major triad. In the key of C, the notes used are C (root), E (major 3rd) and G (perfect 5th), with an added B (major 7th). Its abbreviation is Cmaj7 or CΔ.

DIMINISHED SEVENTH

The diminished 7th is usually referred to simply as a diminished. It is formed by adding a diminished 7th note to a diminished triad. In the key of C, this adds the note A to C, E♭ and G♭. Its abbreviation is C dim or C°.

BLUES USING SEVENTHS

Try playing along to Backing Track #4 using barred dominant 7th chords. The fret positions for G7, C7 and D7 are all shown on the staff below.

Once again, you are likely to find that you struggle to keep the 4th finger under control. And if you do, it can be at the expense of maintaining both the 3rd finger position and a strong 1st finger barre.   **5/4** ▶

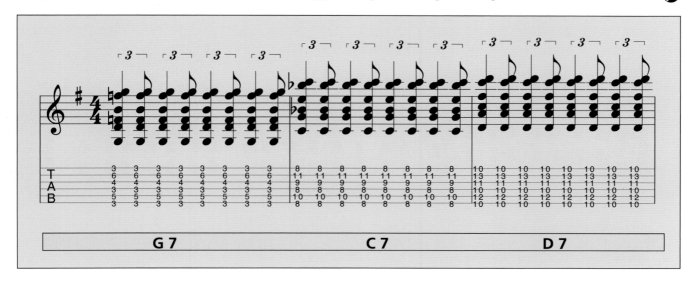

BLUES WITH NINTHS

The NINTH series of chords is created by adding a major 2nd an octave above a chosen 7th chord. In this way, the three most common 7ths – dominant, minor and major – all have their own equivalent 9ths.

Referred to as a NINE, the dominant 9th is formed by adding the major 2nd above the octave to a dominant 7th chord. In the key of C, the chord comprises the notes C (root), E (major 3rd), G (perfect 5th), B♭ (minor 7th), and D (major 2nd/9th). Its abbreviation is C9.

Minor 9th chords are created by adding a major 2nd above the octave to a minor 7th chord. In the key of C, the chord comprises the notes C (root), E♭ (minor 3rd), G (perfect 5th), B♭ (minor 7th) and D (major 2nd/9th). Its abbreviation is Cm9.

Major 9th chords are created by adding a major 2nd above the octave to a major 7th chord. In the key of C, the chord comprises the notes C (root), E (major 3rd), G (perfect 5th), B (major 7th) and D (major 2nd/9th). Its abbreviation is Cmaj9 or CΔ9. **5/5** ▶

DOMINANT NINTHS IN PRACTICE

Try playing dominant ninths on top of Backing Track #4. The music below (and across the page) shows a series of 9th chords with a rhythmic emphasis on the third tuple quaver of each group. Begin by just playing the three 9th chords over the rhythm. Afterwards, take a closer look at the last chord of each bar. You will see that it differs from the others within the same bar. This is a neat little R&B cliché where a chord at the end of a bar "leans in" to the first chord of the next bar by playing a semitone lower. This is commonly achieved by sliding the chord into position. **5/6** ▶

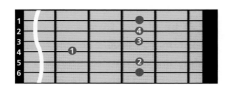

DOMINANT NINTH

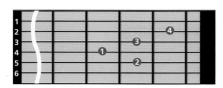

MINOR NINTH

MAJOR NINTH

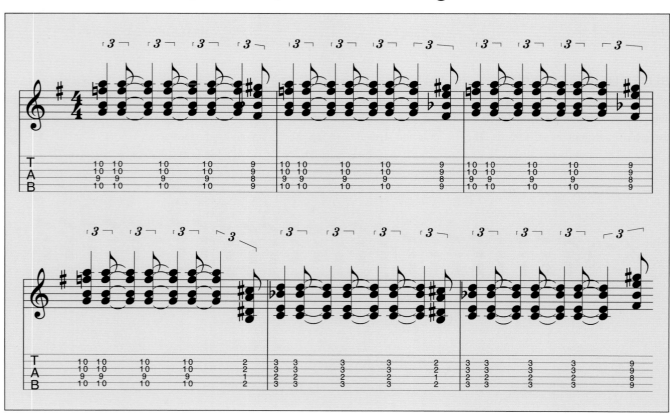

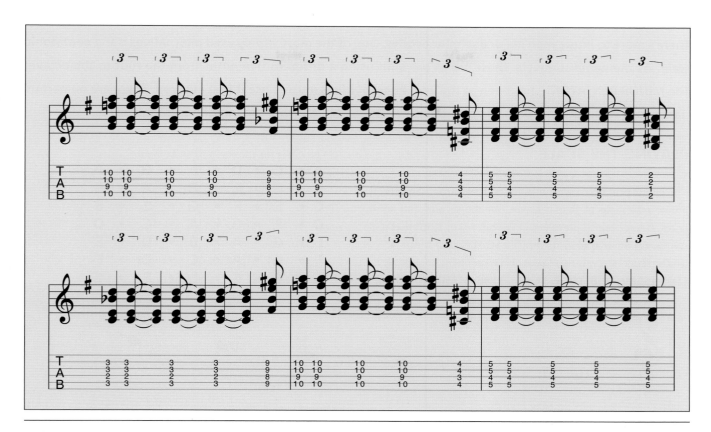

FINAL BAR VARIATIONS

As we have already seen, the classic twelve-bar blues follows the basic format: I-I-I-I-IV-IV-I-I-V-IV-I-V. This is sometimes known as a BLUES TURNAROUND. Within this structure, the last bar of the sequence plays an important part in taking the music back – quite literally turning it around – to the beginning of the cycle in as satisfying a way as possible. Although some blues tunes ignore the chord change, and remain on the root chord (G in our example) for the last bar, ending on the perfect 5th chord (D) does create a very smooth and natural effect.

There are a number of ways the "finality" of the sequence can be made more pronounced by altering the rhythm. In the example above, removing the ties in the last bar, or playing 12 tuple quavers could both be used to dramatic effect – building up a crescendo over the course of the bar would heighten the effect even further.

The staff below (the final two bars of the 12-bar cycle) shows an even more extreme example where the rhythm is quite literally interrupted. Here, the first beat of the final bar is rested, to be followed by a single sustained chord over three beats. This would sound perfectly alright if the final chord being played was similar in type to those being used throughout the rest of the music. However, on this occasion we've thrown in an oddity. This is another member of the seventh family – the SEVENTH AUGMENTED NINTH. Written as D7+9, this chord creates dramatic tension because it contains both a major 3rd and an augmented 9th.

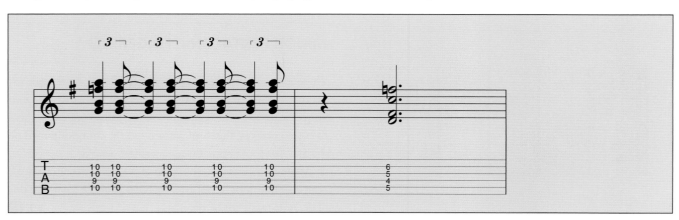

THE MINOR PENTATONIC SCALE

There's more to music than major and minor scales. One of the most widely used alternatives is the pentatonic scale. As the name suggests, these scales are built using a different five notes from the root to the octave. The MINOR PENTATONIC has been at the very heart of blues music since it first evolved. There are numerous classic rock riffs from the past 30 years that have been derived from the minor pentatonic scale.

PLAYING THE SCALE

The minor pentatonic scale uses notes drawn from the natural minor scale, except that it leaves out the second and sixth notes. It has been so prevalent in the history of R&B that it is sometimes referred to as the BLUES SCALE.

The set of intervals that make up a minor pentatonic scale is:
TONE+SEMITONE, TONE, TONE, TONE+SEMITONE, TONE.

The notes for the seven main keys are:

A	•	C	•	D	•	E	•	G	•	A
B	•	D	•	E	•	F♯	•	A	•	B
C	•	E♭	•	F	•	G	•	B♭	•	B
D	•	F	•	G	•	A	•	C	•	D
E	•	G	•	A	•	B	•	D	•	E
F	•	G♯	•	A♯	•	C	•	D♯	•	F
G	•	B♭	•	C	•	D	•	F	•	G

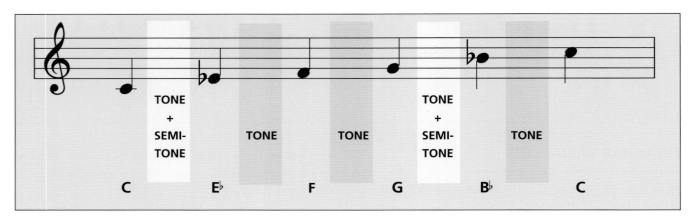

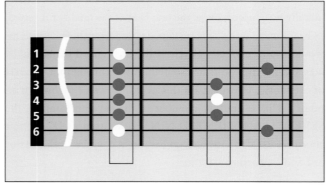

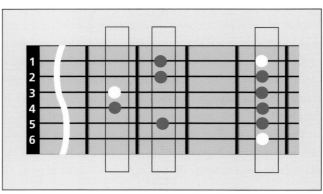

MINOR PENTATONIC FINGERING

Three alternative fingering patterns are shown on the left for playing the minor pentatonic scale in the key of C. The two above begin with the root note on the 6th string and extend over two octaves; the third pattern has the root positioned on the 5th string and plays through a single octave.

Attaining a good understanding of the minor pentatonic scale is an absolute must for all aspiring blues guitarist – without this scale, it just will not be the blues.

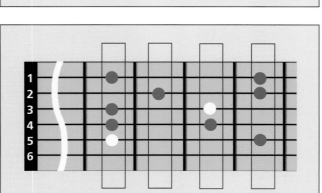

5/7

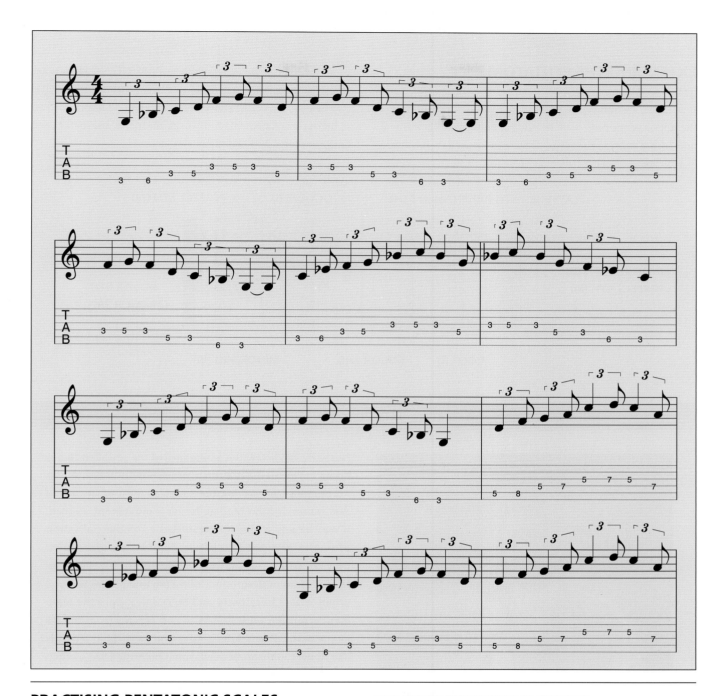

PRACTISING PENTATONIC SCALES

Blues music may not be quite the profound influence on rock that it once was, but from a soloist's point of view a good understanding of the pentatonic scale is still extremely important. So take time out to learn the three fingering positions shown across the page by heart.

Like the other scales you've played, they can all be executed in any key so long as you are familiar with the names of all the notes on the 5th and 6th strings. (And if you still haven't yet learned them, then now would be a good time to hang your head in shame.)

THE MINOR PENTATONIC IN CONTEXT

The music above is a series of little sequences based on minor pentatonic scales in G, C and D. Although it's a good practice exercise in its own right, it was designed to be played along to Backing Track #4.

This is especially useful since it requires scales built on both the 5th and 6th strings to be played. When playing over C and D chords, it would, of course, be possible to repeat the same 6th-string pattern that appears in the first bar (beginning on the 3rd fret) but starting on the 8th and 10th frets respectively. However, playing C and D from the 3rd and 5th frets of the 5th string is a far more economical way of working. **5/8** ▶

EXTENDING THE PENTATONIC

For further flexibility, it's possible to extend the usefulness of the minor pentatonic scale by adding "unrelated" notes – ie, notes from outside the scale. These can be used to produce a wider range of melodies, or simply as PASSING NOTES – notes whose role is simply to connect two notes within a phrase.

The diagram below shows three different additions for you to try out: the flattened 5th (mauve), the major 3rd (pink), and both the major 2nd and major 6th (green).

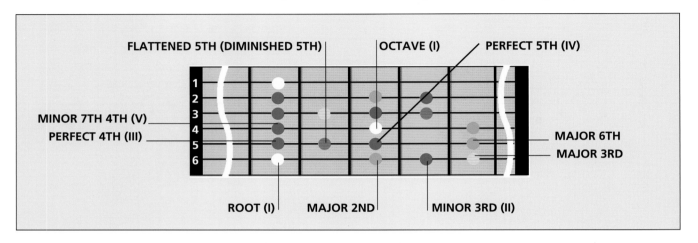

THE BLUES BOOMERS

The early 1960s saw the emergence of the so-called "Blues Boom". The earliest British practitioners were Alexis Korner and Cyril Davies, but the evangelist of the group was guitarist John Mayall. Never a movement as such, it was largely a reaction against the commercialisation of singles-oriented R&B bands. Their stance was purist; they consciously eschewed the pursuit of hit singles in favour of an underground following and album success. Where once Chuck Berry and Bo Diddley were the main men, attention now turned to cult figures from the US like Albert Collins, Albert King and long-dead legends like Robert Johnson. Indeed, some bluesmen were given bizarre second careers quite late in life – all of sudden Howlin' Wolf, by then in his fifties, started getting hits in Europe for the first time and playing to audiences usually less than half his age.

The movement reached its peak of popularity in August of 1967 with the Windsor Blues Festival. This was the ultimate showcase of British blues talent, and featured Mayall, Eric Clapton's Cream (*see left*), Jeff Beck, Ten Years After and Fleetwood Mac.

A parallel trend also existed in the US, launching the careers of, among others, the Paul Butterfield Blues Band, Canned Heat and Johnny Winter.

EXPRESSIVE EFFECTS

There's more to soloing than simply manipulating scales to play a melodic series of single notes. Expressive lead effects such as hammering-on, pulling-off, string bending and vibrato can be used to give your playing a unique or distinctive voice, or allow you to project the "feel" of your music. Some of the basic techniques are discussed over the next few pages.

HAMMER-ON

The HAMMER-ON (or *ligado* as it is called in the classical world) is used in every type of guitar music. It is produced by moving a left-hand finger to another fret further along the fingerboard on the same string, while that string is ringing, hence sounding a higher note. It is shown as two notes joined by a slur with the letter "H" placed alongside.

To try this for yourself: place your 1st finger on the 5th fret of the 3rd string; pick the note; while the note is still ringing "hammer-on" the 7th fret of the 3rd string with the 3rd finger; let the new note sustain.

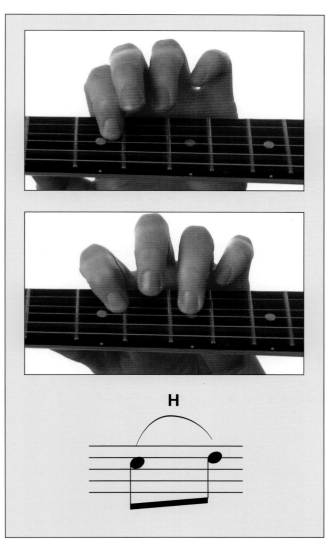

PULL-OFF

The reverse of the hammer-on is known as a "pull-off" – or "descending *ligado*". This effect is produced by playing a fretted note and releasing the left-hand finger to sound a lower note. This is shown in written music in a similar way to the hammer-on, only the letter "P" is used instead.

Here is a pull-off exercise for you to try. Place the 4th finger on the 10th fret of the 6th string (the note D); place the 1st finger on the 7th fret of the 6th string (the note B); pick the note; while the note is still ringing, release the 4th finger, allowing the new note to sustain.

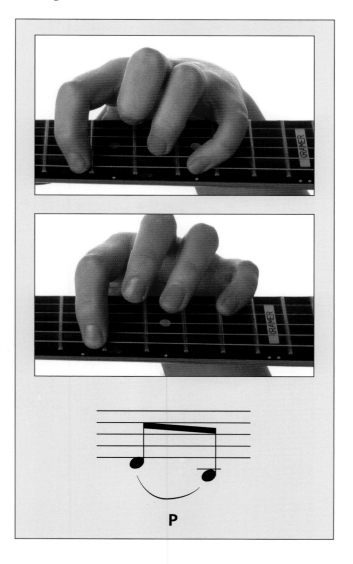

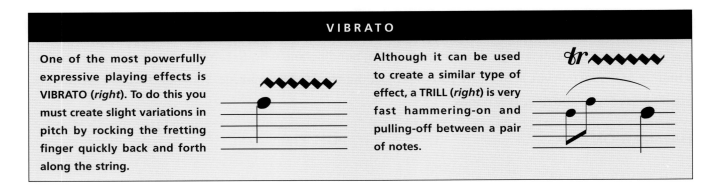

HAMMER-ON AND PULLING-OFF EXERCISES

Three different exercises are shown below. Each bar relates only to chord named below the staff. It's up to you to construct the full version. The first exercise simply hammers-on and pulls-off up and down a pentatonic scale. The second example sees each bar played as two phrases – the curve above the notes is a LEGATO which instructs you to play the phrase as if it were a single movement.

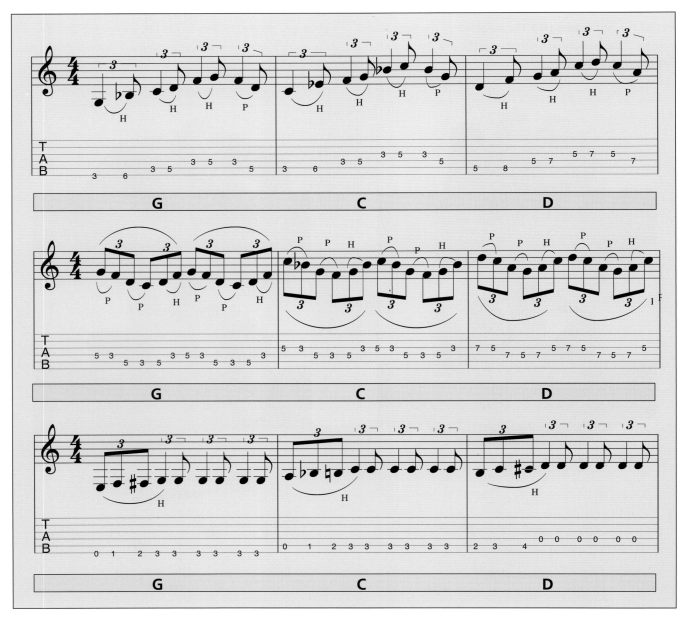

BENDING THE STRINGS

One of the most basic yet effective techniques used by electric guitarists comes from bending the strings. This is usually achieved by playing a note and then bending the string to alter the pitch. It can also be produced mechanically if you have a tremolo arm.

Here is an exercise for you to try. The idea here is to play the note F and bend it up to a G:

- **Place the 2nd finger on the 6th fret of the 2nd string.**
- **Pick the note.**
- **While the note is sustaining, pull the string downward until the pitch increases by a tone.**
- **You should now be playing the note G.**

At first it may be difficult to stop bending at the correct pitch, but this will come with practice. In fact, in some styles of playing a pitch-perfect bend is not even strictly necessary, or even appropriate – a slight flattening of the second note can be very effective in blues playing. Take care, however, not to push the string too far, otherwise you will make the note sharp.

As an alternative, it is also possible to bend the string by pushing upward rather than pulling downward. Which technique you use is a matter of personal preference, although if you bend the top two strings upward, your fretting fingers can easily slip off the fingerboard. Some players find it easiest to pull the treble strings and push the bass strings.

Two different method for notating string bends are shown in the panel on the right.

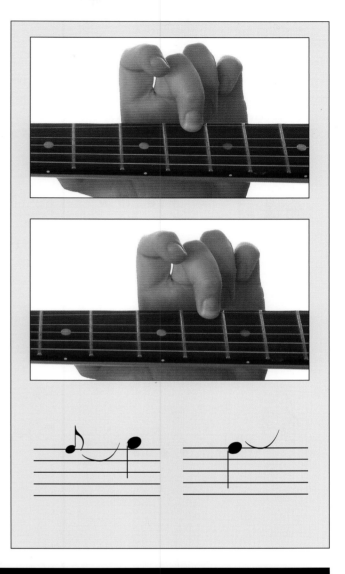

STRING GAUGES AND BENDING

Originally developed by blues and country players to mimic the sound of a bottleneck guitar or, much later, pedal steel guitar, string bending has become a central part of modern guitar playing, where it can provide greater texture to the sound as well as an added emotional dimension. String bending can also be achieved on steel-string acoustic guitars, but its use is extremely limited on classical or flamenco instruments.

The principal factor that will govern the degree to which you can bend a string is its thickness. The different string widths are known as GAUGES and are generally expressed as decimal fractions of an inch. Weighing up the pros and cons of each type is very much a matter of personal taste. You need to balance the fact that lighter strings are easier to hold down and bend, and are less hard on the fingers, with the knowledge that they create a lower volume, shorter sustain, and the degree to which they can stretch makes them more difficult to keep in tune. Some players maintain that heavier-gauge strings simply sound better.

If your guitar uses light-gauge strings – where the 1st string is no more than 0.1 inches thick – you should be able to alter the pitch of a note by at least a tone. On the other hand, the heaviest-gauge steel strings, or nylon strings, may make it almost impossible to reach even a semitone.

Since they are the most pliable, the treble strings are the most commonly used for bending. This is also a common cause of their snapping, so it's always a good idea to keep a good supply of spares in your case.

STRING-BENDING EXERCISE

Here is some more music with which you can accompany Backing Track #4. Again, to save on space that would have been wasted through repetition, we've only notated them for the three different chords used in this track.

In the first example, you take a note and bend it up by a tone. The bar ends with you bending the note and giving it a touch of vibrato as it sustains.

The second example begins with a downward string bend. To do this, BEFORE you pick the note you must bend the string into position. You then pick the note and release the string so that it bends down to the correct pitch.   **5/9** ▶

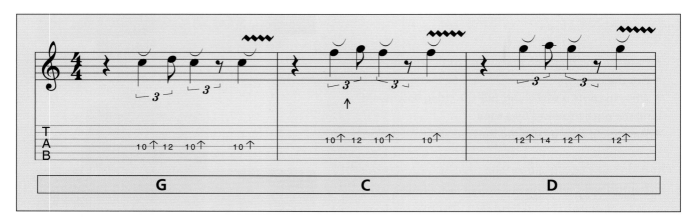

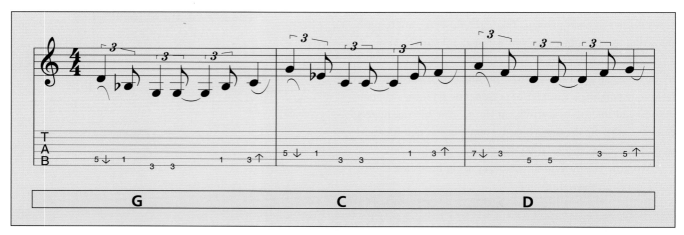

BENDING TO A SECOND STRING

The first of these three exercises is a veritable blues/rock cliché that involves bending a note until it reaches a set pitch, and then playing the same note on a different string. In this example, you play the 10th fret of the 3rd string (F); bend it up by a tone; when it reaches G, pick G on the 8th fret of the 2nd string.   **5/10** ▶

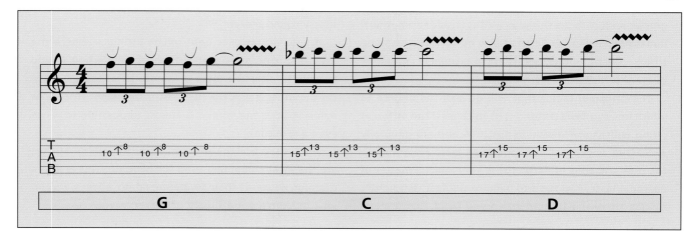

STEVIE RAY VAUGHAN (1954–1990)

Over the past thirty years blues has had quite a specialised audience. But that's failed to prevent a number of very fine guitarists making names for themselves in the wider world. Three names spring immediately to mind: Robert Cray, Duke Robillard and the much-lamented Stevie Ray Vaughan.

Although he had a thorough blues upbringing – he was taught by his elder brother, Jimmy Vaughan of the Fabulous Thunderbirds – Stevie Ray's style gradually evolved, taking in outside influences from the world of jazz and rock. His albums with his band Double Trouble contain some of the finest blues-rock playing heard since Jimi Hendrix was alive.

Running a parallel career as an in-demand sideman, Vaughan looked set for major success when he was killed in a helicopter crash in 1990.

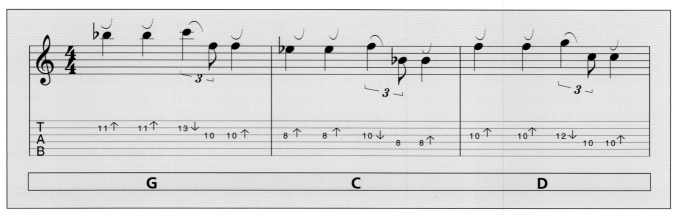

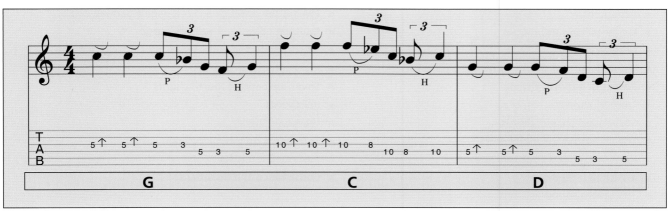

CHAPTER 6
RIFFS AND NOISE

The musical story we'll be following in this chapter begins with the revolutionary forces of Punk Rock and the New Wave, which kicked off during the mid-1970s. Before this period, rock had reached a position that many saw as "growing up". For the first time, joining a band seemed first to require serious study of an instrument. The New Wave made the rock world stand back and reassess itself. It deconstucted the way rock music had evolved and sought to replace sterile self-serving musicianship with simple, raw energy. For the first time since the early days of beat music, kids were rushing out to buy guitars, and – often within a matter of weeks – forming themselves into gigging bands. Although their techniques were primitive, the best of these bands combined power with a natural feel for melody and simple harmony.

A RETURN TO RAW ENERGY

The rules of Punk Rock were simple: no filler, no posing and no nonsense. It was fast, raw and aggressive. A handful of chords and no more than two minutes per song. And if you didn't like it, then too bad (or words to that extent). The recipe was 50% music and 50% attitude.

Punk Rock is often presented as if it all began with the twin axes of the Ramones (*see right*) in New York and the Sex Pistols in London. While these are unquestionably two seminal bands, the real influences appeared several years earlier.

The seeds of the Punk influence can be identified in a number of American bands from the late 1960s. The noise experimentation of the Velvet Underground, the raw power of the Stooges (fronted by Iggy Pop) and the MC5, and the theatricality of the New York Dolls. None of these bands were really terribly popular with mainstream audiences during their lifespans, but all have since become legendary. These were the bands that provided the impetus for the first wave of Punk.

The scenes as they developed in London and New York were actually quite different. The New York scene revolved around the club CBGBs. Although the Ramones were first noticed there, other bands that emerged from the same scene included Talking Heads, Blondie and Television – all great bands, but all also conventionally "musical".

In London, it may have been the Sex Pistols that sparked the Punk movement, but many of the first wave – including such notaries as the Clash – basically evolved out of bar bands from London's so-called "pub rock" scene.

The Punk explosion was over within a matter of months, but the repercussions in the way it affected the evolution of rock and pop music can still be heard today.

IN THIS CHAPTER YOU'LL LEARN...

- Arpeggios
- Finger-picking techniques
- Crosspicking
- Using delay and chorus to fill out a guitar sound
- Suspended fourth chords
- "Add 9" chords
- Suspended second chords
- The chords on the major scale
- Harmonic effects over two strings
- Inverting intervals
- The reverb sound
- Picking the notes of a chord over a backing track
- Multiple voicings in written music
- 12-string electric guitars
- Inversion in practice
- Seven suspended fourth chords
- 6/9 chords
- Harmonic theory
- The chords on the minor scale
- Sustained intervals
- Consonance and dissonance

THE RAMONES AND THE SEX PISTOLS

In 1976, when veteran British DJ John Peel played tracks from the Ramones' debut album on his BBC Radio 1 show, he was showered with complaints from his regular audience – one that tuned in because his was one of the few shows on national radio where "serious" rock music could be heard. Legions of listeners more accustomed to the likes of Pink Floyd and Barclay James Harvest found the sound of a bunch of New York high school drop-outs chanting "Hey ho, let's go" over a thrashed out guitar, distorted bass and pounding toms no less than an insult. Thus, in the UK, a brand new generation gap was born.

The band was the brainchild of guitarist Johnny Ramone (*see right*).

He was joined by singer Joey Ramone, bassist Dee Dee Ramone and drummer Ramone. (They were not real brothers.) Their reputation was formed pounding out 20-minute sets of pure youthful energy at New York's CBGBs club. Surprisingly, perhaps, they were the first of their contemporaries to earn a recording contract. Although their music helped to kick off a brief but significant revolution in rock, they didn't set out with this in mind. They just wanted to be pop stars. According to Johnny Ramone, "*[We] didn't see any difference between what we were doing and the Bay City Rollers*". They were quite alone in this view.

Their 1976 debut album, *The Ramones*, was the definitive punk statement, with songs like "Beat On The Brat", the classic single "Blitzkrieg Bop" and "Now I Wanna Sniff Some Glue" – there were 14 of them on the album, clocking in at under a total of 30 minutes.

The Ramones played in England later that year, their merits dividing music fans and critics alike. It was there they received their first national success, the single "Sheena is a Punk Rocker" charting the following year. The Ramones gave impetus to the nascent British punk scene.

The most infamous band of the period – the Sex Pistols – are remembered as much for their stage-managed petulance and violence as their music. Cleverly marketed by manager Malcolm McLaren, the Pistols were blessed with one truly great asset – a fabulously witty and charismatic frontman, John Lydon – or Johnny Rotten as he would be known to the world.

Before the Pistols even had a record deal, they had featured on the front pages of Britain's influential music press, touted as being the saviours of rock and roll. But although their legendary live shows were noisy and chaotic, in retrospect, if you took away the provocation, you were left with a pretty undistinguished riffing rock sound.

The Sex Pistols achieved national notoriety almost by accident. As a minor news item, they were booked to appear on a London TV news programme to be quizzed about the growing punk rock underground. Live on air, and faced with arrogant presenter Bill Grundy, they let loose with several minutes of foul-mouthed obnoxiousness. Not a single note was played, but this was a defining moment in the evolution of British rock music. The following day, and for pretty much the next year, the Sex Pistols were rarely out of the headlines.

While in the US Punk Rock remained an influential but nonetheless underground scene, in Britain it turned into a full-scale phenomenon, from which some of the greatest bands of this or any other era – for example, the Clash – would emerge.

A NICE BIT OF THRASH

This is a lively piece written in the spirit of modern-day thrashy American bands such as Green Day. The song comprises two eight-bar patterns which each play through twice before changing. You can think of the first eight bars as the verse, and the second eight bars as the chorus section. In traditional style, the verse part is played using "chugging" muted chords; the chorus part is a full-on thrash.

BACKING TRACK #5

Before we get down to the crux of the chapter, get yourself acquainted with Backing Track #5 – you can hear an extract on Track 6/1 of the CD, or the full-length version by playing Track 15. Try to come up with as many ways as you can of playing a simple rhythm guitar accompaniment. Start off by using mostly open-string chords. Now try it using only E-shaped barre chords. Can you hear how different they sound? Because the intervals that make up an E-shaped barre chord are all the same, relative to the root note, there is a consistency of balance that you can't always get with open-string chords.

Try it again, only this time using A-shape barre chords (the root is on the 5th string). Again, even though the same chords are being played, you'll notice that a slightly different musical effect is created.   **6/1** ▶

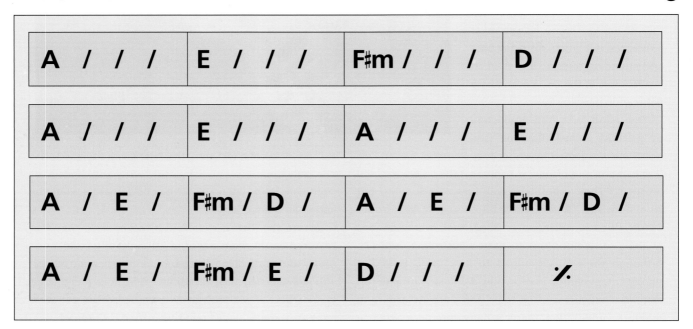

ARPEGGIOS

One the most fundamental aspects of rhythm guitar work is the use of basic chord shapes played not as chords but as a succession of single notes. These are called ARPEGGIOS. The effect can refer to a chord being strummed so slowly that the individual notes are audible, or a series of deliberately played notes.

Across the page there are four arpeggio exercises. Only the first four bars are shown, but you can easily adapt them to play over the entire "verse" section – all you have to do second time around is play the first two bars twice.

To play the first two examples, you can use open-string chords (since we are only playing with the first three strings, you can play F♯ minor with a 1st finger barre on the 2nd fret). The pick directions are shown above the staff – try to follow these carefully. In the first example, you are simply playing notes on the beat. The second exercise breaks up the notes to create a more interesting rhythm.

Examples three and four are based around E-shaped barre chords. Pay very careful attention to the pick directions, especially in the fourth exercise – if you don't follow them your pick won't be in the right place to play the right notes.

(IMPORTANT NOTE: when you use arpeggios the effect is of a gradual build-up of notes on top of one another. This is not shown on the staves because "technically correct" notation would appear unnecessarily complex and messy. For example, although the first note in the first exercise is a crotchet, in practice it sustains for the entire four beats of the bar; the second note is also a crotchet, but that sustains for the remaining three beats of the bar, and so on.)   **6/2** ▶

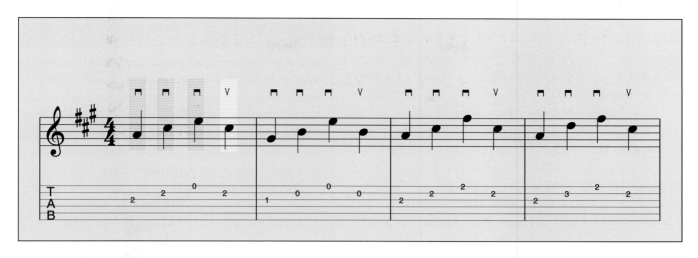

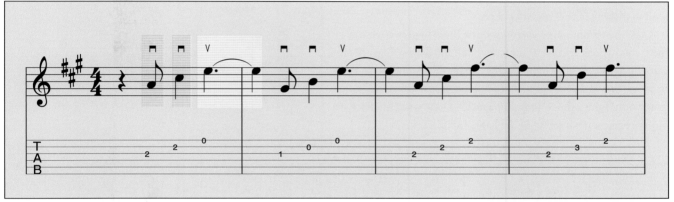

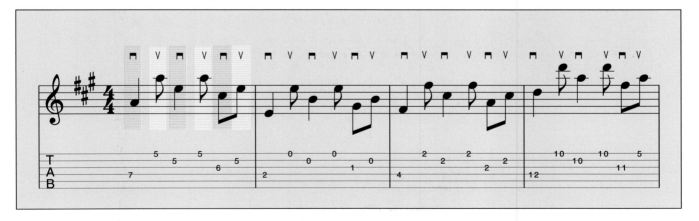

FINGER PICKING

We've only briefly touched on the subject of striking the strings with the fingers rather than a pick. Although this is a classical technique, many electric players in rock use their fingers when playing arpeggios.

Below are two exercises that you can use to practise your fingerpicking technique. Don't be too surprised if they sound familiar – they're the previous two exercises with pick directions replaced by fingering directions. These are very simple to follow. The letters refer to the Spanish names for each finger. They are: P – *pulgar* (thumb); I – *indice* (1st finger); M – *medio* (2nd finger); A – *anular* (3rd finger). In the rare cases when the 4th finger is used in picking, it is denoted by E or X.

Classical technique tends toward the three fingers covering the treble strings and the thumb covering the bass strings. We can afford to be a little more flexible, so on the second exercise there are two independent sets of fingering instructions for you to try out. Take a quick look at page 25 if you want to check out the correct positioning of the hand and fingers.

4 BEATS + 4 BEATS = 4 BEATS?

You may come across written music where at first glance the durations of the notes in the bar don't seem to add up to the values described in the time signature. In the bar below, it appears that although the time signature is 4/4 there are two minims (four beats) and four crotchets (four beats). The differing stem directions tell us that they are two VOICES playing at the same time. The first crotchet is played at the same time as the first minim; the second minim plays at the same time as the third crotchet.

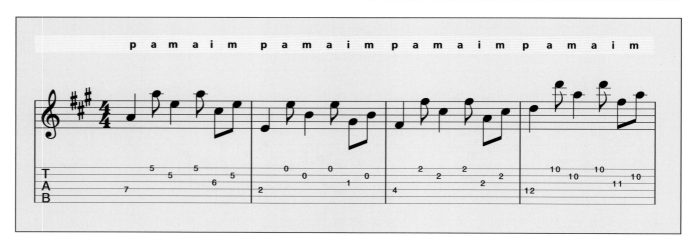

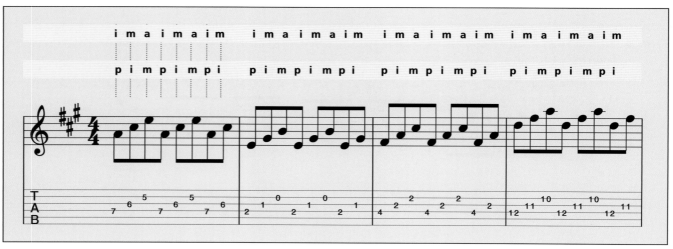

DOUBLING UP

The next two exercises step up the pace, and are played as sets of quavers – this means that you have to play a note on every half beat. For both staves, the music has been written for the chorus section of the track, so the chord changes have also been doubled up. You should find it quite demanding to manage both fingering and chord changes at this pace. This time there are both pick directions and fingering directions. Although you're bound to find one easier than the other, it's worth becoming adept at both picking and fingering.

Once you've worked through all of the exercises you should be able to play arpeggios for the entire backing track. **6/3**

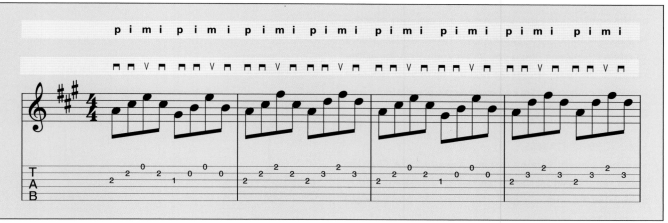

CROSSPICKING

In spite of our modern context, some of the exercises shown here are examples of a country bluegrass technique called CROSSPICKING. This is where the notes are picked (sometimes using just the fingers, but a pick can also be used) in a constant pattern. It is very effective when used on an acoustic guitar to accompany a singer since the volume of single notes can fill out the sound more powerfully than simply strumming chords.

The key to effective crosspicking is to establish a pattern and stick with it throughout the song. This can add unity to the different parts of the song. An arpeggio is an example of crosspicking.

The basic crosspicking patterns are usually referred to as ROLLS. The most common is the forward roll – others include the backward roll and the forward/reverse roll.

The pioneer of the forward roll was Earl Scruggs, the bluegrass banjo pioneer. It simply involves picking across the strings from the bottom to the top using a consistent pattern, even when the whole pattern moves to a different set of strings. The fourth exercise on page 113 is an example of forward roll crosspicking.

When crosspicking, it can be especially effective (and emphatic) to start the forward roll on the root note of the chord you are playing.

FILLING OUT THE SOUND

We've already seen how it's possible to fill out the sound by picking the chords as single notes. Now let's look at some hardware approaches to creating a fuller sound.

When recording it's easy enough to bolster the sound by doubling up the rhythm guitars – playing each part twice on different tracks. A different approach to this is to use a guitar with twice as many strings – a 12-string guitar.

The 12 strings are not fitted across the bridge so that they are equidistant from one another, but are run together in closely strung pairs. This reverts to the principles on which the first guitars were originally strung.

The standard tuning for a 12-string guitar has the two strings that make up each course tuned to the same note. The overall tuning is the same as for a standard guitar. The top two strings are simply doubled up. The remaining four courses consist of standard-gauge strings, and thinner strings tuned one octave higher.

You can buy sets of the strings for the instrument, or you can customise regular sets. The tuning is shown in the panel on the right. For the octave courses, it's common practice to have the thinner string above the fatter strings. This is so when strumming down you know you will strike all the strings (if the fatter strings are first the tip of your pick may miss the thinner strings in each pair). Some players, however, prefer to string each course in the opposite way. **6/4** ▶

SIMULATED 12-STRINGS
Six-string players wanting to mimic the effect of a 12-string guitar can try using a chorus pedal. This delays and gently modulates the original signal, giving the effect of a bigger sound. When recording, it's even more effective if you pan the original signal and the treated signal to opposite extremes of the stereo spectrum.

1	Standard 1st string E
2	Standard 1st string E
3	Standard 2nd string B
4	Standard 2nd string B
5	Standard 3rd string G
6	G one octave above standard 3rd string G (use standard 1st string tuned up to G)
7	Standard 4th string D
8	D one octave above standard 4th string D (use standard 1st string tuned down to D)
9	Standard 5th string A
10	A one octave above standard 5th string A (use standard 3rd string tuned up to A)
11	Standard 6th string E
12	E one octave above standard 6th string E (use standard 4th string tuned up to E)

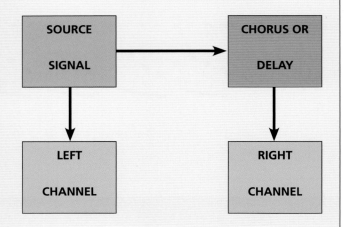

INVERSION IN PRACTICE

We'll conclude our fingerpicking excursion with a neat little exercise that will not only tax your fingers but give you a practical illustration of the contrasting sound of inverted chords. (Take a look back to page 86 if you need a reminder of what inversion means.)

Using just the top three strings, you will hear the same chord played four times along the fingerboard in different inversions. To play each bar you have to play the first minim and first crotchet simultaneously with the thumb and 3rd finger respectively; play the second crotchet with the 2nd finger while the minim is still sustaining; play the third crotchet/second minim (which is the same note) and then the fourth crotchet.

The first four bars are all versions of E major: bar 1 is a first inversion; bar 2 is a second inversion; bar three is the root version; bar 4 is a first inversion one octave above bar 1. The same pattern of inversions follows from there: F♯ minor (bars 5-8); G♯ minor (bars 9-12); A major (bars 13-16).

If it's a real challenge you're looking for, try this exercise using the hybrid pick/finger technique described on page 25. In this case, the pick plays the notes marked "P"; the "i" notes are played by the 2nd finger; the "m" notes by the 3rd and the "a" notes by the fourth. **6/5** ▶

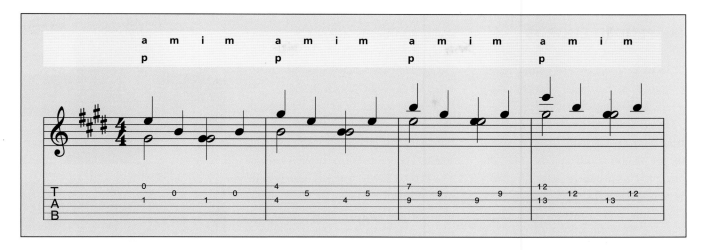

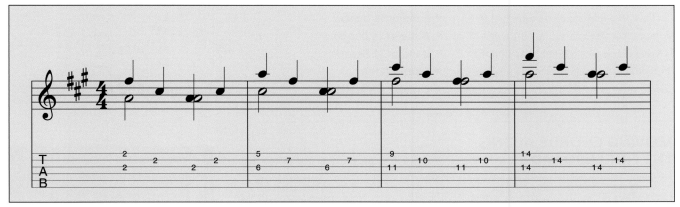

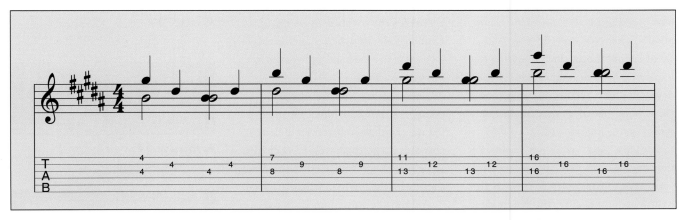

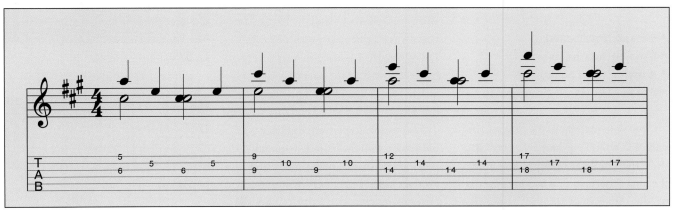

SUSPENDED CHORDS

Now we're going to start adding to our ever-growing chord vocabulary by taking a look at SUSPENDED chords.

By replacing the major 3rd in a major triad with a perfect 4th, the basic sound of the major chord can be radically altered. This produces what is called a SUSPENDED 4TH.

On the right you can see a chord diagram for E suspended fourth (or E SUS 4, as it is usually called).

This principle can also be applied to a dominant seventh chord, in which case it is known as a SEVENTH SUSPENDED FOURTH (or 7 SUS 4). To play an open-string version in E, simply remove the 2nd finger from the diagram. A famous suspended 7th chord can be heard on George Harrison's opening chimes to "A Hard Day's Night" by the Beatles.

The movement from the suspended chord back to its equivalent major or dominant 7th chord is a very common sound. This kind of progression is known as a FULL CLOSE, and has been widely used through the ages in all types of music, from classical to heavy metal. Try this exercise to hear the effect:

- E major (4 beats);
- A major (4 beats);
- B major (4 beats);
- E sus 4 (2 beats);
- E major (2 beats).

E Suspended 4

MOVING CHORDS ALONG THE FINGERBOARD

Once you are familiar with just a few basic open-string chord voicings you have access to a wide range of interesting possibilities. Not only do you have a set of simple chords, but by adding the barre you have access to these chords in any key. One further option is to use these basic chord shapes at different points on the fingerboard.

Perhaps the simplest way of introducing lush new sounds to your chord vocabulary is to play with the basic E major shape. Try this progression playing standard barre chords:

- E major (four beats);
- B major (four beats);
- A major (four beats);
- E major (12th fret) (four beats).

This time play the same progression only WITHOUT the barre. To play "B", slide the whole E major shape along the fingerboard so that the 1st finger is on the 8th fret of the 3rd string; the 2nd finger is on the 9th fret of the 5th string; the 3rd finger is on the 9th fret of the 4th string. Now strum across all six strings. It sounds nice, doesn't it?

To play the A chord, move the entire position down by two frets; for the octave E chord, move the hand up by seven frets from the A chord.

These chords can be improved by taking the root note along for the ride. Use the chord diagram for A add 9 (right, above) as a template for the other chords. What you are playing in effect is a barre chord with the top two strings left open.

Among the most famous bands to experiment with this approach was the American folk-rock band the Byrds. The effect was heightened by their pioneering use of electric 12-string guitars – every "jangly" artist of the past two decades has in some way been influenced by this band.

It's possible to perform a similar type of exercise with the basic A major and D major chord shapes: both can sometimes produce fascinating, unpredictable and inspiring results.

6/7

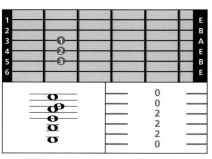

A add 9

F♯ minor 11

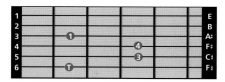

D 6/9

D sus 2

Since the contents of each chord obviously changes when you omit or alter some of the notes, the chord names will also change. We won't worry about this just for the moment. For now, just learn the chord shapes shown on the last page and try them out as suggested below over the verse section of the backing track. (Note: for the purposes of this exercise, D 6/9 and D sus 2 are interchangeable – even though they are very different chords.)

In the music below you can use these new chord shapes to play arpeggios. Notice the pick directions: downstrokes are used as the notes are played from bottom to top; upstrokes are used when playing top downward.   **6/8** ▶

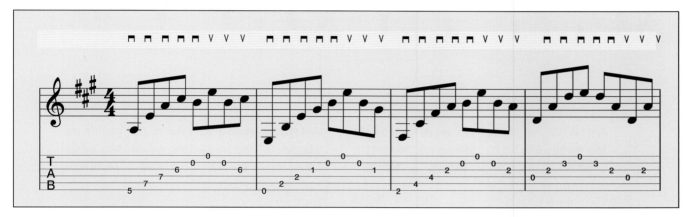

ALTERED BASS NOTES

Moving chord shapes around as above can create somewhat ambiguous voicings. POLYTONAL chords, for example, are those which contain the basic elements of two different chords played at the same time. Similar is the sound of a chord when played over a bass note other than the root.

To hear this effect, try this experiment with an open D major shape:

- Play the top four strings of a D major chord.
- Now play the top three strings with E on the 2nd fret of ● the 4th string (this will require rearranging fingers).
- Now play the top three strings with F# on the 4th fret of the 4th string.
- Finally, repeat with G on the 5th fret of the 4th string (this one's a bit of a stretch).

HARMONY

By now you will have figured out for yourself that there are certain types of chord sequence that sound more pleasant when played together than others. We can investigate this link by building triads on each degree of the major scale. You will see (and hear) that there is a particularly strong link between the chords on the first, fourth and fifth degrees. This is clear from the number of popular songs of the past century that have been based around these chord relationships.

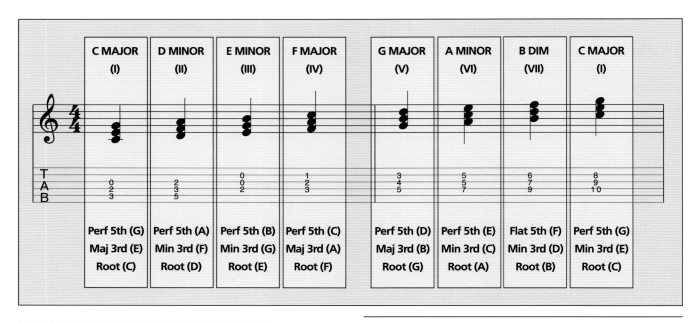

C MAJOR (I)	D MINOR (II)	E MINOR (III)	F MAJOR (IV)	G MAJOR (V)	A MINOR (VI)	B DIM (VII)	C MAJOR (I)
Perf 5th (G)	Perf 5th (A)	Perf 5th (B)	Perf 5th (C)	Perf 5th (D)	Perf 5th (E)	Flat 5th (F)	Perf 5th (G)
Maj 3rd (E)	Min 3rd (F)	Min 3rd (G)	Maj 3rd (A)	Maj 3rd (B)	Min 3rd (C)	Min 3rd (D)	Min 3rd (E)
Root (C)	Root (D)	Root (E)	Root (F)	Root (G)	Root (A)	Root (B)	Root (C)

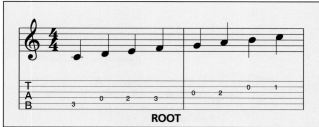

ROOT

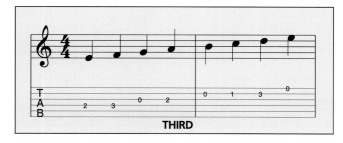

THIRD

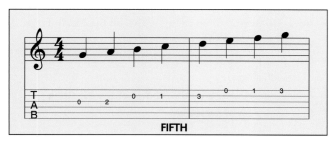

FIFTH

THE MECHANICS OF HARMONY

Just as each step of the major scale has its own "degree" and name, so too have the triads. Indeed, they are named after the degrees on which they are constructed. Although they are not all major triads, if you play the sequence through you will hear that it has the "quality" of a major scale about it. **6/9** ▶

BREAKING DOWN THE TRIADS

If you split those triads up into roots, thirds and fifths – as shown on the left – you have the basis of practical harmonic theory. There is harmony in all music, from the most angelic of choirs to the thrashiest of metal bands. Any time you detect something "melodic" going on at the same time as (but differing from) a song's main tune, you are hearing harmony. It may be a counter-melody, chordal effects built up on different instrumentation, or backing vocals – most of the elements of a typical recording are in some way providing examples of harmony.

Understanding how to create a "third" harmony, and then a "fifth" harmony, is not only central to a composer's skill but essential for any creative musician. It enables you to deviate from the most obvious musical paths and come up with ideas of greater sophistication. **6/10** ▶

PUNK, NOISE AND BEYOND

Although by the start of the 1980s the music industry had lost interest in the wider commercial appeal of Punk, successive generations of disaffected youth have continued to latch on to the evergreen appeal of very basic, loud, thrashy guitar music.

In America, during the early 1980s, the "hardcore" scene emerged, spearheaded by bands such as Black Flag and the Dead Kennedys. At the same time, a politically infused scene emerged around the band Crass. Brutally primitive in sound, Crass could sell enough copies of their singles to top the singles charts – but since their sales were made in specialist shops, they never did.

The spirit of Punk returned to the mainstream in the early 1990s when bands from the Seattle grunge scene, notably Nirvana and the Smashing Pumpkins, fused punk attitude with traditional rock and metal forms with enormous commercial success.

But there seems to have remained a lucrative market for bands that can provide a short, sharp musical shock. The most successful "Punk" band of the past two decades

are Green Day. Although American, their music quotes directly from British bands of the late 1970s such as the Clash and Stiff Little Fingers. They may be a thrashy and noisy, but Green Day's songs are also imbued with an extra ingredient – a good memorable tune. Others followed in the wake of Green Day, among them "boyband" Punks like McFly and Busted, who thrashed up standard "safe" themes for teens. You only need to listen to the adverts on kids' TV channels to hear how mainstream the classic Punk sound has become.

A more interesting offshoot of the '80s hardcore scene saw bands such as Sonic Youth adding "noise" to the equation. Contemporary equivalents include Lightning Bolt *(see above)*, a drum and bass noise duo who create an awesome live sound. Another modern relative is the drone metal of bands such as Earth, Boris or Sunn 0))) *(see left)*, the latter of whom has a sound that could be characterised as playing a single heavily distorted chord and letting it sustain for as long as possible – as simplistic as that sounds, it can create an astonishingly powerful impact.

MINOR TRIADS

You can also build triads from each degree of the minor scale. However, because of the differences between the natural, melodic and harmonic minor scales, the triads used are variable. An example is shown here for the key of C.

SCALE DEGREE	CHORD	NOTES
I	C Minor	(C, E♭, G)
II	D Diminished	(D, F, A♭)
	D Minor	(D, F, A)
III	E♭ Major	(E♭, G, B♭)
	E♭ Augmented	(E♭, G, B)
IV	F Minor	(F, A♭, C)
	F Major	(F, A, C)
V	G Minor	(G, B♭, D)
	G Major	(G, B, D)
VI	A♭ Major	(A♭, C, E♭)
	A Diminished	(A, C, E♭)
VII	B♭ Major	(B♭, D, F)
	B Diminished	(B, D, F)

HARMONY IN PRACTICE

Let's now put some of those harmonic ideas into practice. We're going to play a solo and then build up third and fifth harmonies over the top.

The first four bars of music represent a simple but effective lead line that can be used to accompany the "verse" section of the song. Work out the notes and when you're happy with your performance, play it along with the backing. It's important that you get the notes right… well, that should always be true, but especially so in this case as errors will wreck the harmonic effects we produce.   **6/11** ▶

The second line of music is a "third" harmony for the main line. For the first two bars the logic behind the harmony is very obvious – it mimics the major or minor 3rd notes in the triads built on the major scale. The notes in A major are: A, B, C♯, D, E, F♯, G♯, A. If we build triads on these scales they will be: A major, B minor, C♯ minor, D major, E major, F♯ minor, G diminished, E major. Therefore, the 3rd notes from those triads will be: C♯, D, E, F♯, G♯, A, B, C♯. Things deviate a little at the end of the third bar where instead of going with the obvious harmony we raise the note by a tone. The reason for this will become clear when we add the third part.   **6/12** ▶

HARMONY ON TWO STRINGS

As a slight aside, here is another harmony exercise for you. In this example, the fingering for the two lines above has been rewritten so that they can be played together at the same time on two adjacent strings. Each of the pairs of notes that make up the interval are separated by one or two frets, so the big task facing your fingers is getting them used to these shifting movements. Mastering these intervals can add a dimension of dynamism to your playing.   **6/13** ▶

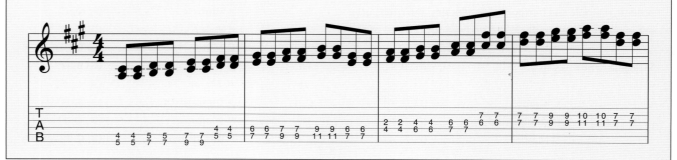

FIFTH HARMONY LINE

Here is the final part of the harmony. Once again, for the first two bars the notes are drawn from the notes of the triads built on the major scale – in this case, the fifth. Now that we've added the third line, you can see that the two notes used at the end of the third bar have maintained the interval used in the second line. Whereas the previous notes all use "first/third/fifth" harmonies, this uses the root, perfect fourth and major sixth. So why does it still work? The reason is that it creates a movement from an A major triad (A, C♯, E) to an F♯ minor triad (F♯, A, C♯). These chords have a special relationship in that F♯ minor is the RELATIVE MINOR of A major.   **6/14**

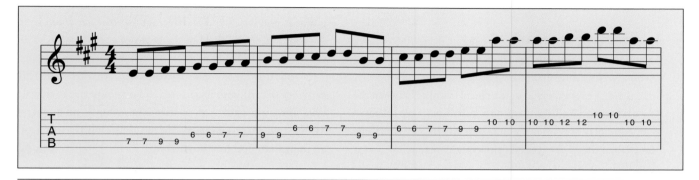

SUSTAINED INTERVALS

Playing just two well-chosen notes instead of a chord can be used to emphasise certain notes or rhythms – usually combinations of the root, third and fifth. There are numerous variations we can build from this idea. One is to alternate "sustained" intervals.

If you remember that the sustained fourth chord was so called because the major third was replaced by a perfect fourth, we can do the same thing with an interval of the root and major third.

In the example below, the shift is emphasised by the tied note. You can work out your own variation to play over the "chorus" part of the backing track.   **6/15**

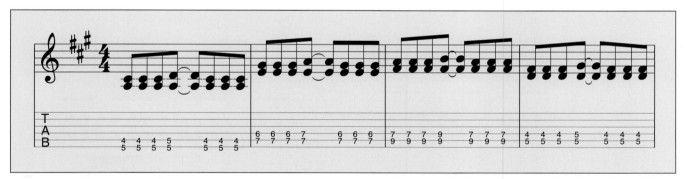

WORDS OF WISDOM

Still not convinced that this theory is any use? Here are the thoughts of a couple of great jazz musicians – what they have to say applies to musicians regardless of genre.

"I spent a lot of time teaching myself theory and harmony so I could be free to express myself on the instrument. I learned what relatives and substitutes could be played against a root of a chord, like E minor related to G, and so forth. I've gathered all this knowledge because for ten years all I've done is play jazz, every day."

George Benson

"Everyone should practise lots of scales. Actually, I feel there are only scales. What is a chord if not the notes of scale hooked together? There are several reasons for learning scales: one, the knowledge will unlock the neck for you – you'll learn the instrument; second, if I say I want you to improvise over G maj 7 + 5 and then go to E aug 9-5, then to B maj 7-5 – well, if you don't know what those chords are in scale terms, you're lost. It's not all that difficult, but you have to be ready to apply yourself."

John McLaughlin

MORE INVERSION

At the risk of labouring a point, it can't be stressed enough that a good understanding of inversion is a very powerful tool for any creative musician. The knowledge it provides is endlessly flexible and can be used to create fascinating solutions to musical problems.

INVERTING THE INTERVALS

Although we've touched on this earlier, here is a practical example of inverting intervals.

In the first example below, the chord changes between the first and second and the third and fourth bars are reflected in an extremely economical guitar part which only shifts one note. When the backing track is playing A major, the guitar plays the root and perfect fifth in A major (A and E); in the second bar, when the backing is playing E major, the guitar simply shifts one finger to play on the 4th fret of the 6th string. The two notes are G♯ and E – if we invert them, then we can see that they are also playing the root and perfect fifth, this time in E major. Playing with such smooth transitions can

completely alter the feel of a piece of music. Compare that movement to playing the 6th string/open and 5th string/2nd fret over E major.

A similar kind of progression is made between bars three and four. Over F♯ minor the guitar plays the root and perfect fifth (F♯ and C♯). This time, the note on the 5th string is raised by a semitone, which means that over the D major chord the guitar is playing F♯ and D. Invert those notes and you have the root and major third of the D major scale. It really is all so terribly logical.

Notice that there are also accent marks on this staff. This provides the riff with its rhythm. If you count out in double time (because each bar is made up wholly of quavers) "ONE-two-three-ONE-two-three-ONE-TWO", you'll get an immediate feel for the rhythm.   **6/16** ▶

PLAYING THE EXERCISE AS SINGLE NOTES

We'll end with effectively the same guitar part played as a series of alternating single notes. Notice, however, how the flavour of the original part with the notes played together is still very much in evidence.   **6/17** ▶

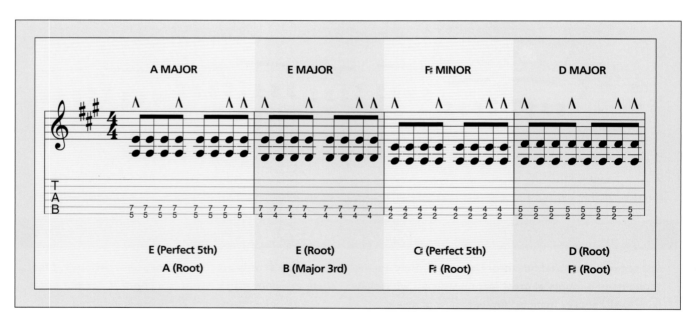

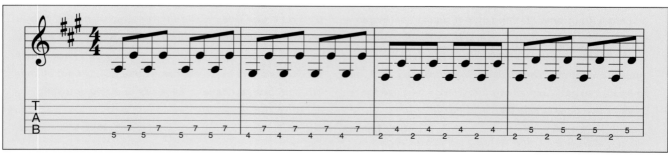

WHY DO SOME NOTES JUST "WORK"?

As you have been working through this chapter, you will no doubt have become aware that some harmonies sound more pleasant than others. The musical terms used to describe these effects are CONCORD and DISCORD. Although these words are sometimes used very loosely to describe whether a piece of music is pleasing to the ears, they also have very specific meanings.

Any interval between two notes can be described in terms of being either CONSONANT or DISSONANT. There are two distinct categories of consonance. PERFECT concords are the four "perfect" intervals: unison (the interval between two notes of the same pitch), perfect 4th, perfect 5th and the octave. The IMPERFECT concords are the minor 3rd and minor 6th intervals.

All other intervals, including those that are augmented or diminished, are deemed to be dissonant. Concords and discords are usually discussed in terms of their musical "stability" – using words like "open", "sharp", "soft" and "mild". This state can be slightly complicated for the interval between a root and perfect 4th, which can in some contexts be consonant or dissonant. Similar is true for the augmented 4th/perfect 5th (also called a "Tritone") which has an ambiguous nature. Indeed, in ancient times you could quite literally find yourself in trouble with the church for using these intervals – they were referred to as the "*Diablo in musica*" – the Devil in music!

C-C	OPEN CONSONANCE
C-D♭	SHARP CONSONANCE
C-D	MILD DISSONANCE
C-E♭	SOFT CONSONANCE
C-E	SOFT CONSONANCE
C-F	CONSONANCE OR DISSONANCE
C-F♯/G♭	NEUTRAL OR "RESTLESS"
C-G	OPEN CONSONANCE
C-G♯/A♭	SOFT CONSONANCE
C-A/B♭♭	SOFT CONSONANCE
C-B♭	MILD DISSONANCE
C-B	SHARP CONSONANCE
C-C	OPEN CONSONANCE

REVERBERATION

Another electronic effect which is important to many guitarists is REVERBERATION. This is a natural acoustic effect caused by a sound bouncing off the surrounding environment – typically walls, ceilings and objects – before finally fading away. It is heard as a part of the original sound. If you think of the effect of walking through a tunnel, you'll know the sound – each footstep you take can be heard swirling around as the sound hits the walls.

The density of the reverberation is in the fact that the sound is created from many different components. Firstly, the listener hears the sound directly from its source; then there are the early reflections, such as the first "bounces" off the wall; finally, there are the later reflections – clearly the bigger the room, the more late reflections there are likely to be. In this way, a complex new sound is created, the effect of which lingers on a while after the direct sound has passed.

In early studios, reverberation was still created naturally. Specially built reverb chambers fed signals through loudspeakers which were then picked up by microphones spread out around the room. Reverberation is now invariably produced electronically. When added to a guitar signal, "reverb" creates the warm, ambient effect of the sound spreading out.

ARTIFICIAL REVERB EFFECTS

Simulated reverb effects were originally created in the 1950s using a small spring that was vibrated by the audio signal. Many guitar amplifiers came with a spring reverb built in to the amplifier head. Over the next two decades, electronics manufacturers attempted a variety of analogue recreations of the sound, but these generally sounded like a very poor imitation of the real thing.

It was during the early 1980s that digital reverb first appeared. Initially, units cost several thousands of pounds, and were only found in the smartest studios. But they were a revelation, allowing engineers the luxury of programming parameters based on the attributes of natural reverberation – the size, shape and sound-damping features of an imaginary room. Digital technology is now so cheap that reasonable quality reverbs are available for not much more than the price of a foot pedal.

CHAPTER 7
FUNK AND STUFF

Although so often it's the melodic side of guitar work that garners the praise – the soloing, in other words – the importance of rhythm playing in most forms of rock music cannot be overstated. It may be the drums and bass guitar that underpins the groove, but it is the rhythm guitar which more often than not provides the real harmonic structure. In this chapter we will first be looking at the role of the rhythm guitar in the context of a 1970s-style funk backing. Although you may not consider funk to be strictly a sub-set of "rock" music, over the years it has crossed over in numerous areas. Certainly many of the techniques and sounds from funk have permeated through to modern-day rock – think of such creative artists as Beck and Eels, and listen to how funk/hip-hop grooves are an integral part of many of their tracks. Taking advantage of the repetitive E9 chord sequence used in this chapter's backing track, we conclude with a section on single-note solo "licks" of varying degrees of complexity.

RHYTHM OR LEAD? OR BOTH?

When the idea of the electric beat ensemble started to dominate popular music in the 1960s, the lines of demarcation were often quite carefully drawn. If a band had two guitarists, the more accomplished of the pair usually handled the single-note "lead" work, leaving the other to provide "rhythm". Consequently, many an aspiring young guitarist growing up during the 1960s and '70s was drawn to the glamour of the solo, ignoring the important role that the rhythm player brings to music of all kinds: check through any guitar magazine's poll during this period and you'll find it filled up with an impressive list of players noted for their lead guitar abilities.

That past two decades have seen this imbalanced viewpoint redressed. These days we are much less likely to be bowled over by soloing alone. Lead and rhythm guitar are now viewed less as separate entities, but rather as being interwoven skills that all players should seek to attain. As such, guitarists who are more oriented toward "rhythm" (in its traditional sense, that is – ALL guitarists, of course, have to be able to play with rhythm) are more likely to have their work acknowledged.

This means that figures such as Steve Cropper and Jimmy Nolen – both of whom made gloriously measured contributions to hundreds of classic Stax and Motown soul hits of the '60s – are now widely appreciated for the spartan tastefulness of their playing, and the "space" that it creates within their music.

IN THIS CHAPTER YOU'LL LEARN...

- The importance of rhythm guitar
- Vamping chords
- Seventh augmented ninth chords
- Hammering chords
- Funky rhythms
- Octave soloing
- Hybrid pick and fingers technique
- Melodic intervals

- The history of funk
- Alternative ninth chords
- Sliding chords
- The wah-wah pedal
- Funk licks
- Picking with the thumb and fingers
- Harmonic intervals

THE ROOTS OF FUNK

Funk has its roots firmly in the history of R&B and soul music. During the 1950s, a small group of artists began to evolve a new sound that fused the raw power of R&B with gospel-style vocals. It was a recipe that found widespread popularity at the end of the decade when Ray Charles hit the charts. It wasn't until Berry Gordy's Detroit-based Tamla Motown stable started enjoying national success in the early 1960s that this music began to take on the "soul" label. A variation of the same influences also emerged at the same time in other parts of the United States, such as the Stax label and studios in Memphis, Tennessee.

It's difficult to say when the term "funk" emerged, at least as far as soul music was concerned. The word was known as a black slang expression for body odour, and had some kind of musical connotation as far back as 1907, when Buddy Bolden wrote "Funky Butt Hall".

The first big funk hit was in 1968 when Sly and the Family Stone released "Dance to the Music". It provided a template for much of the funk that would follow: a strong beat, powerfully incisive bass line and rhythm guitar playing on the semiquaver with rhythmic patterns created by muting techniques.

As listenable as the sound might have be, it had one function above all others – it had to be danceable. This music was critical to the evolution of "disco" clubs – a strange new concept where punters danced to recorded music rather than live bands.

The decade that followed was funk's most important period. For many, the story really begins in 1970 with the release of James Brown's ten-minute workout "Sex Machine". Other important artists to follow included George Clinton's P-Funk ensembles – namely Parliament, Funkadelic and Bootsy's Rubber Band – Curtis Mayfield, the Brothers Johnson and, the slickest and most successful of them all, Earth, Wind and Fire.

By this time, musicians in other fields were also beginning to integrate some of funk's mannerisms into their own work. Thus was born jazz-funk – driven by the success of Herbie Hancock's *Headhunters* album. Rock bands of the period also began to get in on the act. Critics' favourites such as Little Feat, featuring the excellent guitar work of Lowell George, and Steely Dan both brought elements of funk rhythms into their sound.

As funk became increasingly commercialised it eventually evolved into the "disco" phenomenon, which gripped the mid-'70s. The finest band to emerge from this much-maligned form were Chic, a vehicle for guitarist Nile Rodgers and bass player Bernard Edwards. Their songs may have been of the lightweight "get down and boogie" variety, but the subtly shifting rhythm guitar work and powerfully memorable bass lines are certainly worthy of study by players of any genre. Their work reached its widest audience in 1983 when they gave David Bowie a funky makeover with the multimillion-selling *Let's Dance* album.

Since then, a fusion of funk and metal has seen a number of interesting bands emerging in the US. The first to become prominent were Living Colour, with their 1988 hit "Cult of Personality". Founded by guitarist Vernon Reid, they were unusual in that they were a black rock band. The Red Hot Chili Peppers have been by far the most successful funk-rockers. Formed in the early 1980s, they struggled for most of the decade to find an audience for their sound – a task not helped by drug problems within the band. However, they hit their stride in 1991 with multimillion-selling *Blood Sugar Sex Magik*.

GETTING FUNKY

One way or another, funk has been around since the late 1960s, crossing over into rock during the years that followed. Funk has also had an indirect influence on the path of rock and pop music over the past decade. The whole dance scene was built on a collision between relatively cheap and accessible technology and stolen James Brown samples. Since the early 1990s, dance music has made massive inroads into all kinds of unlikely areas, most notably in the DJ/Heavy Rock crossover of Nu Metal at the end of the 1990s.

INTRODUCTION

E13 / / /	D13 / / /	C13 / / /	D13 / / /

12-BAR TURNAROUND

E9 / / /	✕	✕	✕
✕	✕	✕	✕
D9 / / /	✕	C9 / / /	B7+9 / / /

INCOMPLETE CHORDS

Certain extended chords – those that use additional notes beyond the octave, such as ninths, elevenths, and thirteenths – are difficult or impossible play over six strings of a guitar. To work, some of those notes simply have to be left out.

The guitarist has to use his or her own skill and judgement to know which notes not to play. The most important aspect of this skill is in ensuring that the resulting chords still retain the flavour of their "full" equivalents. A dominant ninth, for example, is essentially a dominant seventh with a ninth note sitting on the top. It's quite reasonable, though, to omit the perfect 5th note and still produce a chord that sounds as if it is a dominant ninth. The same is even more true

BACKING TRACK #6

This chapter's backing track is a twelve-bar "acid jazz" style funk turnaround in the key of E. The structure is quite simple: there is a jazzy four-bar introduction (*see panel below, left*) after which there follows a repeating 12-bar sequence. The first eight bars of the main sequence are vamped ninth chords; the final four bars conclude the sequence, returning it back to E9.

NEW SHAPES

Let's begin by going over some unfamiliar chords. The introduction uses a series of THIRTEENTHS. A full thirteenth chord in the key of E would consist of a root, major third, perfect fifth, minor seventh, major second (ninth), major fourth (eleventh) and major 6th (thirteenth) note. Unfortunately, that would require seven strings to play, so a compromise is necessary. You can read a little more about this in the box below. The version we have chosen is slightly unusual in that it has no root note – it requires an accompanying instrument (on this backing track, the "root role"

is taken by the bass guitar) to create the correct effect.

MOBILE CHORDS

Two versions of E9 are shown on the right. One of them uses the top four strings; the other uses the 2nd to 5th strings. The advantage of using chords like this is that, like barre chords, they are mobile and can be moved along the fingerboard to play in any key.

A full six-finger version of the top chord is possible, but it requires you to bring your thumb around the neck and on to the 7th fret of the 5th and 6th strings. This is only for those with wide fingerspans and/or narrow guitar necks.

There are also two different versions of B SEVENTH AUGMENTED NINTH, shown below on the right. The chord above is probably best suited to basic funk vamping.

Listen to Backing Track #6 all the way through a few times – a short version can be heard on track 7/1 of the CD (the full-length version is on Track 14). For now just strum the chords gently along with the music until you're used to all the new chord shapes.   7/1 ▶

E9

ALTERNATIVE E9

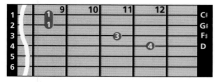
E13

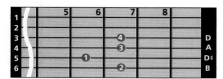
B7 + 9

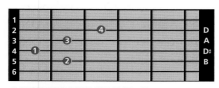
ALTERNATIVE B7+9

---

of elevenths and thirteenths. Whilst a six-note fully voiced eleventh chord may be possible in some keys (albeit with some rather contorted fingering), it's more common to leave out the perfect 5th and major 9th notes as a pair, or even the major 3rd and perfect 5th together.

To execute a full thirteenth chord on the guitar is quite impossible: it requires seven notes. Common omissions include the perfect 5th and major 9th, or the major 9th and the perfect 11th.

But are there any notes that we shouldn't ever leave out? Well, clearly, if we left the major 9th out of a dominant 9th chord, the result would no longer be a 9th – it would be a dominant 7th! But what about the root note? The concept of a "rootless chord" would seem to be something of a nonsense. After all, it's surely the root note that defines

the chord's key. If you look at the first of the three chords used in the introduction to Backing Track #6, you will see that it contains the notes D, F♯, G♯ and C♯. If we think of D as the root, F♯ as the major 3rd, G♯ (or A♭) as the diminished 5th and C♯ as the major 7th, we *could* call this chord D MAJOR 7 FLAT 5. However, if we underpin those same notes with an E and alter their names in relation to an E root, we now find that they are E (root), D (minor 7th), F♯ (major 9th), G♯ (major 3rd) and C♯ (major 13th) – the notes of a thirteenth chord.

This is an example of what is called a CHORD SYNONYM. The simplest synonym change is to take a minor triad and add a note a perfect 4th below the triad's root – this creates a major 7th in the key of the added note.

A sound understanding of harmonic theory is necessary to make such decisions in your playing.

FUNKY VAMPING

VAMPING is term used to describe a phrase or chord progression that can be repeated indefinitely until a vocalist or other soloist comes in.

The essence of funk vamping is in creating a rhythm through accenting notes or chords. This is usually achieved by damping the "unaccented" strings so that they almost make a "clicking" sound rather than an audible chord.

These are the two rhythms used on the backing track. If you count out the accents you will hear that they revolve around groups of three and do not necessarily sit obviously on the beat or off the beat.

Since the notes used are semiquavers, the count in the first example could go: "ONE-TWO-three-four-ONE-two-three-ONE-two-three-ONE-two-three-ONE-ONE-two".

In the second sequence, the count is: "ONE-two-three-ONE-two-three-ONE-two-three-ONE-two-three-ONE-ONE-ONE-two".

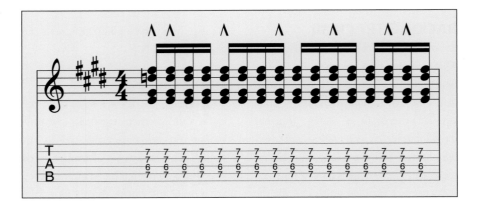

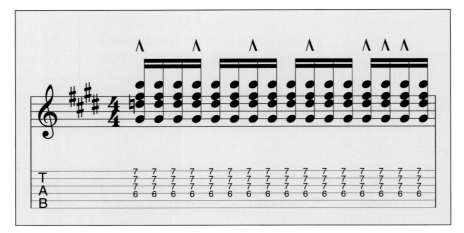

Try playing both of these riffs over the backing track. Don't worry about the accents to begin with – just concentrate on strumming the chords in time. Once you're comfortable with your timing, start getting used to strumming dampened chords. Then you can start working out the accenting.   7/2 ▶

SLIDING CHORDS

While playing funk rhythm guitar, using slide techniques when playing chords can be extremely effective. A commonly used funk cliché (and that isn't meant in any derogatory sense) is to emphasise key parts of the rhythm by sliding into the chord from either a tone or semitone below. This creates an interesting sense of movement.

In this example, although the track is still in the key of E major, the first chord played on the first beat is E♭9. But even though it's played over an E bass line, it doesn't actually create a discordant effect because it's only used momentarily; almost straight away – for the second semiquaver – you slide the chord up by a single fret.

This is an open slide, so the second semiquaver is not actually picked. A second similar slide is used near the end of the bar.   7/3 ▶

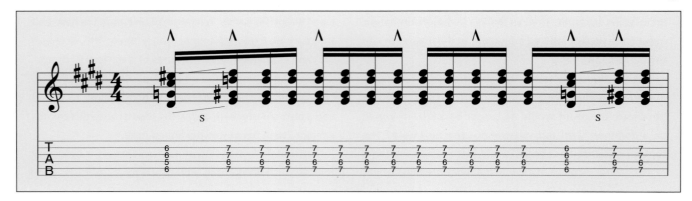

HAMMERING CHORDS

An alternative technique for building movement into the chord progressions is to use a variation on the single-note hammer-on technique. In this example your job is to hammer-on chords. For both of these exercises, you need to play the version of E9 that uses the top four strings (*see page 129, top right*). Before you try out the exercise below, begin by practising the hammering effect at a more leisurely tempo.

Barre the 6th fret by placing the 1st finger across the top four strings. However, instead of positioning the 3rd-finger barre immediately on the top three strings of the 7th fret, YOU FIRST PLAY THE 6TH FRET BARRE. While the chord is ringing you then hammer the 3rd-finger barre on the top three strings. When played over the backing track, the hammer-on is almost instantaneous.

The second exercise is similar except for an unusual change at the end. This is a B9 flattened 13th chord (usually written as B9–13).

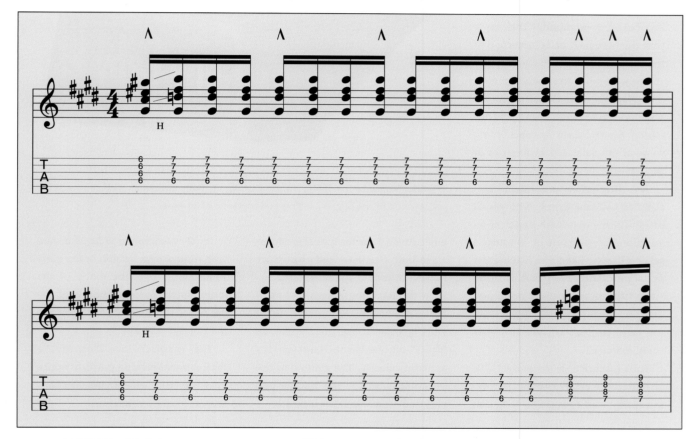

THE WAH-WAH PEDAL

One of the most famous guitar effects is the WAH-WAH PEDAL. This unit is a tone filter which is rocked back and forth inside a foot pedal. It can be used to create different effects.

The wah-wah was developed by Warwick Electronics in the UK, the company that owned the popular Vox brand. It was under this name that the first such pedal emerged at the start of 1967.

Perhaps more than anyone else, Jimi Hendrix was responsible for popularising the wah-wah pedal, his album *Electric Ladyland* providing some of the most expressive uses of the device.

An alternative approach was adopted by Frank Zappa, who would often use his wah-wah pedal as an additional tone control, finding a setting that he liked and leaving the pedal permanently in that position – the filter in most units providing greater resonance (or "Q") than the tone controls of any amplifier could manage.

Funk guitarists in the early 1970s also used the effect heavily; muting the strings and strumming a rhythm

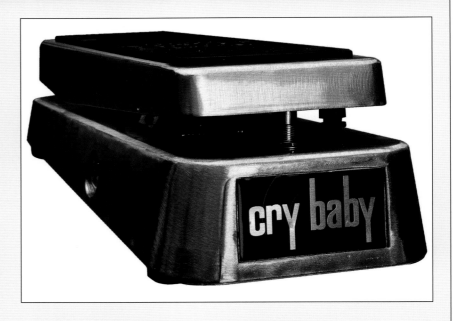

In production since the 1960s, the JIm Dunlop Cry Baby wah-wah pedal is one of the biggest-selling guitar effects of all time.

while rocking the footpedal produces a sound characterised by Isaac Hayes's music for the film *Shaft*.

In the past, manufacturers have also produced automatic wah-wah effects. These are "envelope filters" whose tonal characteristics are controlled by the volume of the incoming signal – the harder you play, the more "wah" you create.

Rarely seen during 1980s, the wah-wah returned to fashion in the early 1990s when used by many of the indie/dance crossover bands of the period, such as the Stone Roses and the Happy Mondays.

The graph below illustrates a typical pedal-rocking pattern: notice how the "full" effect coincides with accents in the written music.

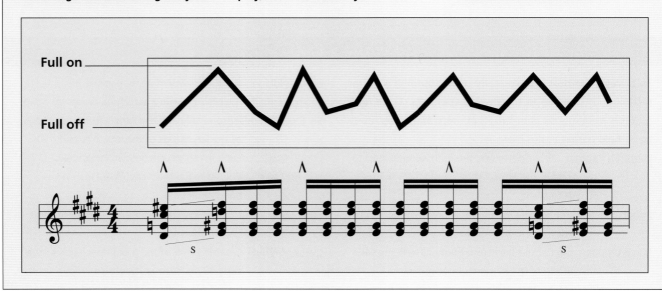

THE LAST FOUR BARS

The final four bars of the track use a descending sequence to conclude the turnaround in a way that returns it to the beginning with a smooth transition.

The first two bars play the chord D9 as quavers. It then descends a further major second to C9. The final chord is B SEVENTH AUGMENTED NINTH (written as B7+9). When reading chord names it is important that you don't misinterpret shorthand terms. A common misconception among novices is that a chord marked "+9" is the same as an "add 9". This is an easy error to make. However, "add 9" means literally the addition of the ninth note to a chord. In this way, B ADD 9 is simply a B major chord with a major 9th added (which is not the same as a "ninth" chord, by the way – that requires a minor 7th to be present somewhere).

The "plus" sign used in this way means that the scale degree following must be AUGMENTED – raised by a semitone. The notes that make up a full B7+9 chord are B (root), D♯ (major 3rd), F♯ (perfect 5th), A (minor 7th), and D (augmented 9th). This version omits the perfect 5th. This chord is heavily used in funk and jazz. It has an unusual, slightly jarring quality to it because of the interval between the major 3rd (D♯) and the augmented 9th (D). When these notes are almost an octave apart, the inherent "discord" is less apparent.

Lets compare these two intervals on the guitar. Begin by playing D♯ on the 6th fret of the 5th string simultaneously with open D on the 4th string. The effect is not pleasant. Now play that same D♯ alongside the higher-pitched D on the 7th fret of the 3rd string. The effect it creates is quite different.

In the four bars shown below, you will notice a different approach to completing the cycle in the final bar. The two opening semiquavers played staccato bring the sequence to a dramatic halt. A neat little lick completes the effect.

When counting the final bar, pay special attention to the rests. Since the first two semiquavers are followed by quaver and crotchet rests respectively, we can tell that the final lick starts exactly on the 3rd beat of the bar. And watch out for those demi-semiquavers in there – you'll certainly need a nimble left hand to pull this one off!   7/4 ▶

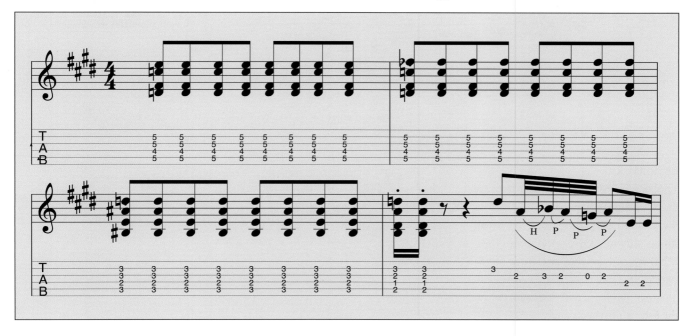

FUNK LICKS

The next few pages are devoted to showing you a few interesting licks that you can play along with Backing Track #6 (Track 16 on the CD). Moving away from rhythm guitar, these are little lead motifs taking up one, two or four bars. Since the backing track plays 12 bars of the E9 chord in each cycle, you can simply repeat the riffs over and over again, or string them together as one rather demanding solo.

Some of these licks are rhythmically quite demanding, so it's a good idea to start off by tapping or counting out the note values on the page. Once you've mastered the timing, work out the notes and then have a crack at playing it along with the backing.

EXERCISE 1

This is a four-bar riff which comprises a pair of two-bar phrases. The first uses an ascending minor pentatonic scale in E; the second "answers" with a descending minor pentatonic scale.

The count for this may look quite tricky on the surface, but if you listen to Track 7/5 of the CD, you'll hear that it's actually a very simple rhythm. The key to figuring it out is in looking at the groups of notes mathematically. Since each one comprises a semiquaver and a quaver, you can think of the emphasis of the rhythm as being on every third semiquaver, so if you count "ONE-ONE-two-ONE-ONE-two-ONE-ONE-two-ONE-ONE-two-ONE-ONE-two-ONE", you should get the feel of it. See, it's not that difficult, really.   **7/5** ▶

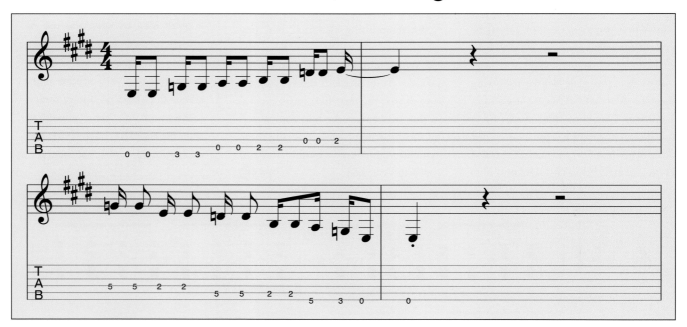

EXERCISE 2

This one is quite a bit trickier because the dotted quaver on the third G♯ throws the rhythm. Try this count to break things down: "ONE-ONE-two-ONE-ONE-two-ONE-ONE-two-three-ONE-two-ONE-ONE-ONE-two". You can hammer the final two semiquavers on the 6th string, if you fancy it.

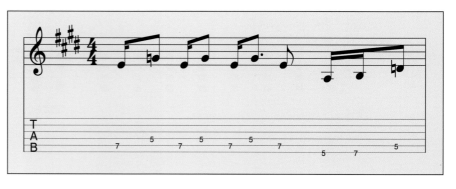

EXERCISE 3

There are two things to watch for here. To begin with, the first three notes of the first bar are played staccato. This gives an added "punch" to the rhythm.

Secondly, there is a group of eight demi-semiquavers at the end of bar two. These are played as a TRILL – very fast hammering and pulling between two notes. The curve beneath the notes is a LEGATO, meaning that the notes should be played as one phrase. **7/6** ▶

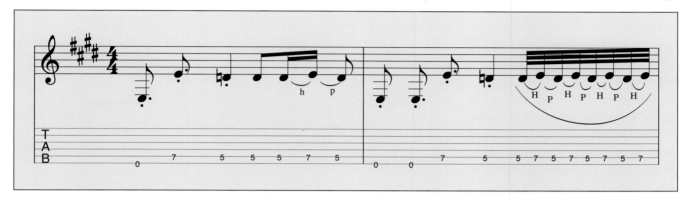

EXERCISE 4

This example begins with a double hammer-on. To do this, you play the 5th fret of the 5th string with the 1st finger, and then hammer-on the 6th fret with the 2nd finger, and then hammer-on the 7th fret with the 3rd finger. Once again, try to make this a smooth single movement. You can hear this example (as well as the two below) on Track 7/6 of the CD.

EXERCISE 5

This exercise kicks off with a double pull-off. This is the reverse of the technique used above. Position your fingers on the string in readiness: the 1st finger is on the 5th fret; the 2nd on the 6th fret; and the 3rd on the 7th fret. Pick the note and then in quick succession remove the 3rd and then 2nd fingers so that three distinct notes can be heard.

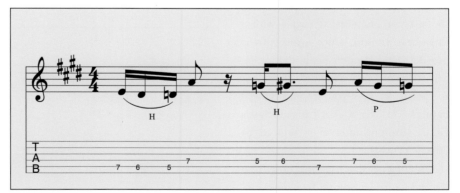

EXERCISE 6

This exercises begins with hammering-on a pair of notes. You need to position the top joint of your 1st finger on the 12th fret of the 4th and 5th strings. Pick both notes together and then hammer-on the 14th fret with your 3rd finger.

For an added little bit of variety you could try a semitone string bend on the penultimate pair.

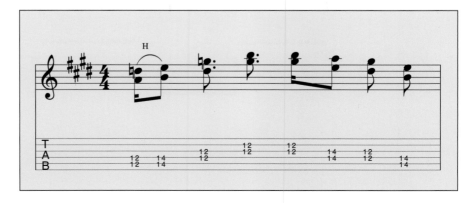

EXERCISE 7

All of the licks shown on this page can be heard on Track 7/7 of the CD.

This exercise makes use of three simple hammered notes. Take care when working out the rhythm, though – the emphasis is off the main beat. **7/7** ▶

EXERCISE 8

The "stuttering" effect of the semiquaver/quaver opening played on the same note has been widely used by many funk (and jazz-funk) musicians. The second half of the bar gives you practice at the art of hammering across strings.

EXERCISE 9

Again, the rhythm kicked off by the opening notes is something of a funk cliché. Broken down into semiquavers, the count goes: "ONE-two-three-ONE-two-three-ONE-two-three-four-ONE-two-ONE-ONE-two-three".

EXERCISE 10

This one (*shown at the foot of the page*), brings together various elements from the last two chapters. It begins with a three-beat vibrato. Once again, this is based around a minor pentatonic scale. The starting note has a bluesy feel about it – this is because you are playing a G natural (G♮) over a chord that includes G♯. A semitone interval is said to be DISCORDANT.

Don't forget that the third note from the end has to be bent up by a tone.

EXERCISE 11

The two riffs across the page are exercises 10 and 11. They can be heard on Track 7/8 of the CD.

The first example begins with an open slide up to a struck note. Place the 1st finger somewhere around the 7th fret of the 4th string. Pick the note, and then IMMEDIATELY slide the finger up to the 9th fret. Do the same thing on the fourth beat, this time sliding up to the 9th fret of the 3rd string.

The downward-pointing curve in the second bar is one of many possible

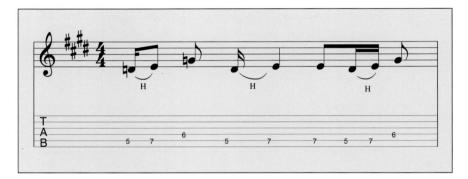

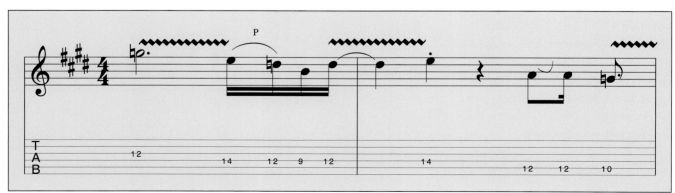

symbols denoting a bend in pitch to a lower note. The TAB indicates the 11th fret on the 2nd string, but what this means in practice is that the 2nd string has to be bent to the same pitch as the note that would be played on the 11th fret – either the 9th or 10th fret depending on the gauge of your strings – before the note is picked. The string is then released.

EXERCISE 12

The bottom exercise on this page is a tricky high-speed sequence of hammering and pulling across the strings, culminating in an upward bend. **7/8** ▶

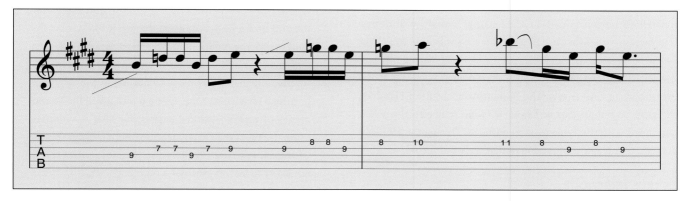

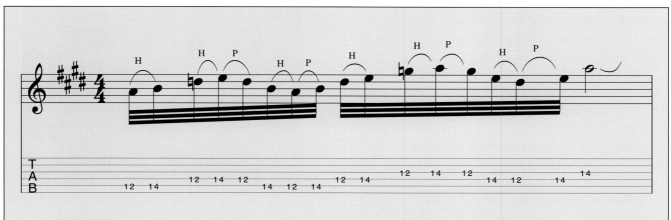

MORE THINGS TO DO WITH THE BACKING TRACK

Backing Track #6 makes an excellent workout tool for the E minor pentatonic scale. Try out these exercises: the first number is the string, the second is the fret. Play using quavers.

FROM THE OPEN 6TH STRING
6/0, 6/3, 5/0, 5/2, 4/0, 4/2, 3/0, 3/2, 2/0, 3/2, 3/0, 4/2, 4/0, 5/2, 5/0, 6/3.

FROM THE 5TH STRING
5/7, 5/10, 4/7, 4/9, 3/7, 3/9, 2/8, 2/10, 1/7, 2/10, 2/8, 3/9, 3/7, 4/9, 4/7, 5/10.

FROM THE 5TH STRING
5/7, 4/5, 4/7, 3/4, 3/7, 2/5, 3/7, 3/4, 3/7, 2/5, 3/7, 3/4, 4/7, 4/5, 5/7, 4/5.

FROM THE 4TH STRING
4/2, 4/5, 3/2, 3/4, 2/3, 2/5, 2/3, 3/4, 2/3, 2/5, 2/3, 3/4, 3/2, 4/5, 4/2, 4/5.

FROM THE 3RD STRING
3/9, 2/8, 2/10, 1/7, 1/10, 1/7, 2/10, 2/8, 3/9, 2/8, 2/10, 1/7, 1/10, 1/7, 2/10, 2/8.

FROM THE 2ND STRING
2/8, 3/9, 3/7, 4/9, 4/7, 5/10, 5/7, 6/10, 6/7, 6/10, 5/7, 5/10, 4/7, 4/9, 3/7, 3/9.

FROM THE 1ST STRING
1/15, 1/12, 2/15, 2/12, 3/14, 3/12, 4/14, 4/12, 5/14, 4/12, 4/14, 3/12, 3/14, 2/12, 2/15, 1/12.

PLAYING WITH OCTAVES

We'll end this chapter with a look at octave lead lines. In essence, this means taking a melodic motif and doubling it up one octave higher. The most famous practitioner of this style of playing was jazz guitarist Wes Montgomery, who was active from the mid-1950s until his death in 1968. Using a mixture of thumb and fingers – he didn't use picks at all – he was able to deliver lyrical passages at considerable speed. However, it's not only jazz musicians who have used this style of soloing: if you listen to the lead break in "All Along The Watchtower" by Jimi Hendrix, the same technique can be heard. It's especially effective when combined with rhythmic picking patterns. During the 1970s, it was often heard in conjunction with a wah-wah pedal.

OCTAVE TECHNIQUE

The simplest way to play octaves is to forget about your pick (although see the panel on the right for an alternative take). You play the low note with the thumb and play the high note simultaneously with the 1st or 2nd finger.

The left-hand fingering is very straightforward. From any fret on the 6th string, the octave can be found two frets higher on the 4th string; from any fret on the 5th string, the octave will be either 2 frets higher on the 3rd string or 2 frets lower on the 2nd string; from any fret on the 4th string, an octave can be found 2 frets lower on the 1st string. These relationships are not consistent across all strings because the interval between the 3rd and 2nd strings is different from the other strings.

PICKY FINGERS

The "octave style" is much easier to play using a thumb and finger, but if you want to integrate it with your regular pick playing you'll need a slight rethink. One approach is to use the pick to play the lower note that would have been struck by the thumb, and use either the 2nd or 3rd finger (or even the 4th if that works for you) to pick the higher note. You need nimble fingers to pull this off, but it can be done with a little practice.

The only minor downside to playing in this way is in getting a consistent tone. Using a pick gives the sound plenty of attack – almost a kind of "click" – whereas using the tip of the finger creates a more mellow sound. Of course, with heavily "effected" electric guitars this is not likely to be too much of a problem.

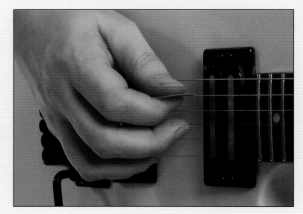

OCTAVE EXERCISES

Before we turn again to Backing Track #6, here are two exercises to get you started. The first illustrates the "two frets up" rule, playing a scale of E major. The second shows the "two frets down" rule, to produce an E major scale one octave above the first.

As with playing barre chords, the left-hand posture is especially significant in that once you have your fingers in position it is a simple matter of retaining that shape and moving the entire hand along the fingerboard.

Both scales can be heard on Track 7/9 of the CD.

OCTAVES IN PRACTICE

Here are three single-bar exercises that you can play along with Backing Track #6 (that's Track 16 on the CD).

Since the root note in this bar is on the 4th string we'll play the octave two frets lower on the 1st string. The big difference between the two approaches is in the fingering. When playing this position, because of the stretch required, the lower note has to be fretted by the 4th finger; the upper note should be held in place by the 1st finger.

There are two slides in this exercise. The first one starts on the second beat (don't forget that the bar begins with a crotchet rest). Place the 4th finger of the left hand on the 14th fret of the 4th string, and position the 1st finger on the 12th fret of the 1st string. Simultaneously, pick the lower note with your thumb and the upper note with your 3rd finger. "Pluck" the strings and immediately slide your entire hand down by two frets so that the new notes are

ringing. Note that you don't pick these new notes.

At the end of the bar, there is an "indeterminate" slide. Over the course of one beat (the notes are crotchets) you should gradually move your hand down

the fingerboard so that the notes descend in pitch. The note should have the effect of fading out during the time it sounds.

The second example is a variation on the same idea. You can hear both exercises on Track 7/10 of the CD.   **7/10** ▶

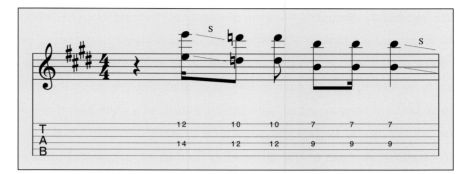

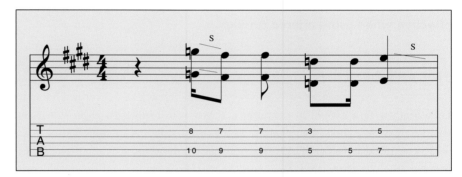

BREAKING UP THE INTERVALS

When two notes are played at the same time, the resulting sound is known as an HARMONIC INTERVAL. When those notes are parted, what you hear is a MELODIC INTERVAL. Depending on whether the pitch of the second note is higher or lower than the first, it becomes either an ASCENDING melodic interval or a DESCENDING melodic interval.

This exercise splits the octave harmonic intervals into ascending melodic intervals. In essence it duplicates an earlier exercise, only this time every alternate note is an octave higher in pitch. To play this with the right-hand fingers requires a slight "rolling" action of the hand. However, since the bar contains only single notes it would be possible to play it using standard pick

techniques. The only way you can really make this work is by alternating your strokes. A downstroke on the 4th string leaves your pick in the correct position to play an upstroke on the 1st string.

The octave style of playing can be used to create attractive and interesting effects in almost any type of music – it's certainly worth spending some time experimenting.   **7/11** ▶

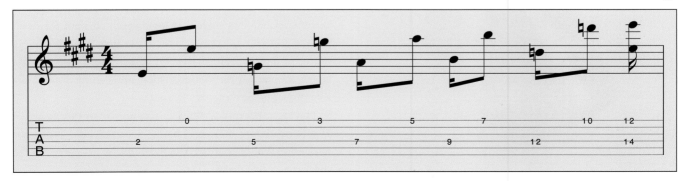

CHAPTER 8
SLIPPIN' AND SLIDIN'

We've already discussed the idea of using the fretting finger to slide between notes on the same string. Now let's take a look at a parallel area: using a glass "bottleneck" or metal slide to achieve the same effect. It all began with early blues guitarists attempting to recreate the expressiveness of the human voice by sliding objects such as knives or glass bottles along the guitar strings. A parallel development took place in Hawaii, which saw the evolution of a style based around playing with the guitar flat on the lap. It was largely the popularity of Hawaiian music in the US during the 1920s which helped to establish the idea of the slide being used in other types of music. Slide playing can be used with standard guitar tuning, where it can be integrated with regular playing techniques, but it is especially effective when using altered tunings.

THE ART OF SLIDE

Let's begin with a couple of definitions. If we were being completely correct about things we would say that a SLIDE is made from metal and a BOTTLENECK from glass. Nowadays, however, the two terms are largely interchangeable, so from now on we'll simply call them all slides. In fact, pretty well anything from a comb to a screwdriver to a beer can could be used to slide across the strings of a guitar. Indeed, some of the

earliest musicians to use this style were known to have used old polished bones to do the job.

So which material produces the best results? Rather like finding a suitable pick, choosing a comfortable slide is important. Slides can be found in a variety of shapes and sizes. Glass produces a cleaner, more "authentic" sound than metal, which can sometimes produce a grazing sound as it moves along the strings. However, the type you use is largely down to the effect you aim to produce and the type of instrument you play. They are relatively cheap items – about as much as a new pack of strings – so it's worth trying as many different types as you can find.

SLIDING IN THE MODERN WORLD

The role of the slide in music has changed somewhat over the decades. If you listen to old pre-war blues recordings by such artists as Robert Johnson, Son House and Blind Willie Johnson you will understand the emotional power of this technique when placed in the right hands. However, like much of the early blues playing, there was less overall concern for note-perfect accuracy on these classic recordings than in simply capturing a great performance. Of course, those bluesmen did largely accompany themselves singing, so the music was wholly a combination of those two factors.

Playing modern-day slide guitar outside of that idiom is a rather different matter. A badly executed slide with poor intonation would be immediately audible when played in the context of a rock band.

MASTERS OF THE SLIDE

Not surprisingly, the most widely admired slide guitar players tend to be vintage blues players.

One of the great masters was Mississippi Fred MacDowell. His story is a classic blues legend. He spent the first 55 years of his life working as an itinerant farm labourer, occasionally playing at night to local black audiences. Discovered in 1959 by archivist Alan Lomax, MacDowell quickly became a popular attraction on the burgeoning US folk circuit and among college audiences.

He recorded his debut album, *Delta Blues*, in 1963, on the eve of his 60th birthday. His style revealed a ferocious playing technique based around the use of a steel slide and bass-string runs executed with staggering dexterity. He gigged and recorded extensively until his death in 1972.

Of course, many other vintage bluesmen played slide with some considerable style – Robert Johnson, Son House and even Muddy Waters.

One of the most famous slide riffs was coined by Elmore James. The octave slide introduction to his hit "Dust My Broom" was the early-'60s wannabee guitarist's equivalent to "Smoke on the Water", "Stairway To Heaven" or "Smells Like Teen Spirit" – EVERYBODY was doing it.

Rock's greatest slide star emerged briefly in the late 1960s. The Allman Brothers Band had been seminal in the development of the "Southern Boogie" sound. Guitarist Duane Allman (*see left*) was already popular with music critics, many of whom found it hard to believe that a young white man could play with so much "soul". Just as the band was beginning to reach a wider audience, Allman was killed in a motorcycle accident. Still lamented almost 30 years later, his most widely remembered work is – ironically, perhaps – a solo he recorded on an Eric Clapton track, Derek and the Dominoes' classic "Layla".

In the modern era, the most noteworthy slide player is arguably Ry Cooder. Over the past 35 years he has played sessions for innumerable noted artists, and recorded many fine albums of his own. A master of pretty well any style of picking you'd care to imagine, the magnificently pure tone of his finest slide playing can be heard on atmospheric film soundtracks, such as *Performance* or *Paris, Texas*.

Another player with a fine reputation for her slide work is Bonnie Raitt. An early disciple of Mississippi Fred MacDowell, she cut nine albums from 1971 until her big commercial break almost 20 years later. Also a well-respected singer and songwriter, Raitt's defining album is *Nick of Time*.

A more recent name to emerge in acoustic slide blues is Kelly Joe Phelps. During the second half of the 1990s, he recorded three brutally spartan albums of haunting atmospheric beauty, peaking with 1999's *Shine-Eyed Mr Zen*. His playing is fluid and seamless, steeped in the great blues tradition. His subsequent work has broadened, departing from this simple format with a small ensemble.

SLIDE TECHNIQUE

The most difficult aspect of slide guitar playing is the fact that you no longer have the frets to provide you with perfect intonation. Therefore, if you are to play in tune – which is usually what we aim for – it is important that the slide always be positioned DIRECTLY ABOVE THE FRET OF THE NOTE REQUIRED. This will take considerable practice to get right, especially as you will be more accustomed to fitting your fingers behind the fret when pressing down on the strings. If the slide is positioned behind the fret, the note will be flat; if it placed ahead of the fret, it will be sharp.

AVOIDING THE BUZZ

In terms of the sound itself, another common problem for novice players is the natural tendency to press the slide too hard against the strings. This is quite natural when you are used to fretting notes, but it usually results in an unpleasant "buzzing" sound, or may even cause actual contact with the frets – which is to be avoided at all costs.

In fact, the slide needs little more pressure than its own weight against the string. Although the fingers behind the slide can be used to dampen fret rattle to a degree, if the "action" of your guitar – the height of the strings above the fretboard – is too low, buzzing may be unavoidable.

To prevent this happening, some guitarists raise the action on their instrument, either by adjusting the height of the strings at the bridge and/or increasing the height of the nut, or zero fret. Frankly, the latter is usually a fairly crude fix, like inserting a thin metal bar just in front of the nut (or zero fret). Take care if trying this out, since you can easily ruin the intonation of your guitar if you're not certain what you're doing.

Players for whom slide is a major part of their sound usually find it more satisfactory to have a separate instrument permanently set up for slide use.

SLIDE EXERCISES

Here are two simple slide exercises to get you started.

First, put the slide on your chosen finger. Position the slide above the 3rd fret, making sure that it is resting on the string directly above the fret. Play the note; while it rings, slowly move the slide along the string (keeping it parallel at all times) until you reach the 5th fret. Now repeat the exercise in reverse. The second exercise is a simple E major scale on the 4th string.   8/1 ▶

BACKING TRACK #7

The backing track for this chapter is made up from two eight-bar sequences. Each one plays through twice before changing. The tempo is slow, and it has been specifically designed to allow you to practise your slide technique. Begin by familiarising yourself with the music – you can hear it on Track 8/2 of the CD.

As you listen to the piece, you may notice a couple of unfamiliar chords lurking in there. Although we've talked previously about major 7th chords (*see page 99*) this is the first exercise that actually features them in practice.

Also in there is the delightfully named F MAJOR 7TH AUGMENTED 11TH. This is not as mysterious or difficult as it may sound – it's simply an F major 7th with the top two strings played open. Although it's a commonly used chord, few players probably know its correct name. **8/2** ▶

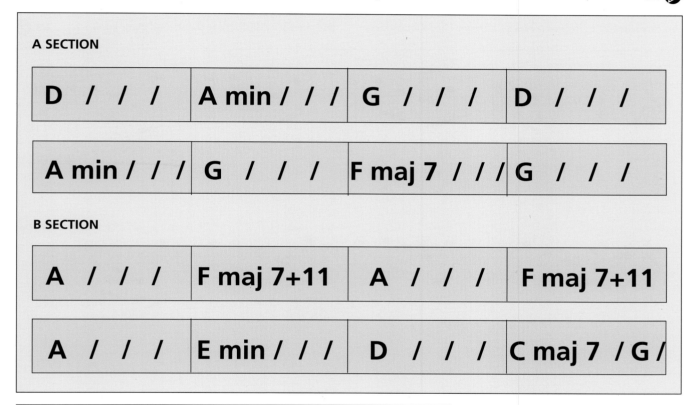

A SECTION

| D / / / | A min / / / | G / / / | D / / / |

| A min / / / | G / / / | F maj 7 / / / | G / / / |

B SECTION

| A / / / | F maj 7+11 | A / / / | F maj 7+11 |

| A / / / | E min / / / | D / / / | C maj 7 / G / |

EXTENDED NOTES

The three additional chords that you need for this track are F major 7, C major 7 and F major 7 augmented 11 (written as F major 7+11). The finger positions are shown on the right. Let's first take a closer look at the last of those chords, and discuss how they're named.

You've already seen chords with names that include "9ths". What does this actually mean? Chord names are derived entirely from the notes they contain. However it's also possible for a chord to include notes from beyond an octave interval from the root. These are EXTENDED notes. To work them out you simply carry on counting scale degrees beyond the octave.

You could view the octave note as both the eighth degree of its scale (hence its name) or the first degree – since the note is the same as the root. Following on from this, we could think of a note one octave above the second degree as the NINTH. Thus, in the key of C major, the note D in the next octave range would be the 9th.

Similarly, the note one octave above the fourth degree is the ELEVENTH. In the key of F major the 11th note is B♭. Since it is an AUGMENTED 11th we need, the extra note has to be B. The other commonly used extended note is the THIRTEENTH.

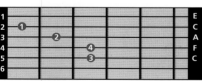

F MAJOR 7

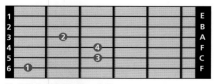

F MAJOR 7+11

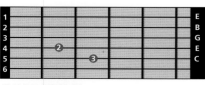

C MAJOR 7

SLIDING ARPEGGIOS

In this exercise, your job is to hold chord positions with the slide and play them as arpeggios – a string of single notes. You can strike the strings either with a pick or with the fingers.

This exercise works because if you hold the slide across any one fret, playing the 2nd, 3rd and 4th strings across creates a major chord (or technically a second inversion of a major chord) whose root is the note on the 3rd string; playing the top three strings in isolation creates a minor chord whose root

is the note on the 1st string. This is useful to know for all rock guitarists – not only for playing slide.

Begin the exercise with the slide over the 7th fret. Observe the half-beat rest and then play the first three notes. Take care to follow the tied note, which sustains beyond the barline into the first half-beat of the second bar. You should keep the slide in position until the end of bar, taking it down to the 5th fret during the first half-beat of that bar.

To play the track in full, play and repeat the first eight bars, and then play and repeat the second eight bars. **8/3** ▶

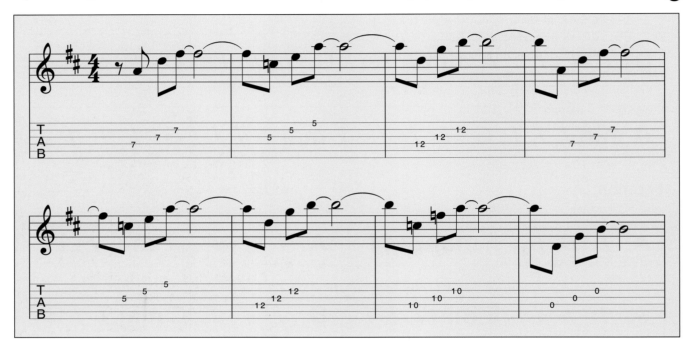

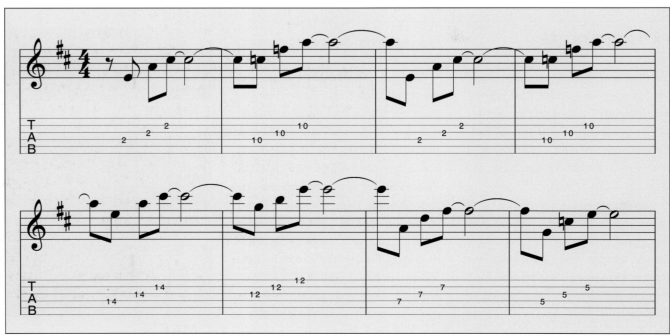

SLIDING CHORDS

Yet again we come up with another reason why it's so important to get to know the notes on the fingerboard, and the way notes work in relation to one another. Not only does it enable you to find any note immediately, or identify the correct positions from which to play barre chords or scales, but it makes possible the identification of a whole new range of simple three-note chords. These can be integrated with single-note work or melodic embellishments.

The box on the immediate right shows you the names of chords that can be played on the 2nd, 3rd and 4th strings simply by placing a barre across the fret. These are second inversion major chords.

The box on the far right shows chords that can be played using a barre on the top three strings. These are first inversion minor chords.

Any basic open string shapes can be reworked along the fingerboard in this way, playing just the fretted notes.

Fret	Strings 2, 3, 4
0	G
1	G#/Ab
2	A
3	A#/Bb
4	B
5	C
6	C#/Db
7	D
8	D#/Eb
9	E
10	F
11	F#/Gb
12	G

Fret	Strings 1, 2, 3
0	Em
1	Fm
2	F#/Gbm
3	Gm
4	G#/Abm
5	Am
6	A#/Bbm
7	Bm
8	Cm
9	C#/Dbm
10	Dm
11	D#/Ebm
12	Em

SLIDES FOR EFFECT

Rather than being a fundamental part of a guitarist's sound, slide guitar is more often than not used as an attractive musical embellishment. Here is an example of how that might work. Each bar features a slide that starts on the third beat and ends on the first beat of the subsequent bar.

Notice that the music doesn't actually start on the first chord of the song, but at the start of the four-beat count-in. This means that on the count of "four", before the band starts playing, you must position the slide on the 11th fret of the 3rd string and immediately begin to slide the F# down the string. Your aim should be to reach the note D on the 7th fret EXACTLY on the first beat of the next bar. Sustain the note for three beats, then quickly bring the slide away from the string and place it on the 9th fret, and carry on. It is important that you only slide the notes linked by the straight line. **8/4** ▶

DELAY EFFECTS

We already briefly discussed chorus effects earlier in the chapter. Now let's take a look at delay effects in general.

Many of the electronic effects used by guitarists are produced by repeating a delayed signal. Delay effects were originally produced by mechanical means, using magnetic tape, but are now almost entirely produced digitally. Different effects can be created depending on the length of the delay. They are shown below measured in milliseconds (500 milliseconds equals half a second).

PHASING (7–12 MS) AND FLANGING (12–20 MS)

When the same signal is played back from two sources at the same time, PHASING occurs. Every sound comprises a soundwave, which passes from peaks to troughs. When two identical signals are slightly out of alignment, and the peaks on one signal tie up with the troughs on another, "phase cancellation" takes place, producing a "sweeping" sound. If the delay is greater, the sweep becomes more dramatic and "metallic", which is called FLANGING.

CHORUS AND ADT (20–35 MS)

Delay effects were originally created by recording a signal on two tape machines and then playing them back at the same time. The inconsistencies in speed and pitch between machines helped to create the overall sound. Digital emulation adds pitch modulation and speed controls to disturb the delayed signal. ADT (AUTOMATIC DOUBLE TRACKING) and CHORUS are two such effects. Adding variations in pitch to a delayed signal can create the effect of doubling up the performance. It's usually employed to beef up vocals or a "thin" guitar sound, and is an effective alternative to recording the same part twice on separate multitrack channels. If used over a rhythm guitar part, it is especially effective when the original signal and the effect are panned to extremes in the stereo spectrum.

Chorus extends this approach, modulating a number of repeats. As the delay is so fast, this creates a full-bodied, rich and sustained sound which is especially effective on chord work.   **8/5** ▶

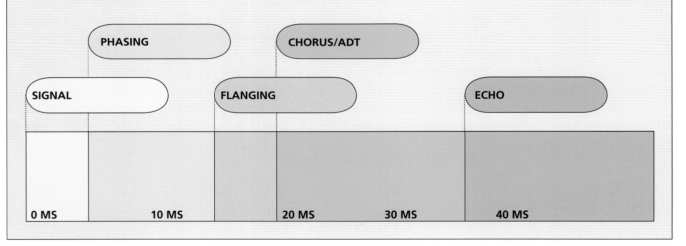

SLIDES WITH VIBRATO

The final exercise in this chapter introduces a new idea: using the slide to create vibrato effects. In the music shown across the page, you are called upon to produce both one- and two-bar vibratos – these are the wavy lines above the notes. This is much more difficult to execute than straightforward fingered vibrato in that the only option you have is to move the slide back and forth delicately along the string. The key here is judging exactly how much to move the slide, and how quickly to do it. There is no correct answer to this – it's a matter of taste. That said, too great a movement either side of the note will just sound like your pitch control is poor.

Another aspect of working with slides on which this exercise focuses is in moving ACROSS strings. It's all well and good working on a single string, but, as we've seen with scales and chords, you can play with greater efficiency by utilising the whole fingerboard. You could play the third bar from the 7th fret of the 6th string, but since your hand is already broadly in position it makes more sense to work on the 5th string.

If you have access to a digital delay effect pedal, this would be a good point to experiment. You can create some beautiful, powerful (and very strange) sounds by combining slide guitar with a chorus effect, "slapback" echo (around 40 ms), or even multiple delays of half a second or more.   **8/6** ▶

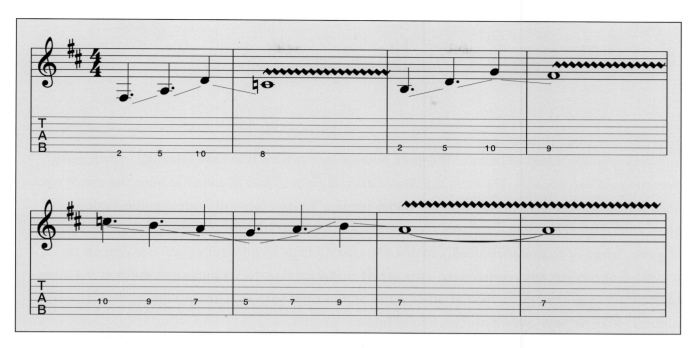

SLIDE POSTURE

Slide guitar was first popularized by the American fad for Hawaiian music in the 1920s and 1930s. This type of music is played on an unusual-looking instrument called a LAP STEEL GUITAR. As the name suggests, the guitar is not hung from a strap or balanced sideways on one of the knees, but sits horizontally across both of the player's knees. Usually, the instrument is tuned to an open G chord (*for more on this see page 164*). The right hand picks the strings, and the left hand moves the slide up, down and across the strings.

Through his work in Hollywood during the 1930s, the best-known practitioner of what is also called the "slack key" style remains Sol Hoopii, but the most influential player was Gabby Pahinui, whose sophisticated work elevated the instrument beyond a novelty.

Some blues slide players also choose to hold their regular guitars in the horizontal position. The most notable exponent, Jeff Healey, plays in this way using a standard Fender Stratocaster electric guitar.

CHAPTER 9
NEW MODES

In this chapter we'll look at some of the more popular innovations that have emerged in rock music over the past two decades. The most significant development in solo playing has been the use of right-hand fret tapping (sometimes also called "finger tapping"). However, with formal guitar tuition now often embracing rock styles – a marked contrast to earlier generations – we have also seen the growth of a new breed of technical virtuoso, capable of powerful high-speed soloing, and drawing on the traditions of classical and modern jazz – the use of modal playing, for example – as much as the blues. Furthermore, a greater awareness of other styles of music has seen rock integrating with other sub-cultures to create new and interesting hybrid forms.

WHATEVER HAPPENED TO HEAVY METAL?

During the early 1970s, heavy rock was the music of choice for most teenage boys. But things began to get a little strange, as groups of serious-minded young musicians tried to imbue their work with classical gravitas. So it was that for several years progressive rock bands – the likes of King Crimson and Emerson, Lake and Palmer – ruled the roost. That was before Punk attempted to sweep it all away, making traditional rock forms desperately unfashionable. But although music journalists stopped writing about them, hard rocking bands like Motorhead, Thin Lizzy and AC/DC and prog rockers like Yes and Genesis still retained legions of followers.

At the start of the 1980s, things started to look promising, as the "New Wave of British Heavy Metal" introduced bands such as Def Leppard and Iron Maiden. However, the saviour of rock music was to be a Dutch-born American guitarist named Eddie Van Halen. He was the first of new generation of virtuoso rockers. A magnificent technician, Van Halen could hammer-on and pull-off notes at an extraordinary pace, introducing to rock audiences the idea of right-handed fret-tapping. He was also one the first to see the potential of the locking nut tremolo system, enabling him to insert dramatic "dive-bomb" pitch bends into his soloing. Oddly enough, one of his finest moments can be heard guesting on Michael Jackson's hit "Beat It". Other supercharged technicians also emerged, including ex-Frank Zappa protégé Stevie Vai, and Joe Satriani.

From the mid-80s, metal has fragmented into different strands. Genres such as "thrash metal", "death metal" and "speed metal" produced such powerful bands as Anthrax, Venom and, above all, the massively successful Metallica – whose lead player Kirk Hammett is also easily deserving of the "virtuoso" tag.

IN THIS CHAPTER YOU'LL LEARN...

- Rock music hybrid forms
- Asymmetric time
- Playing the Ionian mode
- Playing the Phrygian mode
- Playing the Myxolydian mode
- Playing the Locrian mode
- Fret tapping techniques
- Compression and noise gates

- Playing with unusual time signatures
- Introduction to the modes
- Playing the Dorian mode
- Playing the Lydian mode
- Playing the Aeolian mode
- The dance/metal crossover
- Tapping out a scale
- Tapping across the strings

NEW FORMS OF METAL

Although heavy metal was deeply unfashionable for many years, and in some circles, rife for mockery (as seen in the movie *This Is Spinal Tap*, for example), it has shown itself to be a surprisingly durable genre, capable of reinventing itself in any number of interesting ways.

Arguably, metal became a "credible" mainstream cultural entity around the turn of the 21st century with what was briefly known as "Nu Metal". In truth, this was a fairly meaningless term since many of the most popular bands described as such – Korn, Papa Roach, Linkin Park and Slipknot (*see below*), for example – seemed to have little in common apart from what could perhaps be described as a contemporary attitude and musically progressive outlook. Some, like Slipknot, integrated very *un-metal* technology, such as digital samplers and turntables for rhythmic vinyl "scratching" effects – creating a curious hip-hop-infused form of classic speed metal.

Another unexpected trend reversal has been the gradual rehabilitation and acceptance of progressive rock. Reviled for it's technical excess by most of the music press in the wake of punk (even if much of its fan base remained loyal to the cause) younger bands such as Radiohead, Tool, The Mars Volta, Mastodon (*see above*) and Muse have embraced many of prog's defining characteristics, with displays of technical virtuosity, lengthy multi-segmented compositions, shifts in tempo and time signature, not to mention the obligatory lyrical obfuscation. There are now entire prog-related sub-genres – such as mathrock, prog-metal and mathcore – whose exponents feature some of the most musically agile guitarists around.

Other sub-genres have included death metal, black metal (with its controversial church-burning Norwegian wing), power metal (including the brilliant DragonForce) and doom/drone metal (*see page 121*).

Indeed, the second decade of the new millennium looks set to continue as a golden age for metal and its assorted offsprings.

MODERN METAL

Our next track is a thrash metal number which makes use both of atonal keys and changes in time signature. It's a tricky piece to play – at first you may well even find it hard to figure out what's going on.

BACKING TRACK #8

This is just about the most complex piece in the whole book. Backing Track #8 comprises four four-bar segments that you'll need to learn independently before you string them together. The sequence is shown at the foot of the page.

This will be tougher than other tracks to learn because it is ATONAL. This means that the music has no real identifiable tonal centre. Although in three of the segments the chords return to begin on A major, there is nothing else in there to suggest that we could describe the track as being "in" A major.

The most striking aspect of this track is the way in which the time signature alters in parts C and D. Whereas parts A and B are in four-four time, the other two have a time signature of SIX-FOUR. This means that it has six beats in the bar. Listen to Track 9/1 on the CD and see if you can follow it. **9/1** ▶

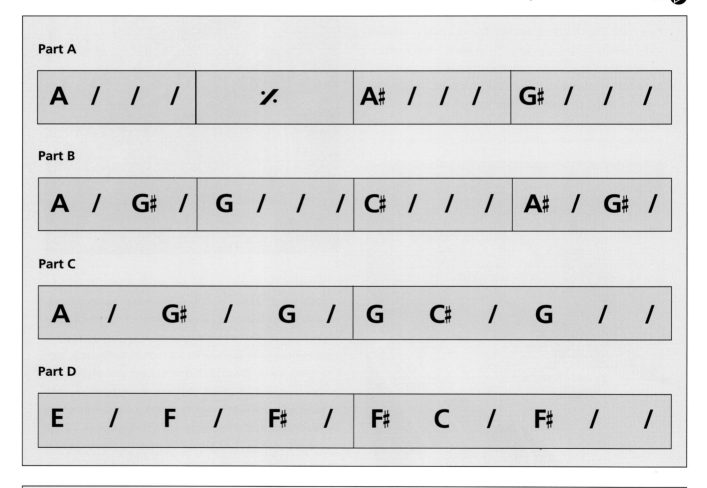

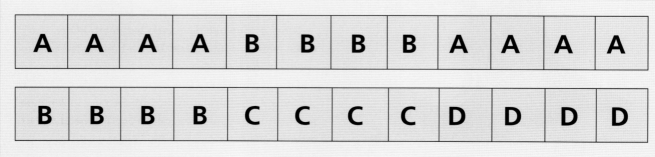

PART A

The music for the first half of the track is laid out in the first set of staves below. The first four bars represent part A in full. The chords can be played using a standard E-shaped barre fingering with roots on the 5th (A), 6th (A♯) and 4th (G♯) frets. You will notice from the staff that only the bottom four strings are being used; to recreate this track's "chugging" effect you don't need to play the top two strings – it just wouldn't sound right. The sound should be distorted in the extreme and preferably heavily compressed. Strike the strings with plenty of right-hand muting – this will help to create the characteristic "grinding" effect of this kind of music.

PART B

Part B is shown in the bottom four bars. Use the same techniques as above, only switching to an A-shape barre on the 5th string for the third bar (C♯). The chord changes between the second and third and third and fourth bars are both particularly disorienting, creating an effect which is menacing or even aggressive.

Parts C and D can be found over the page.

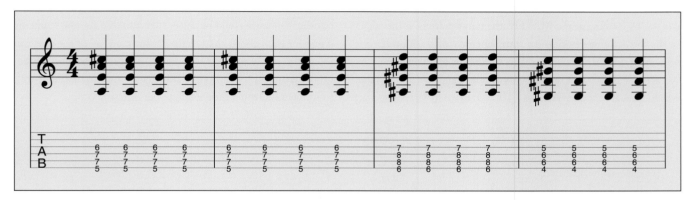

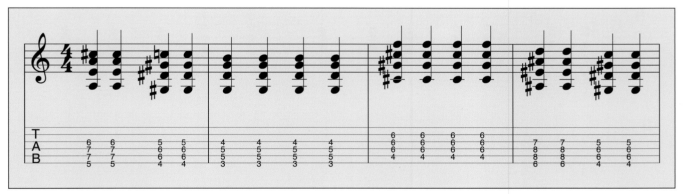

SWITCHES AND KNOBS

It is possible to create some interesting playing effects just using the knobs and switches on your guitar.

Manipulating the volume controls while playing is a classic rock effect. All it requires is a working knowledge of your guitar's controls. Some instruments – the Gibson Les Paul, for example – have volume and tone controls for each pickup; others like the Fender Telecaster have just one volume and tone control covering both pickups.

Try this example for yourself. Cue up the backing track on the CD. Retain the distorted sound suggested above. With just one pickup switched on (make it the lead pickup for a more powerful attack), turn the volume down to zero.

- Play the A major chord.
- Start to play Backing Track #8.
- When the intro count reaches "four", and with the strings still ringing, quickly turn up the volume control so that it reaches "full" on the first beat of the track.
- Almost immediately, turn the volume back down to zero, and then back to full in time for the second beat.

By doing this you create a very simple rhythm of sound fading in and out.

A similar effect with greater attack can be achieved with careful manipulation of the pickup switch.

TIME SIGNATURES IN PRACTICE

Although you should now be very familiar with the idea of time signatures, up until now the only one we've used is four-four (or COMMON TIME). This is quite reasonable in that the overwhelming majority of rock music doesn't deviate from this norm. Now it's time we looked at how some other time signatures work in practice.

SIX BEATS TO THE BAR

Parts C and D of Backing Track #8 are shown below. As you can see by looking at the METER (the two numbers at the start of the music), these both use a time signature of six-four. If you remember what those two numbers mean, this tells you that each bar is made up of six crotchet beats (a time signature of six-eight would indicate six quaver beats). There are two different aspects to the rhythm presented below. Firstly, you need to make sure that your count goes from one to six for each bar. Secondly, however, note the position of the accents. It's almost as if the two-bar sequence could be better split into five discrete segments – one for each chord change. To get the true feel of the rhythm, then, try this count: "ONE-two-ONE-two-ONE-two-three-ONE-two-ONE-two-three". This does sound quite unnatural, so it may take you a little while to get the hang of it.

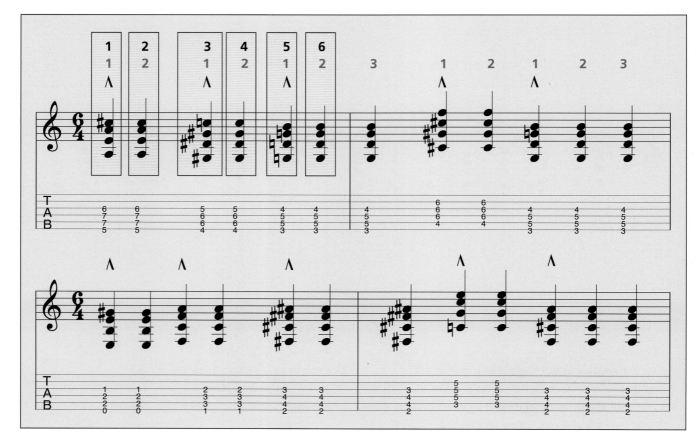

ASYMMETRIC TIME

Although six-four time is technically a COMPOUND time signature (see page 37), the way the accents are positioned gives it a deliberately unbalanced rhythmic effect. This has much in common with ASYMMETRIC TIME – a type of time signature whose number of beats in the bar are not divisible by two or three. The most common asymmetric times comprise five or seven beats in the bar. Eleven- and thirteen-beat time signatures can also be found. Although the music using such rhythms is generally more complex or esoteric in nature, the rhythms themselves are usually accented in such a way that they can be broken down into groups of two, three or four. For example, a piece of music in 5/4 can be heard as a group of two beats followed by a group of three beats, the accents falling on beats one and three. Alternatively, they can be heard as a group of three beats followed by a group of two, with the accents falling on beats one and four. The marks above the staff indicate these accent points.

Below you will see three examples of asymmetric time. Play them through taking care with both the counts and the position of the accents. The chords used are taken from parts C and D of the backing track.

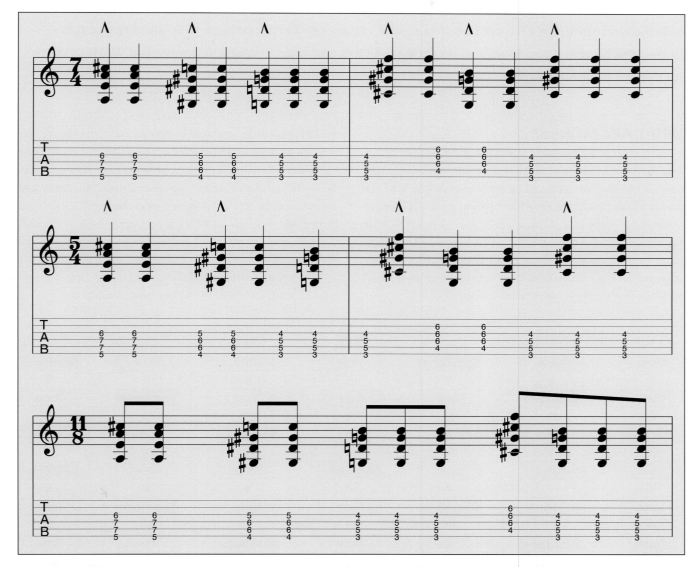

SIX-EIGHT TIME

Counts in sixes are usually far more conventional in rhythmic flavour than those shown in our example. A more typical use would swing along quite nicely: count out "ONE-two-three-TWO-two-three". Although the emphasis of the rhythm would be slightly different, there isn't too much practical difference between "six-eight" and "twelve-eight".

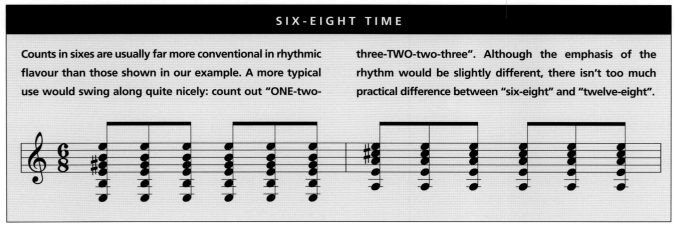

MODAL PLAYING

So far we've played around with the major, minor and pentatonic scales. Another type of scale worthy of serious investigation is called a MODE. There are seven different types of mode. You may be surprised to learn that modes predate the diatonic scales (the major and minor series), which didn't evolve until the 17th century. The modal system can be traced back to Ancient Greek times. During the Middle Ages, it was taken up by the Christian church, where it dominated Western music for several hundred years.

WHAT ARE MODES?

Like diatonic scales, each of the seven modes comprises eight notes from root to octave. The notes used by ALL of the modes equate directly to the white notes of a piano keyboard – hence the notes of a C major scale. However, each mode starts on a different note, even though it uses the SAME eight notes between root and octave. This means that each of the seven modes has a different set of intervals, which means that each also has a unique sound characteristic.

You might now be wondering what practical use this has for you. That's a reasonable question. Originally, the modes were viewed as a fixed series of notes, not a set of relative intervals. Before the evolution of key signatures, musicians knew and understood the nature of each mode. Pieces of music were composed for the mode, which in turn defined the notes used.

Modern usage, however, has reinterpreted a mode merely as a scale with its own unique set of intervals. Therefore it is possible to transpose any of these modes into any key, creating seven new types of scale, each with its own unique characteristics.

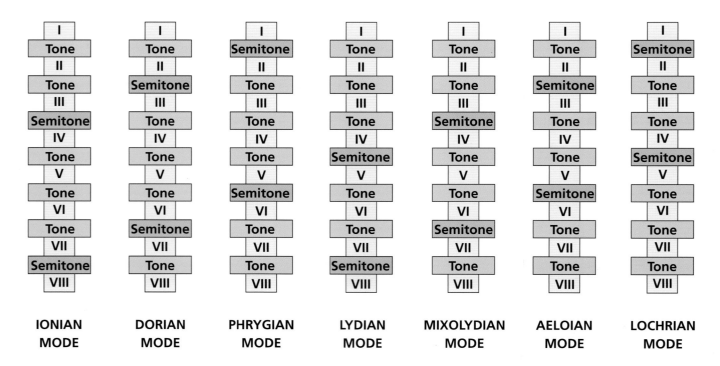

| IONIAN MODE | DORIAN MODE | PHRYGIAN MODE | LYDIAN MODE | MIXOLYDIAN MODE | AELOIAN MODE | LOCHRIAN MODE |

FAMILIAR SOUNDS

The sets of intervals from root to octave that make up the seven modes are shown above, along with their original Greek names.

In fact, only five of the seven modes may be unfamiliar to you. When you play through the set of modes across the page, you should be able to recognise straight away that the Ionian

mode is, in fact, a major scale by another name; similarly, the Aeolian mode uses the same set of intervals as the natural minor scale.

If you've learned to play a variety of major and minor scale positions suggested earlier in the book you shouldn't have too much trouble getting to grips the different modes.

COMPARING THE MODES

Below you will see seven staves. Each one shows the notes of one of the modes. Remember that although the modes were originally fixed sets of notes, we have given them their modern use, and converted them to seven distinct scales in the key of A.

If you look at the TAB below each staff, you will see that it is possible to play the complete scale from the 6th string using a range of just four frets. Remembering the one-finger-per-fret "rule", the number beneath the first note in the scale indicates which finger of the left hand plays the first note: this will allow you to get your hand in the correct position.

One of the most effective ways of getting yourself acquainted with the characteristics of each scale is to play them (or improvise with them) over a drone or PEDAL TONE. This will give you a context for the intervals that make up the scale in relation to the root note. In this example, try to find a reference tone for the note A (the one below Middle C would be best here) and sustain it while you are playing. (A piece of sticky tape holding down the note on an electronic keyboard would do the trick.) A slightly more sophisticated alternative is to play the scales over a droning triad. To do this you need to figure out whether the tonal flavour of each mode is "major", "minor" or "ambiguous" in character. This should become clear when you've played them through on their own a few times. **9/2**

1. IONIAN MODE IN A

2. DORIAN MODE IN A

3. PHRYGIAN MODE IN A

4. LYDIAN MODE IN A

5. MYXOLYDIAN MODE IN A

6. AEOLIAN MODE IN A

7. LOCRIAN MODE IN A

PRACTICAL MODES?

Leaving aside the familiar Ionian and Aeolian modes, let's look briefly at how modes have been used in practice.

The minor DORIAN MODE has been widely used by jazz musicians since the 1950s. A famous use can be heard on the Miles Davis track "So What".

The PHRYGIAN MODE is another minor mode. (You can identify a minor mode by looking for an interval of three semitones between the 1st and 3rd notes.) The Phrygian mode is used extensively in flamenco music.

The LYDIAN MODE differs from the regular major scale, in that the 4th note is sharpened. Composer George Russell helped to kick off the modal fashion in the 1950s, with his work The Lydian Chromatic Concept Of Tonal Organization.

The MIXOLYDIAN MODE creates a mellow, "bluesy" sound, and is the most widely used mode in modern music. It is especially useful in blues and rock playing, where it can almost be interchanged with a minor pentatonic scale.

OTHER INTERESTING SCALES

If you like the exotic flavour of the Locrian mode you may find it worth your while investigating other scales from Eastern Europe and the Far East. Try these for size:

PELOG SCALE
Root – Major 3rd – Perfect 4th – Perfect 5th – Major 7th

INDIAN SCALE
Root – Major 3rd – Perfect 4th – Perfect 5th – Minor 7th

HIRAJOSHI SCALE
Root – Major 3rd – Augmented 4th – Perfect 5th – Major 7th

KUMOI SCALE
Root – Minor 3rd – Perfect 4th – Diminished 5th – Minor 7th

The LOCRIAN MODE is a diminished scale widely used in the ethnic music of Asia and the Middle East.

Below you will find three examples taken from the Dorian, Phrygian and Locrian modes that can be played over part A of Backing Track #8.   **9/3** ▶

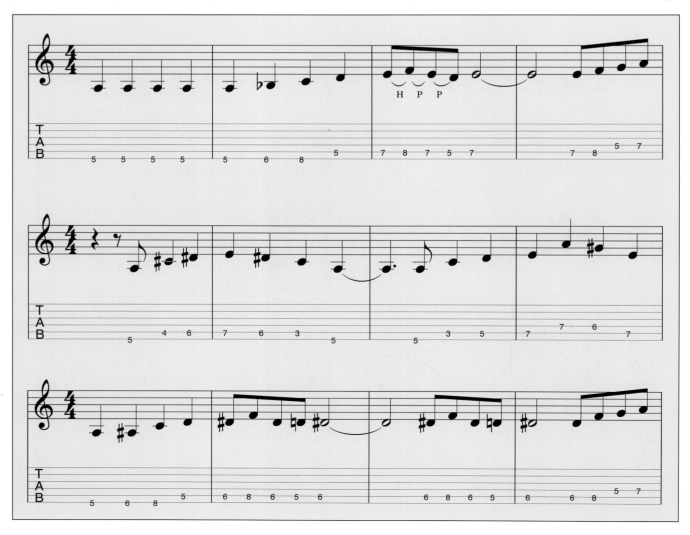

ROCK MEETS HIP-HOP

A 1970s music fan transported forward by almost 40 years might have been in for a bit of a shock at the disparate elements that would eventually become bedmates. Back then, the worlds of the nightclub (disco and funk) and the rock concert were largely mutually exclusive: a self-respecting Deep Purple fan was unlikely to be found boogieing the night to away to Earth, Wind and Fire.

Things gradually changed in the early 1980s when the cheesy disco boom had died, and dance music started to become electronic. Guided by European pioneers such as Kraftwerk, black dance producers in New York and Chicago evolved a new sound that fused these influences with funky rhythms. The result was hip-hop and, later in the decade, house music. Although in the US popularity of these new sounds was largely restricted to metropolitan areas, it quickly hit the mainstream across the Atlantic, eventually spawning the "rave scene". From there, electronic dance music gradually nudged its way into other less obvious forms – guitar-based indie bands such as New Order, Stone Roses and Happy Mondays being among the first to pull large audiences.

In fact, the link between rock and dance does have certain historical precedents in the US. At the end of the

1960s, Sly and the Family Stone – a pointedly multi-racial band – began to mix elements of the two. Their appearance at the Woodstock festival gave them a broad audience. Their template was followed by the "P-Funk" bands lead by George Clinton since the early 1970s. A huge stable of artists releasing numerous albums under a variety of guises – most famously Parliament *(see left)* and Funkadelic – their music was a wild and unpredictable amalgamation of Jimi Hendrix and James Brown.

During the mid-1980s, the link was tentatively re-established when hip-hop band Run DMC sampled Aerosmith's rocker "Walk This Way" with some success. However, it wasn't until the following decade that the two cultures started to merge and create something new. Pioneers of this crossover were American agit-prop rockers Rage Against The Machine. A highly politicized (and fiercely intellectual) bunch, their music was a blaze of powerful metal riffing underpinned by a funky, hip-hop beat and topped by the ferocious rapping of lead man Zack De La Rocha. Guitarist Tom Morello *(see above)* is one the few players of the past twenty years to have evolved a noticeably modern style. He has no qualms about modifying his guitars, one particular innovation being the creation of a simple touch-sensitive output switch – when engaged rhythmically this enables him to make his guitar sound appear as if they are coming from a digital sampler. The band's sound was too uncompromising to capture mainstream audiences of the 1990s, but in an odd quirk of fate, in 2009, following an anti-*X-Factor* campaign on the Internet, Rage Against The Machine found themselves with an unexpected Christmas chart-topping single!

TAPPING FOR SPEED

If it's high-speed lead work you're after, finger tapping is a must. In effect, it's essentially an extension of the standard hammering and pulling effects described on page 105. It became extremely popular in the mid-1980s – so much so that it soon became a tired cliché. It's now viewed as just another technique that most decent players have as part of their armoury.

A BIT OF HISTORY

Finger tapping (or "fret tapping" as it is sometimes known) draws on the single-note hammer-on/pull-off technique. The difference is that it also uses the fingers of the right hand to "tap" out notes along the fingerboard. The note sounds when it is pressed down against the fret.

It's first prime exponents were Eddie Van Halen, Steve Vai and Joe Satriani, who stunned their audiences by delivering solos at breakneck speed. Since then, most rock and metal players have at least experimented with the technique. Interestingly, although finger tapping became a prominent metal style in the 1980s, legendary US session man Harvey Mandel could be heard using the technique on jazz-funk instrumentals at least a decade earlier.

Tapping is one of those techniques that can be appropriated pretty easily, but requires a good deal of skill (and taste) to use effectively. To maximize the effect, a guitar with a low action and good sustain at the top end is important. Extreme levels of compression and distortion can also help to give a consistency of volume to individual notes.

GET TAPPING

The basic tapping technique works in much the same way as hammering on and pulling off – notes are hammered when moving up a scale and pulled off when moving down. The only real difference is that you are using additional fingers from your non-fretting hand. In these cases, the pull-off can be executed with a slight sideways pluck, to give extra volume for the next hammered note.

Here is an example for you try out for yourself:

- Position the 1st finger of the left hand on the 7th fret of the 1st string.
- Place the 1st finger of your right hand near to the 11th fret and pluck the note.
- With the note playing, hammer-on the 9th fret of the 1st string with the 3rd finger of the left hand.
- Pull-off the 11th fret by tapping the string alongside the fret and releasing the finger.
- Pull-off with the other two fingers in a similar manner.

FRET THE FIRST NOTE.

HAMMER-ON THE SECOND NOTE.

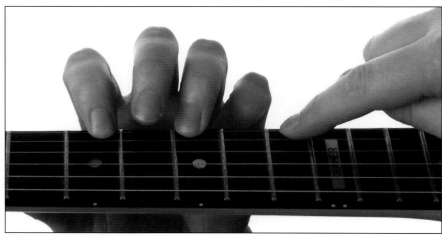

TAP THE THIRD NOTE.

COMPRESSION AND SUSTAIN

A COMPRESSOR is not a sound effect in its own right, but it is often used in conjunction with distortion to enable sustain for a longer period. This is especially useful when hammering-on, pulling-off or fret tapping. Compression units, like the one shown on the right, reduce the volume of sounds above a predefined threshold, smoothing out the DYNAMIC RANGE – the difference between the maximum and minimum volume levels for any signal. The guitar possesses a very wide dynamic range. This means that in the course of playing with other musicians, if your amplifier level remains consistent, the overall signal will be too loud; and at other times it will be lost in the mix.

Compressors are found in every recording studio. Indeed, very few pop or rock recordings are made without the entire mix being compressed during the mastering stage. Although studio compressors need to be of a much higher quality than foot-pedal equivalents, they share many of the same controls, most notably THRESHOLD and RATIO. The threshold control dictates the level of volume above which the compression takes effect – when the overall signal stays below that level, it is left untouched. The ratio control sets the degree to which the signal is to be compressed once the threshold figure has been breached. Many compressors also double up as LIMITERS. This is a cruder form of compression, which simply reduces the gain when a signal exceeds a preset threshold.

Often used hand-in-hand with compression, the NOISE GATE is another effect that doesn't actually alter the sound but is extremely useful. A noise gate is used

to shut out unwanted signals. The reverse of a limiter, a threshold setting on the noise gate dictates the level at which the signal can be heard. Until the signal reaches that point, NOTHING AT ALL gets through. A particularly raw, heavily "effected" solo guitar sound can produce an unavoidable degree of electronic buzzing when the guitar is not actually being played. If you set the noise gate threshold above the buzz it will not be heard. No signal will pass through the gate until the first note is struck, by which time the noise will have been drowned out.

GETTING THE MOST OUT OF EFFECTS

If you read guitar and technology magazines, you can't fail to notice the glossy adverts telling you how much you MUST buy the latest state-of-the-art processing. As tempting as this can be, it's always a good idea to step back and think carefully about how useful any new toy you buy is really going to be to the sound of your music. And effects can be costly, so might also end up saving yourself some cash.

• Take great care with effects that are too gimmicky. Sounds that leap out of the speakers and scream "I AM AN EFFECT" are not usually very versatile. And any effect that becomes fashionable WILL DATE.

• If you do reach into your wallet, when you first buy an effect spend a good deal of time working through all the possible

sound permutations that its parameters will allow. Modern effects units are complex beasts, and they can sometimes generate noises that you might not have expected (or that were not even intended by the manufacturer).

• Before you consider using it live or on a recording, get the novelty value out of the way. However new the sound, you will soon get used to it.

• If you use effects pedals live, invest in a suitable transformer. They are cheap and will save you a fortune in batteries in the long run.

• Buy or make some short patch-bay leads for linking effects. If you use regular-length guitar leads, you will find yourself with a mess of cables all over the stage or studio.

• Finally, don't forget that a bad idea or performance is rarely turned around simply by adding an effect.

TAPPING A SCALE

This exercise should help you achieve some simple tapping effects. They will probably sound much better with distortion and sustain (but then again, what doesn't?).

Here, you're going to tap out an A major scale progression. In each case, you will fret the first note with the 1st finger of your left hand, hammer-on the second note with the 3rd finger of your left hand, and finally tap the third note with the 1st finger of your right hand.

The hardest part of tapping is getting the rhythm right. Because tapping usually takes place at a higher tempo it can be difficult to get the right hand to make that third note and keep in time with the hammering of the first two notes. Take things slowly at first, mastering each bar individually before stringing the whole sequence together.   **9/4** ▶

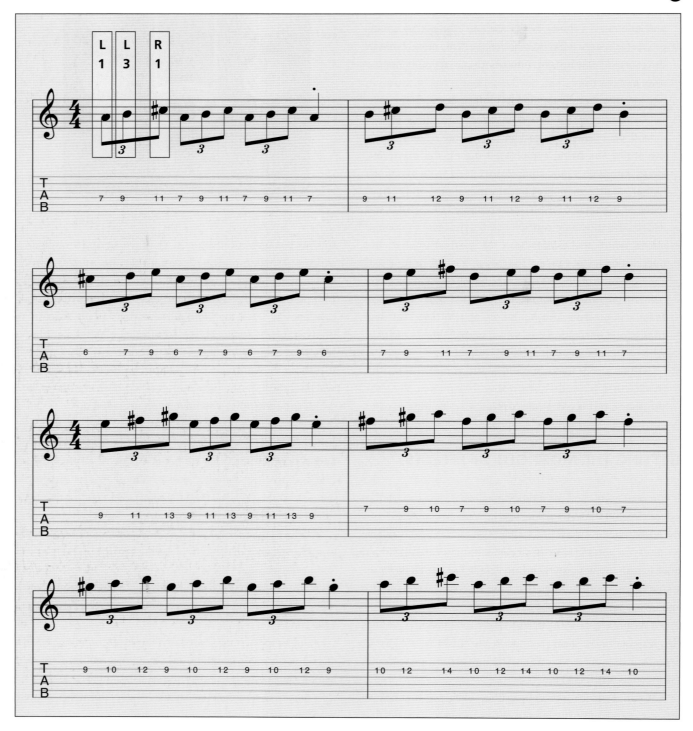

ADVANCED TAPPING EXERCISE

This next exercise is considerably more complex in that not only do you have to concentrate on tapping in time, you also have to vary the notes that are hammered and tapped on the fingerboard.

The first two bars are variations on the first exercise. As before, the first two notes of every group of triplets are played by the 1st and 3rd fingers of the left hand respectively; the third is played by the 1st finger of the right hand.

In the third bar, the tapping alternates between the 12th and 13th frets. When this kind of effect is played at speed it can sound very impressive indeed (if high-speed playing is your thing, that is).

Don't forget that the tapping motion isn't strictly the same as hammering: for it to work effectively you really need that little sideways pluck or else you may find it hard to match the volume of the two notes fretted by the left hand. **9/5**

TAPPING ACROSS THE STRINGS

The exercises we have shown have all been about tapping notes on the same string. For a more strenuous workout, try a tapping exercise that moves *across* the strings.

Take, for example, the first bar of the exercise below. Take the same fret positions, but begin by playing them on the 1st string. When you get to the end of the bar, play the same fret positions on the 2nd string; and then the 3rd string, and so forth.

To take this to the limit, play the entire exercise below using the same fret positions on each string. Play all four bars on the 1st string, and then on the 2nd string, and so on.

This kind of practice will enable you to tap away in any direction you choose.

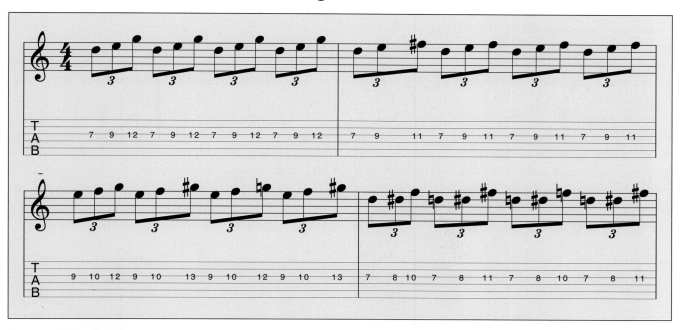

DIVE-BOMBING

A powerful effect sometimes used by rock guitarists in conjunction with tapping is the DIVE-BOMB pitch bend. This is when a tremolo arm is used to reduce the pitch by amounts of more than five or six semitones. A tremolo arm is a mechanical device fitted to the bridge mechanism which can produce variations in pitch when manipulated. In fact, the term "tremolo" is something of a misnomer – it would be more accurate to call them "vibrato arms", but nobody does that.

The early tremolo arms – the old-style Bigsby and Fender systems – were never really intended to enable pitch variations of any more than a semitone. All that was required was enough to create a neat vibrato "twang". These effects can be heard on early guitar instrumentals by the Duane Eddy, the Shadows, or by the surfing bands of the early 1960s.

The problem with these "trems" was that if they were overused they would put the guitar out of tune. The answer to this problem was provided by a guitarist/engineer named Floyd Rose (see page 23). He produced a system where the strings were locked between the nut and the bridge, making it possible to detune strings to a point where they were laying slack on the body, but would then return to perfect intonation when pressure was taken off the arm.

CHAPTER 10
TASTE FOR ADVENTURE

Although over the years rock music has presented itself as "giving the finger" to the establishment, most of the music – and techniques to produce that music – has been largely mainstream, even if sometimes not quite as formal as conservatory tutors might prefer. But there are those who have gone out of their way to experiment with both their playing and composition, taking alternative approaches to making music with the guitar. This chapter focuses a little on some of the less orthodox playing techniques, such as alternative tuning systems, harmonics, hardware-driven music or other methods for striking the strings.

YOUR IMAGINATION IS YOUR LIMIT

Think about the construction of the modern guitar. The basic acoustic classical guitar has changed little in 150 years; after a flurry of experimentation in the mid-20th century, not much has changed *dramatically* in the world of the electric guitar since the 1950s.

And how about our own behaviour? We routinely tune our guitars in the way we have been taught, but why should we accept that they even have to have six strings? The answer is that not everybody does. In the 1920s, Gibson made an abortive attempt to boost the bass register of the guitar, producing a so-called "harp guitar". In the 1940s, jazz guitarist George Van Eps developed a seven-string instrument with a lower bass string tuned to B. This went into production for a short while. In the 1980s, Steve Vai collaborated with the Ibanez company to manufacture the seven-string Universe guitar.

Like previous attempts, only a small number of guitarists felt inclined to take the challenge.

STRINGING AND TUNING

Although strings come in many sizes and materials, they are designed to produce a consistent sound over around four octaves. A number of experimental musicians have tried variations on the traditional approach, with varying degrees of success. Perhaps the best known artist to work in this area is composer Glenn Branca, who is noted for the sounds produced by his guitar orchestras. Many of Branca's works have been performed in large-group settings comprised principally of electric guitars. The individual instruments, however, are either re-strung or retuned so that they can be played over a limited register or range of notes. At its most dramatic, the guitar is restrung so that ALL of the strings are identical and are tuned to the same note. Shifts in pitch are made by playing barres with the 1st finger.

ALTERNATIVE PICKS

The trusty pick is not the only device which can be used to strike the strings. Literally any object can be brought into contact with the strings, some of which may well create interesting or unexpected sounds. This is not a terribly new idea – 30 years ago Led Zeppelin's Jimmy Page could be seen performing "solos" by scraping the strings of his guitar with a violin bow.

The strings of an amplified guitar are highly sensitive, making them responsive to the most subtle of dynamic shades, so any object with a slightly abrasive surface can be used to vibrate the strings. Equally, some interesting percussive sounds can be achieved by striking the strings with different objects, such as a comb, light sandpaper, brush, drum sticks, gnarled metal, "Bulldog" clips clamped to the string and then plucked, paper threaded between the strings, and cloth threaded between the strings. The edge of a rotating sanding attachment can make some fascinating sounds, although the results may be somewhat unpredictable, and your guitar may be placed in danger.

THE EXPERIMENTAL GUITARIST

Guitar players have always had a tendency to experiment. The guitar was, after all, the first popular musical instrument to "go electric". Even though country musicians are often thought of as being a pretty conservative bunch, it was the likes of Les Paul and Merle Travis who pioneered the solid-body electric guitar – without that innovation, rock music as we know it could certainly not exist.

Les Paul was also a popular guitarist, recording many hits during the 1940s with his wife Mary Ford. Most of these songs were recorded in a home-built studio where Paul pioneered the concept of multitrack recording – something that we all now take for granted. His one-man band – featuring multi-layered, multi-harmony guitar parts – baffled music buyers of the time, who wondered how such a thing could be possible.

Of course, if historians of pop culture are to be believed, the 1960s was a time when it was almost *de rigueur* to be experimental. Fuelled by the widespread availability of the drug LSD, the middle of the decade saw the birth of what came to be called "psychedelia". The impetus came largely from the city of San Francisco, where improvisational band

the Grateful Dead did a pretty good job of producing the aural equivalent of an "acid" trip. They would play for hours on end to audiences for whom the notion of time must have lost some of its meaning.

The UFO club in London was the home of Britain's psychedelic revolution. The figureheads of this scene were the early Pink Floyd (*see below*), then led by guitarist, singer and songwriter Syd Barrett. The music conjured up dream-like soundscapes, and most of their songs could be turned into extended jams if the mood caught them. Barrett's "free-form" guitar work was central to the overall sound – the long improvised passages and soaring sustained echo and reverb effects can be heard on tracks such as "Astronomy Domine" and "Interstellar Overdrive" from their debut album *Piper at the Gates of Dawn*. Shortly afterward, fuelled by a ferocious intake of LSD, Barrett's mental health went into freefall. Forced to quit the band, after two unpredictable solo albums he became rock's most famous recluse until his death in 2006. With replacement guitarist Dave Gilmour, Floyd went on to become one of the most popular bands of all time.

OPEN TUNING

We have a tendency to view the "standard" tuning for the guitar – E, A, D, G, B, E – as something of an absolute. And yet it was not until the end of the 18th century that six strings became the norm, and the tuning system that we use today became standardised. There have, however, always been those who have been prepared to experiment and try out their own variations.

ALTERED TUNINGS

A wide variety of alternative tunings exist. While they are more often than not used with steel-string acoustic guitars, they can equally be applied to electric instruments.

OPEN TUNINGS are the most widely used alternatives to the standard tuning method. They are so-called because the strings of the guitar are tuned to a chord.

One such open tuning is OPEN G. If the strings are played across the chord G major will be heard. Open D, A and E tunings are also heard from time to time.

G / / /	C add 9 / / /	G7 / / /	C add 9 / / /
D / / /	⁒/.	C / / /	⁒/.

OPEN G TUNING

To play the next set of exercises along with Backing Track #9, you'll have to tune your guitar to open G. To do this you must retune the 1st, 5th and 6th strings so that they are lowered by a tone. From bottom to top, the notes should be: D – G – D – G – B – D.

Musicians of surprisingly disparate styles have used this particular tuning with great success: blues masters such as Robert Johnson recorded much of his work using open G; in his early years, Muddy Waters only used open G – if he wanted to play in a different key he would fit a capo to his guitar. Other fans include folk pickers Leo Kottke and James Taylor.

In the rock world, Jimmy Page and Keith Richards have made extensive use of open G tuning – in fact it's the ONLY way you can reproduce classic Rolling Stones sounds such as the opening chords to hits like "Brown Sugar" or "Jumping Jack Flash".

The simplest way to use the open G tuning is with a barre. If you play the strings without fingering any frets, you will hear the chord G major. It clearly follows, then, that if you hold a 1st-finger barre over the 2nd fret you will be playing an A major chord. This simple approach to playing full six-string chords makes open-string tuning very popular among slide players.

CHORDS WITH OPEN G TUNING

Open tuning can be used effectively as a source of alternative chord shapes by fretting notes around the open strings. Although there is the obvious issue of having to learn a whole new set of shapes, experimentation can yield fascinating and unexpected results.

To accompany Backing Track #9, there are two open-string chord shapes you need to learn. They are a C major chord with an added 9th (C ADD 9) and a G dominant 7th. Both shapes are shown on the right.

1ST	D	(DROP 1 TONE)
2ND	B	(STANDARD)
3RD	G	(STANDARD)
4TH	D	(STANDARD)
5TH	G	(DROP 1 TONE)
6TH	D	(DROP 1 TONE)

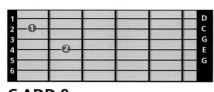

C ADD 9

G7

PLAYING WITH BACKING TRACK #9

There are five different chords needed to play along with this chapter's backing track – a medium paced rocker. The chords for the first four bars are shown below.

To play G major you simply play across the open tuning – there is no fretting necessary at all. Chords don't come any easier.

C add 9 should also be easy enough for you to play, since it uses the same fingering as an open A minor 7 in standard tuning. Start off by practising just the chord change, alternating between G and C add 9.

G 7 is played using the 3rd frets of the 2nd and 4th strings. With a little practice, the four-bar sequence should become a very natural hand movement. At first you can play the chords as semibreves, as shown in the music below, before graduating to playing quavers on every half-beat.

The two other major chords are played by using 1st-finger barres across all six strings: a 5th-fret barre creates C major; a 7th-fret barre creates D major. **10/1** ▶

THE OPEN A MINOR SEVEN SHAPE

The second chord shown below is a classic rock shape. Although it's A minor 7 when played in the open string position, when only the three fretted strings are played it produces an inverted major chord.

SLIDE EXERCISE

To show you how effective open-string tuning can be with a slide, let's try a couple exercises using open G tuning and Backing Track #9. The first will concentrate on playing chords, the second on crosspicking the notes of the same set of chords.

SIMPLE CHORDS

Play each chord as a semibreve on the first beat of every bar.

Bar 1 – Start with the slide poised over the 12th fret. Play across all six strings. This chord is G major

Bar 2 – Move the slide down to fret 5. Play across all six strings. This chord is C major.

Bars 3 and 4 – Repeat bars 1 and 2.

Bars 5 and 6 – Move the slide up to fret 7. Play across all six strings. This chord is D major.

Bars 7 and 8 – Move the slide down to fret 5.

Once your slide positioning is accurate you can concentrate on the right hand. Build up speed so that you are playing a crotchet chord on every beat.

CROSSPICKING

This time, try playing the notes of the chords as a series of arpeggios. Begin by picking a note on every beat, and then progress to a note on every half-beat.

Start with the slide poised over the 12th fret (or if you feel like a bit of variation, why not instead slide up from the open strings).

Pattern 1 – Play each bar in consistent forward-roll crosspicking pattern. Start with the 6th string, and pick crotchets to the 3rd string. (*See page 115 if you're confused about crosspicking terminology.*)

Pattern 2 – Forward-roll crosspick crotchets from the 4th string to the 1st string.

Pattern 3 – Backward roll from the 1st string to the 4th string.

Pattern 4 – Backward roll from the 3rd string to the 6th string.

Patterns 5 to 10 – Forward/reverse rolls. (In all examples, the number represents the string played on each beat):

Pattern 5 – 6/1/2/3	**Pattern 6** – 6/4/5/3
Pattern 7 – 4/2/3/1	**Pattern 8** – 1/2/3/6
Pattern 9 – 4/1/2/3	**Pattern 10** – 5/3/6/4

EXAMPLES OF ALTERED TUNING

Here are some fine examples of altered tunings used in recordings. As you will notice, there are several guitarists who make use of different systems. That's not so surprising: once you get a taste of the rich or unusual sounds made possible by alternate tuning, it becomes a part of your everyday armoury.

The songs are shown below along with the tuning system employed. Where those systems have not been shown in the book, the tunings have been included from the bottom to top.

Will Ackerman	Childhood and Memory	
		(FACCGB♭)
Allman Brothers	Little Martha	(Open D)
Chet Atkins	Yellow Bird	(G6)
The Beatles	Dear Prudence	(Drop D)
Ry Cooder	FDR In Trinidad	(Drop D)
	Available Space	(Open G)
Doobie Brothers	Black Water	(Drop D)
Nick Drake	Road	(DGDDAD)
John Fahey	Revolt of the Dyke Brigade	
		(CGCGCE)
Michael Hedges	Lenono	(FADGBE)
	Ragamuffin	(DADGAD)
	Rickover's Dream	(CGDGBC)
Robert Johnson	Milkcow's Calf Blues	(Open G)
Jorma Kaukonen	Water Song	(Open G)
Leo Kottke	Jesu, Joy of Man…	(Open G)
Peter Lang	As I Lay Sleeping	(Open D)
Led Zeppelin	Black Mountain Side	(DADGAD)
	Bron-Y-Aur Stomp	(Open G)
	Going to California	(Drop D)
Joni Mitchell	Big Yellow Taxi	(Open D)
Bonnie Raitt	Write Me a Few of Your Lines	
		(Open G)
John Renbourn	John's Tune	(G6)
	Old Mac Bladgitt	(Open G)
	Pelican	(DADEAD)
Pete Seeger	Livin' In The Country	(Drop D)
Steven Stills	Suite Judy Blue Eyes	(EEEEBE)
	4+20	(E♭E♭E♭E♭B♭E♭)
James Taylor	Country Road	(Drop D)
	Love Has Brought Me Around	
		(Open G)

OTHER ALTERED TUNINGS

Open G is not the only alternative to standard tuning. A further small selection is shown below.

OTHER OPEN TUNINGS

Tuning can be varied to produce open chords in other keys, most commonly D and E.

1ST	D	(DROP 1 TONE)	E	(STANDARD)
2ND	A	(DROP 1 TONE)	B	(STANDARD)
3RD	F♯	(DROP 1 TONE)	G♯	(RISE SEMITONE)
4TH	D	(STANDARD)	E	(RISE TONE)
5TH	A	(STANDARD)	B	(RISE TONE)
6TH	D	(DROP 1 TONE)	E	(STANDARD)

DROP D

This can provide harmonically rich alternative sounds, especially for songs based around the key of D. Experiment with standard chord positions – just to see how they sound.

1ST	E	(STANDARD)
2ND	B	(STANDARD)
3RD	G	(STANDARD)
4TH	D	(STANDARD)
5TH	A	(STANDARD)
6TH	D	(DROP 1 TONE)

DADGAD

Folk guitarist Davey Graham introduced this tuning after having travelled to Morocco and played with local musicians. The lower strings are often used to create a "droning" effect.

1ST	D	(DROP 1 TONE)
2ND	A	(DROP 1 TONE)
3RD	G	(STANDARD)
4TH	D	(STANDARD)
5TH	A	(STANDARD)
6TH	D	(DROP 1 TONE)

DROP G (OR G6)

Effective for songs in G, this tuning works well because the bottom two strings can be used as drones, but the top four strings can be used to play standard open-string chords.

1ST	E	(STANDARD)
2ND	B	(STANDARD)
3RD	G	(STANDARD)
4TH	D	(STANDARD)
5TH	G	(DROP 1 TONE)
6TH	D	(DROP 1 TONE)

PLAYING WITH DELAY

We've already looked at how delaying an electric guitar signal can create interesting effects such as phasing, flanging, chorus and echo. Let's now take this idea one step further and see how technology can be used to create complex harmonic structures.

MULTILAYERED GUITARS

It was in the early 1960s that it first became possible for guitarists to create delay effects. The British-built WEM Copycat and its US counterpart, the Echoplex, used tape-recorder technology and loops of magnetic tape to repeat signals. With experimentation, guitarists discovered that by covering up or removing the erase head from the unit, lush soundscapes could be built up. By the 1970s, guitarists such as John Martyn and Queen's Brian May had made this multi-layering effect a part of their fundamental sound – the latter using multitrack recording to build up what amounted to a guitar orchestra.

In the early days, the biggest problem faced by musicians working with delay was in the control of the timing. The most sophisticated units had "varispeed" dials which could alter the length of the delay, but it was difficult to set precise values.

Nowadays, with the onset of affordable digital technology, even the most humble units are capable of creating delays that can be set to two decimal places of milliseconds. Delay or echo plug-ins designed for computer-based recording systems can go

one step further, linking delays to the tempo of the track with near-perfect precision.

Here's a practical example you can try for yourself. The top staff is a simple minor pentatonic scale played in G. Set your digital delay line so that there is a delay of a single beat. Make sure that the FEEDBACK control is set to minimum. This controls the number of times the signal is repeated: with it set to minimum you will hear only one repeat. Now if you play the four bars, the sound you hear will be a combination of the first and second staves; on the second beat, while you are playing B♭, the delayed signal will be playing G. If you turn up the feedback so that it repeats twice, you will hear the top three staves played together. **10/2** ▶

Now half the delay speed so that it takes two beats to repeat. You will hear the first and third staves playing together: when you play the third beat (C), the signal will also play back the first beat (G). **10/3** ▶

If you half the delay speed again, you will get a single bar delay (top and bottom staves). **10/4** ▶

Listen to the examples on the CD to hear how these delays can be used to create attractive and complex harmonic structures.

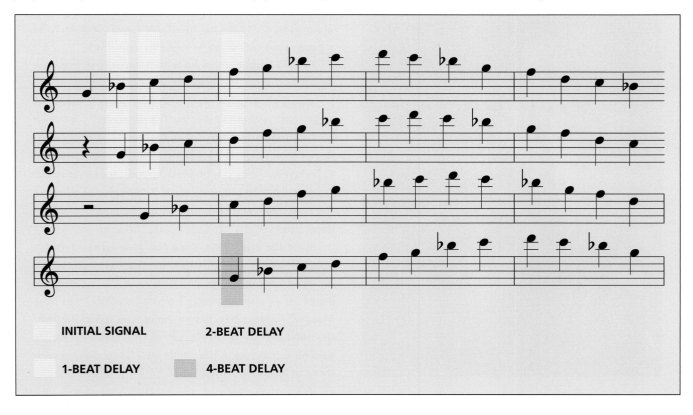

INITIAL SIGNAL   **2-BEAT DELAY**

1-BEAT DELAY   **4-BEAT DELAY**

HARMONICS

The term HARMONIC refers to the bell-like sounds you can get by damping specific frets on the guitar's fingerboard. You have already encountered harmonics briefly in the tuning section (*see page 23*), and while it's true to say that for a great many players that is the whole extent of their knowledge and use, it's worth taking things a little further since they can provide you with some very useful playing effects.

HOW DO HARMONICS WORK?

Each time you strike a guitar string, the precise sound you hear is the result of a number of different components which, when taken together, are referred to as the HARMONIC SERIES. The dominant sound you hear is known as a FUNDAMENTAL. This is the string vibrating along the full length of the fingerboard between the bridge and the nut, and consequently the element which defines the pitch of the note. However, there are further components that can also be heard. These result from shorter frequencies vibrating along different parts of the string. These frequencies are always strict multiples of the fundamental, and are known as harmonics or OVERTONES. The balance between the various harmonics and the fundamental is what creates the tonal characteristics of an acoustic note produced by any musical instrument.

THE HARMONIC SERIES

You can hear a harmonic in isolation by playing a note muted by the left hand at specified points on the fingerboard. The easiest one to produce is an octave harmonic. Place the tip of one of your fingers gently on top of any of the strings EXACTLY above the 12th fret. Make sure that you don't actually hold the string down against the fret. Now pick that string. All you should

ROBERT FRIPP: MAINSTREAM EXPERIMENTALISM

Robert Fripp is one of the few guitarists with an experimental bent to have a created music that has gained mainstream success. The popularity of his band King Crimson – the name of which has now been active with various personnel for over 30 years – has given a wider audience to some of his more esoteric work than pretty well any other "left-field" guitarist. This fact alone has made him an important influence on several generations of guitarists and experimental musicians.

Formed at the end of the 1960s, King Crimson was one of the most worthwhile of the progressive rock era. It was largely the carefully balanced playing of Robert Fripp that set them apart from needlessly flashy contemporaries. His guitar work stood out because there always seemed to be a good reason for what he was playing.

In 1973 Fripp hooked up with Brian Eno, with whom he made the ground-breaking *No Pussyfooting* album. Effectively a solo guitar work, with synthesiser "processing" by Eno, the system – known as "Frippertronics" – involved passing magnetic tape across the heads of two linked Revox tape recorders, enabling lengthy loops of sound to be layered, thus creating lush soundscapes over which Fripp could then play solo parts. Fripp later abandoned the tape recorders, switching instead to powerful digital delay lines.

Since the mid-1990s, Fripp has focused much of his energy on teaching at his Guitar Craft schools, which promote an alternative philosophy of the instrument, including an altered tuning – which he refers to as New Standard Tuning ("NST"). From the bottom string upwards, the notes are: C – G – D – A – E – G. This system is slowly gaining acceptance in the guitar world, especially among those of an experimental bent.

hear is a bell-like tone. This is the harmonic, the fundamental having been muted by your finger.

The pitch of the harmonic that you hear depends on the mathematical divisions of the string that are resonating. By muting the fundamental at the 12th fret you divide the string in half. This causes the string to resonate in two equal measures – the distance between the nut and the 12th fret being identical to the distance between the 12th fret and the bridge saddle (the point at which the bridge comes into contact with the string). This is known as a FIRST HARMONIC, and creates a note which is identical in pitch to the note fretted on the 12th fret.

Other types of harmonic are also possible: the SECOND HARMONIC divides the string into three equal segments; the THIRD HARMONIC causes the string to vibrate in four equal lengths; and the FOURTH HARMONIC divides the string into five equal lengths. You can see the notes that this produces in the diagram on the right.

HARMONICS IN PRACTICE

With a good knowledge of the fingerboard, and the points at which harmonics can be created, it becomes possible to integrate them into your general playing. If you want to hear some fine examples of harmonics in practice – albeit on a bass guitar (although the principles are the same) – listen to the album *Jaco* by Jaco Pastorius, which makes extensive use of harmonics – indeed, his composition "Portrait of Tracy" is almost entirely played using harmonics.

FRETTED HARMONICS

It's actually possible to play harmonics (or FAKE HARMONICS, as they are sometimes called) for any note on the fingerboard. The left hand frets notes in the conventional way, while the right hand simultaneously mutes the string with the 1st finger of the right hand and plucks the note either with the thumb or 4th finger. To pitch a note in this way requires a good working knowledge of the fingerboard. By fretting a note you are, in effect, creating a new "nut" position – the harmonics are played relative to the shift between the nut or zero fret and the fretted note.

To see how this works, position the 1st finger on the 2nd fret of the 2nd string. Now place the 1st finger of the right hand lightly on the string above the 14th fret and pluck the note with the thumb of the right hand. This produces a first harmonic of C♯. Similarly, with the left hand still in position it is possible to hear second harmonics – the note G♯ – on the 9th and 21st frets, and a third harmonic (C♯) on the 7th fret.

HARMONICS ON THE FINGERBOARD

The diagram below shows the position of the different harmonics on the fingerboard. Note that to produce a 5th harmonic the finger needs to be position between the 3rd and 4th frets, NOT directly above the 3rd fret.

Fret	1	2	3	4	5	6	Harmonic
0							
1							
2							
3	B	E	A	D	F♯	B	5th
4	G♯	C♯	F♯	B	D♯	G♯	4th
5	E	A	D	G	B	E	3rd
6							
7	B	E	A	D	F♯	B	2nd
8							
9	G♯	C♯	F♯	B	D♯	G♯	4th
10							
11							
12	E	A	D	G	B	E	1st
13							
14							
15							
16	G♯	C♯	F♯	B	D♯	G♯	4th
17							
18							
19	B	E	A	D	F♯	B	2nd

APPENDIX i
TAKING GOOD CARE

Unlike most other modern-day musical instruments and technology, a high-quality guitar of any kind is not likely to depreciate too much in value. This is one good reason why we recommend that you buy the best instrument you can afford when learning. But even if you don't have a precious investment to protect, simply taking a few simple measures, such as cleaning the components, changing the strings, checking the way it's been set up, and storing or transporting it in the safest possible way, will help you to get the maximum enjoyment and playability from your guitar.

STRINGS AND THINGS

Steel strings are used on electric, electro-acoustic and "folk" acoustic guitars. Differences among steel strings are generally characterised by the STRING WRAP. While the top two strings (and sometimes the 3rd when using ultra-light-gauge strings) are invariably a single thread of wire, the remaining strings comprise a wire inner core with a second piece of wire wound tightly around the outside. The nature of the wrapping has a direct impact on the sound and playability of the strings. There are three common types of winding: roundwound, flatwound and groundwound, and each of these types has its own characteristics.

ROUNDWOUND STRINGS

The most commonly used strings on electric and acoustic instruments, these strings are wound using conventionally shaped round wire, giving the characteristic ridge-like feel.

FLATWOUND STRINGS

Most commonly used on arch-top acoustic guitars, flatwound strings feature a core enveloped by a flat ribbon of metal. When tightly wound, this gives a feel as smooth as one of the treble strings. This allows the fingers to move along the strings without creating the characteristic acoustic "squeak" that can accompany roundwound strings.

Flatwound strings have one clear disadvantage in that the sound they produce is somewhat duller in tone than that found with roundwound strings, and they also have a tendency to crack, making them the least long-lasting of the three types.

GROUNDWOUND STRINGS

An attempt to provide the tonal advantages of roundwound with the playing advantages of flatwound, groundwound strings use conventional round windings which are then ground down so that the surface is partially flat.

STRING WEAR

Strings don't last forever: they wear out or they break. This can sometimes be a result of applying too much tension when bending notes or striking the strings particularly hard with the right hand. Strings also lose their stretch with time and use. This is largely a result of salt from the sweating pores of the fingers causing rust. When strings have worn out they lose their shine and the crispness of their sound. Some players change their strings before every gig.

You can make your strings last longer by cleaning them after each use. Wipe them down with a lint-free cloth every time you've finished playing. "Snapping" is also a way that some players get rid of build-ups of dirt and grime form the underside and windings of the strings. This involves pulling the string away from the fingerboard and letting it snap back into position.

One old trick used by musicians of limited means is to remove the strings and boil them in water. This removes the grease and grime and improves the tone. But the benefits are temporary, and you won't get away with more than two or three boilings. Additionally, treble strings, once removed, are apt to kink and snap around the nut and machine head when you are trying to refit them.

CHANGING STRINGS

There are a number of different string-securing mechanisms that you may encounter, all of which require slightly different changing techniques. In all cases, whatever type of instrument you use, whenever you fit new strings they need to be "stretched". To do this, pull the string a few inches away from the fretboard and then release it. If the pitch has dropped, retune it and repeat. Keep doing this until the string stays broadly in tune. Do this for all the strings.

Every one of a new set of strings has a "ball end" attached. This is a tiny disk of metal around which one end of the string is wrapped and secured. The opposite end of the string is threaded through a hole behind the bridge, pulled through and held in position by the ball. With the exception of locking-nut systems, most electric guitar strings are secured either by an independent tailpiece or are passed through the body of the instrument from the back into an all-in-one-bridge unit *(see right, above)*.

Most electric and steel-string guitars use the same kind of system for securing strings at the machine head. The capstan to which the string is attached usually stands out vertically from the headstock. Strings can be passed through a hole in the side of the capstan. The end is then passed around and under, trapping it in place when the machine head is tightened *(see right, below)*.

LOCKING-NUT MECHANISMS

Changing strings can be arduous with locking-nut systems. The strings are clamped in place at the bridge saddle, using an Allen key. Therefore, the ball ends must first be cut away with a pair of pliers. On tremolo systems, because the tension of ALL of the strings alters when one string is removed, fix a block of wood or pack of cards in place beneath the bridge mechanism, to prevent it from rocking back and forth.

The strings are wound on to the machine heads in the conventional way. Once the strings are all in place, the block supporting the bridge should be removed. The strings are then tuned, and locked in place at the nut using an Allen key. Fine tune with the adjusters on each bridge saddle.

STORAGE AND TRAVEL

If your guitar is not going to be used for any length of time, you should pay some attention to the way in which you keep it stored. Apart from protecting the instrument from knocks and scrapes, the main consideration is to avoid the instrument being exposed to wide variations in temperature or humidity. This is especially important for delicate acoustic instruments, where a sudden change of climate can alter the action, distort the woods used, damage glue joints, and cause cracks in the finish. For this reason alone, guitars shouldn't be stored in lofts or basements, or close to radiators or other hot water pipes.

It's always a good idea to store your guitar in a sturdy case (*see above*), although some guitarists favour hanging their instruments from walls. This is less recommended, as it will inevitably suffer from a heavy build-up of dust. If you insist on hanging your guitar (and it can admittedly be convenient, especially where shortages of floor space are concerned), it's a good idea to buy specially made fixtures and fittings. Finally,

never hang your guitar in direct sunlight – it can damage the bodywork, causing the colour to fade and the wood to distort.

Before storing the instrument, always give it a thorough cleaning, to prevent tarnishing or rusting of the metal parts. Always detune the strings so that there is no tension stress placed on the joints between the neck and the body.

TRANSPORT

If you intend moving your guitar around in a car, van or by rail, your instrument is at all kinds of risk. You should ALWAYS keep your guitar in its case and lay it down longways, either on its back or side. This will prevent it falling over. Avoid placing heavy items on top, such as amplifiers, PA systems or drum kits. Even the sturdiest of flight cases has its limits.

Travelling by air poses enormous potential risks. Although regulations will vary from one airline to another, if at all possible, arrange in advance to take your guitar on board as hand luggage. Whatever you do, however, DON'T EVEN CONSIDER putting it the cargo hold without a sturdy, metal flight case – you can be guaranteed that a standard plywood case will be smashed, and your guitar badly damaged. Even though some airlines offer a separate hold for delicate items, the above warning still applies.

If you travel around with your guitar on a regular basis, you should give serious thought to obtaining insurance cover. This is expensive, though – sirens wail and red warning lights flash ever time a musician walks through an insurance company's doors! But it should help to protect your investment.

FLIGHT CASES

To give your guitar even the most basic protection, it should have its own flight case. These come in a wide variety of shapes and sizes. The most basic cases are made from padded plastic or fabric, and zip around the outside of the guitar. They are very cheap and offer you the barest minimum of protection. To be honest, it is just as effective to wrap your guitar up in an old thick blanket, if less neat and tidy.

The sturdiest cases have a hard shell, usually made from plywood or a strong plastic. The insides are padded to keep the instrument in place, and lined with fake fur to protect the body finish. These cases are ideal for most everyday protection.

If you are playing in a touring group or regularly travelling with your guitar, a metal flight case is a necessity. Such cases are fitted with aluminium side panels and thick metal corner units. While they offer great protection, they can be very expensive, sometimes costing as much as a guitar itself, and they usually triple the weight of the entire package. They also invariably cause damage to any thing or body with which they accidentally come into contact.

KEEP IT CLEAN

The various parts of the guitar can be cleaned using a wide variety of agents. Most modern guitars are finished in cellulose and as such can be cleaned with care using any regular household sprays or creams. Avoid those cleaning agents that contain silicone or wax, as they can sometimes cause discolouration to the finish and give the instrument an unpleasant, sticky feel. Under NO circumstances should you use abrasive cleaning fluids, as these will damage the finish. Most music stores sell a variety of specialised cleaning fluids *(see right)*, so if in doubt it is advisable to use one of these.

CLEANING THE STRINGS

Keeping your strings clean not only makes the guitar feel more pleasant to play, but it can make the strings last a good deal longer. The most effective cleaning method is to take a dry, lint-free cloth, pass it between the strings and fingerboard, and drag it the full length of the strings between the bridge and the nut. Some players favour the use of string-cleaning fluids *(see right)*.

CLEANING THE FINGERBOARD

Fingerboards with a synthetic varnish can be cleaned in the same way as the body. Many guitars have oiled ebony or rosewood fingerboards. These should be given a thorough cleaning every time you change the strings. A neat trick here is to apply some lemon oil to the wood and leave it for around five minutes. This should then be cleaned off using a dry cloth – lemon oil also feeds the wood, preventing it from drying out.

CLEANING THE FRETS

Dirt from the fingers often builds along the edge of the frets. This should be removed with a gently pointed object, such as a nail file or toothpick. The grime should come away quite easily, so don't scratch too hard, otherwise you will damage the fingerboard.

HARDWARE

Keeping the guitar's metal parts – machine heads, pickups, bridges, and tremolo arms – clean is the most effective way of preventing rusting or other tarnishing effects. A regular domestic chrome-cleaning agent will work here. Electrical cleaning sprays should be used on the pickup switches to prevent them sticking or clicking. It can also be used to clean the controls, keeping their operation smooth.

SETTING UP

There are number of simple alterations that can be made to an instrument to suit the preferences of a player.

ACTION
The simplest modification is to adjust the height of the strings above the frets. The further away they are, the more pressure needs to be applied by the left hand to fret the notes. For fast solo work, a low action is more suitable. To measure the action, take a steel rule with fine gradations and place it on top of the 12th fret. Measure the distance to the bottom of the string. Setting the action is not usually conducted with scientific precision. More often than not, guitarists choose the lowest action possible without causing fret buzz. The height of the strings is altered by changing the height of the bridge.

On most electric guitars, each string has its own saddle which can be raised by turning a small control screw in a clockwise direction.

INTONATION
If you make a dramatic alteration to the action, you are effectively changing the distance between the nut and the bridge. However small this adjustment is, it can alter the intonation of your guitar. You can test the intonation by playing an open string and then comparing it to the note played on the 12th fret. If the latter is not EXACTLY one octave above the open string, your guitar will go out of tune the further you play along the fretboard. If the note at the 12th fret is sharp, the string is too short and must be lengthened by moving the saddle back.

APPENDIX ii
CHORDS ON THE MOVE

An expansive chord vocabulary, and an understanding of the way in which chords are constructed, is perhaps the most useful capability that a guitarist can acquire. It provides composers and songwriters with a more sophisticated palette from which to draw. It also provides arrangers with valuable lessons, such as the importance of understanding the way different voicings and inversions work.

IT'S ALL IN THE ROOT

This Chord Finder is not like a regular chord dictionary in that it doesn't simply aim to show you basic chord shapes arranged for every key. What you will find over the next few pages is a selection of mobile chord shapes with root notes on either the 5th or 6th strings. Once you have learned these shapes, if you know the names of the notes on the 5th and 6th strings you will be able to play any of them in any key. Thus, although there are 54 different chord shapes shown,

NAMING THE INTERVALS		
NOTES IN THE KEY OF C	INTERVAL NAMES	SCALE DEGREE ABBREVIATIONS
C	Root note	I
D♭	Minor 2nd	ii
D	Major 2nd	II
E♭	Minor 3rd	iii
E	Major 3rd	III
F	Perfect 4th	IV
F♯	Augmented 4th	iv+
G♭	Diminished 5th	v-
G	Perfect 5th	V
G♯	Augmented 5th	v+
A♭	Minor 6th	vi
A	Major 6th	VI
B♭♭	Diminished 7th	vii°
B♭	Minor 7th	vii
B	Major 7th	VII
C	Octave	I

they can in fact generate almost 600 different chords.

Not all of these chords can be strummed across all six strings, but most of them use a combination of four or more strings. Some work better if they are played with the fingers rather than a pick – especially those built on a 6th string root that do not play the 5th string.

WORKING OUT CHORDS

Let's just briefly go over the way chords are built, since it's such a fundamental aspect of understanding music.

The chord's key is defined by its root note. Although in the majority of cases the root will be the lowest-pitch note in the chord, THIS NEED NOT BE THE CASE. A chord is defined by the notes it contains. Each of these notes can be named in relation to their intervals from the root. These are shown in semitone steps in the panel on the left – this example uses the key of C. Let's consider the chord C MAJOR SEVENTH. Why is this so named? Simple: it's a C major triad with the addition of the major seventh note in the scale of C major. If you check the notes in the panel you'll see that means C (root), E (major 3rd), G (perfect 5th) [these are the components of a C major triad] with the addition of B (major 7th).

While there are chords that use the 2nd, 4th and 6th degrees of the major scale, where they are past an octave from the root they are said to be EXTENDED, and so become the 9th, 11th and 13th degrees. Let's now work backward and try naming a chord from its notes. Imagine that you stumbled on a chord in C made up from the notes C, E, G♭, B♭ and D♯. They can all be named in relation to the root: C is the root; E is the major 3rd, G♭ is the diminished 5th, B♭ is the minor 7th, and since D♯ is extended beyond the octave, that becomes a 9th raised by a semitone – an augmented 9th. So it is a C seventh chord with a flattened 5th note and a sharpened 9th note. That makes it C SEVENTH DIMINISHED FIFTH AUGMENTED NINTH, or C7-5+9 for short.

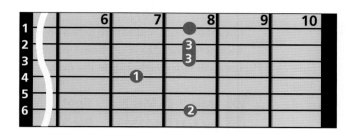

C MINOR SIXTH
(6TH-STRING ROOT ON THE 8TH FRET)

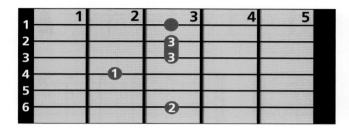

G MINOR SIXTH
(6TH-STRING ROOT ON THE 3RD FRET)

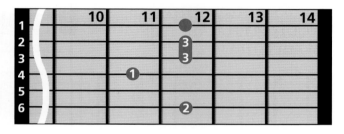

E MINOR SIXTH
(6TH-STRING ROOT ON THE 12TH FRET)

HOW TO USE THE CHORD FINDER

The chord diagrams in this section represent an overhead view of the fingerboard. The red circles indicate that a note has to be fretted – the white number inside indicates which finger should do that job. Circles that are not numbered indicate that the note is optional. None of the chords over the next four pages are open-string, so ONLY THE STRINGS THAT ARE FRETTED WITH THE LEFT HAND SHOULD BE PICKED BY THE RIGHT HAND.

Beneath each chord you will see the name as well as the scale degrees from which that voicing is constructed. Chords can have a variety of names or abbreviations, so a list is provided for you in the panel below.

NAMES AND ABBREVIATIONS					
C major		C	C minor ninth	C min 9	Cm9
C minor	C min	Cm	C suspended fourth		C sus 4
C dominant seventh	C seven (seventh)	C7	C dominant eleventh	C eleven	C11
C major seventh	C maj 7	CΔ	C minor six/nine		Cm6/9
C minor seventh	C min 7	Cm7	C six/nine major seventh	C 6/9 maj 7	C 6/9Δ7
C minor diminished fifth	C minor flat 5	Cm-5	C minor eleventh	C minor 11	Cm11
C diminished 7	C dim	C°	C dominant thirteenth	C thirteen	C13
C seventh diminished fifth	C 7 flat 5	C7-5	C minor thirteenth		Cm13
C seventh augmented fifth	C 7 sharp 5	C7+5	C seventh augmented ninth		
C major seventh augmented eleventh				C 7 sharp 9	C7+9
	C maj 7 sharp 11	CΔ7+11	C minor six/nine	C min 6/9	Cm6/9
C minor/major seventh		C min/maj 7	C major seventh augmented fifth		CΔ7+5
C major sixth		C6		C major 7 sharp 5	
C minor sixth	C min 6	Cm6	C seventh augmented fifth augmented ninth		C7+5+9
C major ninth	C maj 9	CΔ9		C 7 sharp 5 sharp 9	
C dominant ninth	C nine (ninth)	C9	C ninth diminished fifth	C 9 flat 5	C9-5

SIXTH-STRING ROOTS

All of the chords shown here are built from a root on the sixth string. This means that if you know the names of each note on the sixth string any of these chords can be played in any key. The names of the chords are shown along with the relationship of each note to the root (in this case, the key of C). <u>DON'T FORGET THAT YOU SHOULD ONLY PLAY THE STRINGS MARKED WITH A DOT.</u>

Chords are built and named based on the relationship to the root note of each note used. These relationships remain consistent, whichever note on the sixth string is chosen as the root.

1	Min 7	Maj 7	Root	Min 2/♭9	Maj 2/9	#9
2	Per 4/11	#4/#11/♭5	Per 5	#5/♭13	Maj 6/13	Min 7
3	Min 2/♭9	Maj 2/9	Min 3/#9	Maj 3	Per 4/11	#4/#11/♭5
4	#5/Min 6	Maj 6	Min 7	Maj 7	Root	Min 2/♭9
5	Min 3	Maj 3	Perf 4/11	#4/♭5	Per 5	#5/Min 6
6			Root	Min 2	Maj 2	Min 3

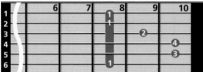

MAJOR (Root, Per 5, Root, Maj 3, Per 5, Root)

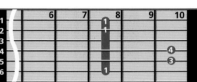

MINOR (Root, Per 5, Root, Min 3, Per 5, Root)

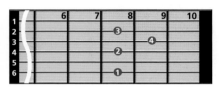

SEVENTH (Root, Min 7, Maj 3, Per 5)

MAJOR 7TH (Root, Maj 7, Maj 3, Perf 5)

MINOR 7TH (Root, Min 7, Min 3, Per 5)

MINOR 7 FLAT 5 (Root, Min 7, Min 3, Dim 5)

DIMINISHED 7 (Root, Dim 7, Min 3, Dim 5)

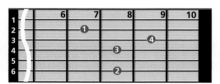

7 FLAT 5 (Root, Min 7, Maj 3, Dim 5)

7 SHARP 5 (Root, Min 7, Maj 3, Aug 4)

MAJOR 7 SHARP 11 (Root, Maj 7, Maj 3, Aug 11)

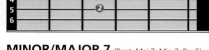

MINOR/MAJOR 7 (Root, Maj 7, Min 3, Per 5)

MAJOR 6 (Root, Maj 6, Maj 3, Per 5)

MINOR 6 (Root, Maj 6, Min 3, Per 5)

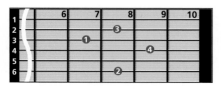

MAJOR 9 (Root, Maj 7, Maj 9, Per 5)

NINTH (Root, Maj 3, Min 7, Maj 9, Per 5)

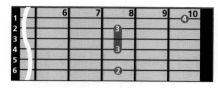

MINOR NINTH (Root, Min 7, Min 3, Per 5, Maj 9)

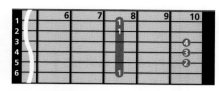

SUS FOURTH (Root, Per 5, Root, Per 4, Root)

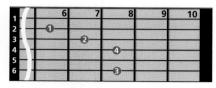

ELEVENTH (Root, Min 7, Maj 9, 11)

MINOR 6/9 (Root, Maj 3, Maj 6, 9, Per 5)

6/9 MAJOR 7 (Root, Maj 3, Maj 6, 9, Per 5, Maj 7)

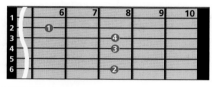

MINOR 11 (Root, Min 7, Min 3, 11)

THIRTEENTH (Root, Min 7, Maj 3, 13)

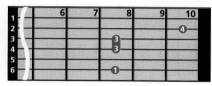

MINOR 13 (Root, Min 7, Min 3, 13)

7 SHARP 9 (Root, Maj 3, Min 7, Aug 9, Per 5)

MINOR 6/9 (Root, Maj 6, Aug 9, Per 5, 9)

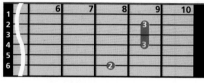

MAJOR 7 SHARP 5 (Root, Maj 7, Maj 3, Aug 5)

MINOR FLAT 6 (Root, Min 6, Min 3, Per 5)

MINOR/MAJOR 9 (Root, Maj 7, Aug 9, Per 5, 9)

7 ♯ 5 ♯ 9 (Root, Min 7, Maj 3, Aug 5, Aug 9)

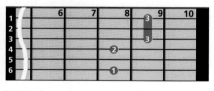

7 ♯ 5 ♭ 9 (Root, Min 7, Maj 3, Aug 5, Dim 9)

13 FLAT 9 (Root, Min 7, Maj 3, Aug 5, 13, Dim 9)

7 FLAT 9 (Root, Min 7, Dim 9, Per 5)

CHORD FLAVOURS

Most of these chords do not use all six strings. For Thirteenth chords it is impossible to play a full chord as this would require seven strings. The art of playing these chords on the guitar is to create the right flavour by missing out the least useful notes. For Eleventh chords, the 5th and 9th notes are often not used; Thirteenth chords often also leave out the 11th notes.

9 FLAT 5 (Root, Min 7, 9, Dim 5)

13 SHARP 9 (Root, Maj 3, Min 7, Aug 9, 13)

FIFTH-STRING ROOTS

The chords shown here are built from a fifth-string root note. Although these chords are less harmonically versatile than their sixth-string counterparts – they can, at most, only be played on five strings – they are actually easier to use. This is because many of the chords shown on pages 176-177 have a central string (usually the 5th) which must not be played, making strumming across the strings a tough proposition.

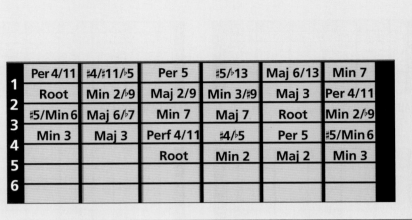

	Per 4/11	#4/#11/b5	Per 5	#5/b13	Maj 6/13	Min 7
1	Per 4/11	#4/#11/b5	Per 5	#5/b13	Maj 6/13	Min 7
2	Root	Min 2/b9	Maj 2/9	Min 3/#9	Maj 3	Per 4/11
3	#5/Min 6	Maj 6/b7	Min 7	Maj 7	Root	Min 2/b9
4	Min 3	Maj 3	Perf 4/11	#4/b5	Per 5	#5/Min 6
5			Root	Min 2	Maj 2	Min 3
6						

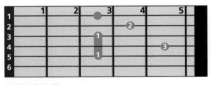

MAJOR (Root, Per 5, Root, Maj 3, Per 5)

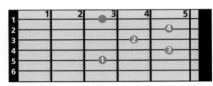

MAJOR SEVENTH (Root, Per 5, Maj 7, Maj 3, Per 5)

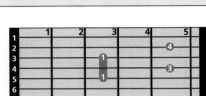

SEVENTH (Root, Per 5, Min 7, Maj 3)

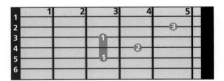

MINOR 7 (Root, Per 5, Min 7, Min 3, Per 5 [optional])

MINOR 7 FLAT 5 (Root, Dim 5, Min 7, Min 3)

DIMINISHED 7 (Root, Dim 5, Dim 7, Min 3)

7 FLAT 5 (Root, Dim 5, Min 7, Maj 3)

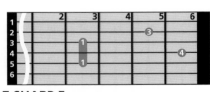

7 SHARP 5 (Root, Aug 5, Min 7, Maj 3)

MAJOR 7 SHARP 11 (Root, Aug 11, Maj 7, Maj 3)

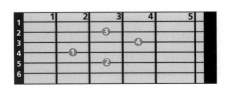

MINOR/MAJOR 7TH (Root, Per 5, Maj 7, Min 3)

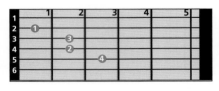

MAJOR 6TH (Root, Maj 3, Maj 6, Root)

MINOR 6TH (Root, Maj 6, Min 3, Per 5)

MAJOR 9TH (Root, Maj 3, Maj 7, 9)

NINTH (Root, Maj 3, Min 7, 9, Per 5)

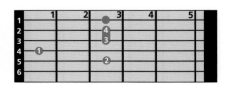

MINOR NINTH (Root, Min 3, Min 7, 9, Per 5)

ELEVENTH (Root, 11, Min 7, 9, Per 5)

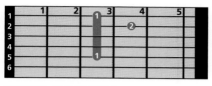

MINOR ELEVENTH (Root, 11, Min 7, Min 3, Per 5)

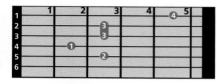

THIRTEENTH (Root, 11, Maj 3, Min 7, 9, 13)

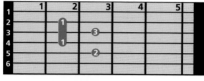

SEVEN FLAT NINE (Root, Maj 3, Min 7, Dim 9)

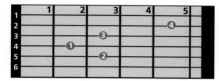

SEVEN SHARP NINE (Root, Maj 3, Min 7, Aug 9)

SUS FOUR (Root, Per 5, Root, Per 4)

CHORD TEST

Here is a **SERIOUSLY** challenging exercise. It's far and away the toughest exercise in the book, and you can bet that the vast majority of your favourite guitarists would be completely clueless if asked to do it. It will only work if you have carefully studied the chords over the past four pages. Below you will see a list of chord names. They are all voicings taken from this section, only this time the chord types have been prefixed by a key. Your job is to work through the list and play them **WITHOUT** looking them up. For the best results, set up a constant beat – a metronome or drum machine running at a steady 100 bps should do the trick. Work through the chord list, playing on the first beat of every bar and sustaining for four beats before seamlessly changing to the next chord in the list. Good luck!

1.	E major	22.	C major	43.	C♯ minor 7-5	64.	C minor 13
2.	C minor	23.	C♯ 7+5-9	44.	G minor 6	65.	B major 7+11
3.	B major	24.	A minor/major 9	45.	A 6/9 major 7	66.	A♭ minor 13
4.	F♯ minor	25.	B minor 11	46.	B♭ minor 13	67.	G major 7
5.	B♭ minor 7	26.	C minor 7	47.	G major	68.	C♯ major 9
6.	A 6	27.	F7-5	48.	C♯ major 7	69.	D♭ minor 9
7.	F diminished 7	28.	A11	49.	B♭ minor 9	70.	A6
8.	D7+5	29.	F♯ 13	50.	G6	71.	B♭ minor 7
9.	A7-5	30.	F minor 7-5	51.	B♭ diminished 7	72.	G♯7-5
10.	C 9	31.	B minor 6	52.	A♯ 7+5-9	73.	B11
11.	A♯ minor 9	32.	G 6/9 major 7	53.	B♭7+5-9	74.	F♯ 13
12.	D7+9	33.	A minor 13	54.	F♯minor 11	75.	B♭ minor 7-5
13.	F 13	34.	D minor/major 7	55.	C minor 7	76.	B minor 6
14.	G minor 11	35.	C minor-6	56.	G♯7-5	77.	D♭ 6/9 major 7
15.	B♭sus 4	36.	A major 7+11	57.	C13-9	78.	A♯ 7+5-9
16.	F minor 6/9	37.	D major	58.	D♭minor 13	79.	B♭7+5-9
17.	G13-9	38.	E minor 7	59.	A7+5	80.	G♯7-9
18.	E♭minor 13	39.	G♯ minor 9	60.	C7-5	81.	C 13+9
19.	C7+5	40.	C♯7+9	61.	D♯ minor 9	82.	G♯9-5
20.	D7-5	41.	E 13	62.	B minor 13	83.	A♯7+9-13
21.	A♯ minor 9	42.	G♭ minor 11	63.	A minor/major 7	84.	C minor 13

APPENDIX iii
BACKING TRACKS

BACKING TRACK #1

E / / /	⁄.	D / / /	⁄.
A / / /	⁄.	E / / /	D / / /

BACKING TRACK #2

A / / /	⁄.	G / / /	⁄.
C / / /	⁄.	D / / /	⁄.
A / / /	⁄.	G / / /	⁄.
C / / /	⁄.	D / / /	⁄.
Em / / /	⁄.	C / / /	⁄.
D / / /	⁄.	G / / /	⁄.
Em / / /	⁄.	C / / /	⁄.
D / / /	⁄.	⁄.	⁄.

BACKING TRACK #3

Part A

| G A / / | / / / / | G A / / | / / / / |

| G A / / | / / / / | C G G G | A / / / |

Part B

| E♭ / / / | / / / / | B♭ / / / | / / / / |

| F / / / | / / / / | G / / / | / / / / |

BACKING TRACK #4

| G / / / | ✗. | ✗. | ✗. |

| C / / / | ✗. | G / / / | ✗. |

| D / / / | C / / / | G / / / | D / / / |

BACKING TRACK #5

| A / / / | E / / / | F#m / / / | D / / / |

| A / / / | E / / / | A / / / | E / / / |

| A / E / | F#m / D / | A / E / | F#m / D / |

| A / E / | F#m / E / | D / / / | ✗. |

BACKING TRACK #6

Introduction

| E13 / / / | D13 / / / | C13 / / / | D13 / / / |

Main section

| E9 / / / | ∕. | ∕. | ∕. |

| ∕. | ∕. | ∕. | ∕. |

| D9 / / / | ∕. | C9 / / / | B7+9 / / / |

BACKING TRACK #7

Part A

| D / / / | A min / / / | G / / / | D / / / |

| A min / / / | G / / / | F maj 7 / / / | G / / / |

Part B

| A / / / | F maj 7+11 | A / / / | F maj 7+11 |

| A / / / | E min / / / | D / / / | C maj 7 / G / |

BACKING TRACK #8

Part A

| A / / / | ∕. | A♯ / / / | G♯ / / / |

Part B

| A / G♯ / | G / / / | C♯ / / / | A♯ / G♯ / |

Part C

| A / | G♯ / | G / | G | C♯ / | G / / |

Part D

| E / | F / | F♯ / | F♯ C / | F♯ / / |

| A | A | A | A | A | A | A | A | B | B | B | B |

| B | B | B | B | C | C | D | D | C | C | D | D |

BACKING TRACK #9

| G / / / | C add 9 / / / | G7 / / / | C add 9 / / / |

| D / / / | ∕. | C / / / | ∕. |

APPENDIX iv
GLOSSARY

ACCENT

A dynamic playing effect that places an emphasis on specific notes or chords within a sequence, making them louder or creating rhythmic effects.

ACCIDENTALS

Symbols used in written music to raise or lower the pitch of a note: the sharp (♯) raises the pitch by a half-step or semitone; the flat (♭) lowers the pitch by a half-step or semitone; the double sharp (𝄪) raises the pitch by a step or tone; the double flat (♭♭) lowers the pitch by a step or tone; the natural (♮) is used to cancel a previous accidental.

ACOUSTIC GUITAR

Guitar which does not require the use of amplification.

ACTION

The height between the strings and the frets on the fretboard. The higher the action, the harder it becomes to fret notes.

ADAT

Popular digital multi-track recording format created by US company Alesis. The system uses standard Super-VHS video format cassettes.

ADT

Automatic Double Tracking. An electronic delay effect that simulates the sound of two instruments playing the same part.

APPOGGIATURA

An ornamental note used to indicate a bend in pitch.

ARCH-TOP

Steel-string acoustic guitar with an arched top.

BOTTLENECK

A glass or metal bar dragged along the strings to alter the pitch. Also the name given to the technique and style of playing with a bottleneck.

BRIDGE

A mechanical device fitted to the body of an electric guitar which supports the strings and controls their height and length. On an acoustic guitar, the part into which the strings are set.

CAPO

A movable nut or zero fret which can be clamped at different positions along the fingerboard, allowing open strings to be played in alternative keys.

CHORD

The sound of three or more notes played at the same time. Two notes played simultaneously can create a chordal effect (although technically this is known as an interval).

CHORUS

Electronic delay effect that simulates more than one instrument playing the same part. Variations in pitch and time can be used to create a richer, thicker effect.

COMPRESSION

Electronic processing effect that equalises the dynamic range of sounds passing through it.

DAMPING

Playing technique which mutes one or more strings by deadening the natural ring with either of the hands. The opposite of accenting.

DAT

Digital Audio Tape. Universal two-track mastering standard which has largely replaced the analogue format.

DELAY

Digital simulation of natural reflected sounds, such as echo.

DISTORTION

Electronic effect created by heavily boosting the volume in the preamp stage of the amplifier. Can also be achieved using external effects units.

DREADNOUGHT

A large-bodied, steel-string acoustic guitar.

ELECTRO-ACOUSTIC GUITAR

A guitar that can be played acoustically or plugged into an external amplifier.

FEEDBACK

A sound produced when amplified sound from a loudspeaker causes a string to vibrate.

FINGERPICKING

Right-hand playing technique where the strings are plucked by the thumb and individual fingers.

FLAT-TOP GUITAR

A steel-string guitar with a flat soundboard.

FRET

Metal strips placed at intervals along the fingerboard.

FRET TAPPING

Playing technique where both left and right hands are used to fret notes on the fingerboard.

FUZZ BOX

See distortion.

GUITAR SYNTHESIZERS

Guitars with in-built synthesizer systems for dramatically altering the sound, or equipped with MIDI to control external synthesizers, drum machines, or processing effects.

HEADSTOCK

The uppermost part of the guitar neck, where the machine heads are mounted.

HUMBUCKERS

Twin-coil electronic pickups that produce a thick or "fat" sound favoured by many rock guitarists.

MACHINE HEAD

Mechanical device for controlling the tension, and therefore pitch, of a string.

MIDI

Musical Instrument Digital Interface. Electronic protocol language that allows computers, synthesizers, drum machines, sequencers and other suitably equipped electronic units to communicate with one another.

NOISE GATE

Electronic effect which cuts out all noise until it receives a signal passing a preset threshold.

NUT

The string supports positioned at the top of the fingerboard.

OCTAVE

An interval of 12 semitones (or half-steps using American terminology). Doubling the sound frequency of any note has the effect of increasing the pitch by an octave.

PA SYSTEM

Stands for Public Address system. Amplification system used when performing to an audience.

PEDALS

Foot-controlled electronic units placed between the output of the guitar and the input of the amplifier, which can be used to process the sound in a variety of different ways.

PICK

Object used for striking the guitar strings – usually made from plastic. Also known as a plectrum.

PICKUPS

Electro-magnetic transducers that convert string vibration into electrical impulses, which are then amplified and played back through a loudspeaker. Pickups are either single-pole or twin-pole; the latter are also known as "humbuckers".

PLECTRUM

See pick.

RESONATOR

Type of acoustic guitar with in-built metal resonator which increases volume and sustain. Also known as a Dobro.

RIFF

A repeated sequence of notes.

SCRATCHPLATE

A plastic plate fitted to the soundboard to protect the guitar body. Also known as a pickguard.

SOUNDBOARD

The front of the guitar on which the bridge is mounted

TEMPO

The speed at which a piece of music is played. Usually measured in beats per minute (bpm).

TIME SIGNATURE

Two numbers shown at the beginning of a piece of music, indicating the beats, and their value, within a bar.

TREMOLO ARM

See vibrato arm.

TRUSS ROD

Metal rod that passes beneath the fingerboard of the guitar and prevents the neck from being distorted by natural string tension.

VIBRATO ARM

Mechanical device that can alter the pitch of a string while playing – sometimes wrongly referred to as a "tremolo arm". Vibrato is also a playing technique where a finger of the left hand is used to create a minor fluctuation in pitch.

VOLUME PEDAL

Foot pedal connected between the guitar and amplifier, allowing the volume to be altered without using the controls on the guitar.

WAH-WAH PEDAL

Foot-operated effect unit that can either be rocked back and forth to produce a "wah" sound, or fixed in one position as a tone control.

ZERO FRET

Fret found on some guitars directly in front of the nut, controlling the action – the height of the strings – at the top of the neck.

INDEX

surf music 161
suspended fourth chords 118
suspended second chords 118
sustain 12, 159
sustained intervals 123

T

Tablature 26, 29
Talking Heads 110
Tamla Motown 127
Tarrega, Franscesco de 6
Taylor, James 166
TC digital delay line 168
teardrop pick 24
Television 110
tempo 34, 37, 185
Ten Years After 104
Them 77
Thin Lizzy 148
third harmonic 169
This is Spinal Tap 149
thrash 112
three-chord tricks 31
threshold 159
thumb position 20
ties 54
time Signature 36, 151, 185
   comparing 94
   five-four time 151
   six-four time 151
   six-eight 152
timing 34
timing skills 34
tone control 8, 9, 13, 27, 44
tones 60, 60
Tool 149
Torres, Antonio de 6
Townshend, Pete 82
T Rex Squeezer 159
transistor 11, 90
transporting guitars 172
transposition 69
travel 172
Travis, Merle 7, 163

treble clef 28
tremolo arm 8, 148, 161, 185
triads 30
   augmented 98
   construction 120
   diminished 98
   major 98
   minor 98
   on the major scale 120
   on the minor scale 121
trill 106
triple time 36
truss rod 185
tuning 22, 164–167
   with harmonics 23
   altered tuning 164
   DADGAD tuning 166
   drop D tuning 166
   drop G tuning 166
   G6 tuning 166
   open D tuning 166
   open E tuning 166
   open G tuning 164
   open tuning 164
   slack key 147
   standard 27
tuple time 94
turnaround 101
twang 161
twelve-bar blues 94
twelve-string guitar 116

U–V

upstrokes 24, 25, 48,148
USB 11
Vai, Steve 158, 162
valves 10–11, 90
vamping 130
Van Eps, George 162
Van Halen 37
Van Halen, Eddie 158
Vanilla Fudge 76

Vaughan, Jimmy 109
Vaughan, Stevie Ray 109
Veeder, Larry 131
Velvet Underground 37, 110
Venom 148
Verve, the 37
vibrato 106, 146
vibrato arm 161, 185
vihuela 6
volume 35
volume control 8, 9, 13, 150
volume pedal 185
Vox AC30 10

W–Z

wah-wah pedal 14, 132, 185
waltz time 36
warping 12
Waters, Ethel 92
Waters, Muddy 7, 90, 93, 97
"Wedding March" 62
wedge pick 24
White, Robert 131
Who, the 82
whole notes 35
whole-tone scales 58
Windsor Blues Festival 104
Winter, Johnny 104
wolf notes 12
writing a song 43
Yardbirds, the 7, 41, 59, 77
Yes 148
Zappa, Frank 44, 132, 148
zero fret 78, 185

BIBLIOGRAPHY

Craig Anderton *Home Recording For Musicians*
(AMSCO, 1978)

Tony Bacon *The Ultimate Guitar Book*
(Dorling Kindersley, 1991)

Derek Bailey *Improvisation* (Moorland, 1980)

Terry Burrows *The Complete Encyclopedia
Of The Guitar* (Carlton, 1998)

Terry Burrows *KISS Guide to Playing the Guitar*
(Dorling Kindersley, 2001)

Terry Burrows *Play Rock Guitar*
(Dorling Kindersley, 1995)

Terry Burrows *Play Country Guitar*
(Dorling Kindersley, 1995)

Terry Burrows *Total Guitar Tutor* (Carlton, 1998)

Terry Burrows *Total Keyboard Tutor* (Carlton, 2000)

Richard Chapman *The Complete Guitarist*
(Dorling Kindersley 1993)

Ralph Denyer *The Guitar Handbook* (Pan, 1992)

Chris Everard *The Home Recording Handbook* (Virgin, 1985)

Hugh Gregory *1000 Great Guitarists* (IMP, 1992)

Mark Hanson *The Alternate Tuning Guide For Guitar*
(AMSCO, 1991)

Juan Martín *El Arte De Flamenco De La Guitarra*
(United Music, 1982)

Fred Miller *Studio Recording For Musicians* (AMSCO, 1981)

Don Randall *The New Harvard Dictionary Of Music*
(Harvard University Press, 1986)

Darryl Runswick *Rock, Jazz and Pop Arranging*
(Faber and Faber, 1992)

Erik Satie *A Mammal's Notebook: Collected Writings...*
(Atlas, 1996)

Aaron Shearer *Classic Guitar Technique*
(Franco Colombo, 1963)

Nicolas Slonimsky *Thesaurus of Scales and Melodic Patterns*
(Scrivener's, 1947)

Happy Traum *Flat-pick Country Guitar*
(Oak, 1973)

Harvey Turnbull *The Guitar*
(Bold Strummer, 1991)

Jason Waldron *Progressive Classical Guitar* (Koala, 1992)

ACKNOWLEDGMENTS

The author would like to thank Lorna Russell and Adam Wright at Carlton Books for their work on this book. Above all, thanks to Mike Flynn for his rigorous music checking.

This book is dedicated to Junior.

PICTURE CREDITS